DARIUS GUPPY

with
Nicholas Davies

ROLL THE DICE

BLAKE

Published by Blake Publishing Ltd,
3 Bramber Court, 2 Bramber Road, London W14 9PB, England

First published in Great Britain 1996

ISBN 1 85782 1599

Cover photograph by Mauro Carraro

Inside illustrations used courtesy of Phil Coburn, News International,
Press Association and the *Daily Star*

British Library Cataloguing-in-Publication Data:
A catalogue record for this book is available from the British Library.

Typeset by BCP

Printed in England by Clays Ltd, St Ives plc

1 3 5 7 9 10 8 6 4 2

To my darling wife

'Revenge is a kind of wild justice,
which the more man's nature runs to it,
the more ought law to weed it out.'

Francis Bacon

The author wishes to thank many friends and family members for their help and support. In particular, Michael Alexander for his general advice and for providing a haven where much of the work was done; Nicholas Davies, for his editing of the manuscript and his ability to control some of the author's wilder instincts; Chris Berry for his assistance in getting the author out of jail; his friend Mohammad for setting a fine example of optimism and quiet determination; Tasneem Osmani, David Price and Jonathan Crystal for all manner of legal advice; Steve from Dixieland for the use of his laptop without which this book would never have been written; Charles Spencer for his steadfast loyalty; and the author's parents for access to various family archives. Above all, the author wishes to thank his wife for her great encouragement and for showing such remarkable courage.

CONTENTS

I

Stuart 'Baddie' Phillips was my first major challenge in life. Strong, wiry, with short fair hair and aquamarine eyes, Baddie Phillips would cause me to grow up quickly. He was fast on his feet, quick to the punch and he could throw stones with remarkable accuracy. Everyone in the playground knew who Phillips was and his classmates would gather around him, follow him wherever he led and fall silent whenever he spoke. We were both five years old.

I had only been at the French Lycée in London's South Kensington for a matter of weeks when I realised that someone had to challenge this boy. Most afternoons, during recreation time, he would gather a number of followers around him and then run wildly at groups of boys, shouting at them as he charged with his gang, scattering the boys in every direction. Those who stood their ground would be surrounded, punched and then pushed aside.

I admired Baddie Phillips. He had a certain quality about him, which to my young mind was irresistible for he seemed to fear no one and yet he was quiet and generally showed little sign of bravado. However, his supremacy in the playground could not be permitted to continue.

For some weeks I had watched Phillips cause havoc among my classmates, but none of them seemed capable of standing up to this boy who, though no taller than the rest, commanded their respect through sheer charisma and courage. So I began to join my classmates whenever they ventured out into the playground, determined to stand my ground when the attacks took place.

Invariably, Baddie Phillips would lead from the front, shouting and screaming as he charged towards us. Having made up my mind that I would not retreat, I was pushed to the ground and took a couple of punches and kicks during the first few attacks. The blows, however, never really hurt but rather encouraged my determination not to yield.

The more I stood my ground, refusing to turn and run, the more I knew that the day would come when Phillips and I would slug it out. It happened one October afternoon after school before our parents came to collect us.

The fight lasted no longer than a few minutes with Phillips' classmates cheering on their champion and mine gathered behind me, waiting to see whether I could indeed topple Baddie. We traded punches before falling to the ground, rolling over and over, pulling each other's hair and punching each other whenever possible with our puny, flailing fists.

As we fought, more boys, as well as girls, came to see the fight, forming a circle and jostling each other to get a better view. Suddenly, the noise stopped and we both looked up, knowing instinctively that a teacher had arrived.

'Get up, get up this instant the two of you!'

I remember obeying the command, pulling up my socks, looking at the dirt on my clothes and walking into the circle of my classmates, hoping to disappear into the crowd and escape the attention of the teacher.

It seemed that I had acquitted myself adequately. The following day, as I walked into the playground, my classmates gathered around me, waiting to see what I would do. It was the ultimate anti-climax. Nothing happened.

Phillips' group didn't charge. They simply assembled opposite us, murmuring and pointing while we stood our ground ten yards away. From that point on, while fights would occasionally break out and sometimes our rivals would charge, no one would turn and run. Instead, we kept our positions and fought.

Phillips and I would become friends and it seemed that he came to admire me as I admired him. Our scrap in the playground had been an honourable draw and months later, he had the grace to accept this. In fact, we soon became such good pals that within a short time we were playing marbles together. These games, however, were contested with great intensity and determination, neither of us wanting to lose a single marble to the other, especially the large, three-coloured ones.

It was three years later that I encountered another serious personal challenge in the playground. This came in the form of a good-looking young boy, a Spaniard by the name of Miguel, who had taken to bullying my brother Constantine, who was a year younger than me.

Unknown to me, because my brother had not complained about it, for most of the school year Miguel, a strong, quite stocky lad who wore long shorts to below the knee, had been chiding, pinching and hitting Constantine, who my family always called 'Couscous' after the Moroccan dish. Even at the age of eight, I realised that Couscous had a more gentle quality about him than me. Most of the time he seemed almost angelic — kind, generous and never spiteful.

One afternoon during the summer term, a young friend of Couscous ran up to me in the playground and told me that Miguel was hitting my brother. I rushed off in search of them both and found them in the playground lavatory. I was determined that Miguel would be taught a lesson and grabbed him, pulling him outside. He said nothing and tried to fight free. I smashed him in the face and blood gushed from his nose. I was very angry that Miguel had picked on my brother and continued to hit him, but Couscous intervened and begged me to stop. I looked at him and saw the appeal in his face, turned to Miguel, pushed him to the ground and walked away. Miguel never touched my brother again.

From an early age, I had always felt responsible for my younger brother. My mother had instilled in me a profound sense of family, telling me that if anything happened to her it would be my responsibility to care for young Constantine.

That incident made me realise that I had a temper that I could never ignore and that it seemed I was quite capable of hurting someone if I felt they deserved a beating.

I loved the holidays. I felt free and began believing that nothing was beyond me. Most days I would roam the Chelsea streets around my home getting into as much mischief as possible, smoking cigarettes, climbing drain pipes, clambering into other people's gardens and spending much of the day on the World War II bomb-site at the end of Shawfield Street, off the King's Road.

Once, my mother found me eating some chewing-gum that I had pinched from the little corner store off St Luke's Street. I told her that I had taken it from the shop and she smacked my hand, ordering me to return it immediately, apologise to the man who owned the shop and hand over the 3p for the Wrigley's chewing gum. I felt bad on two counts: first, because I had been caught stealing by my mother and I considered that I had let her down and second, because I had taken from someone who had very little money. From that moment, I was determined I would never steal again. At that age, though, I had hardly heard of the word 'motive' and certainly had little idea what it meant.

I adored my mother. I thought she was beautiful and I loved the way she would comfort me, holding me in her arms and talking gently in her quiet Persian accent. She was a folk singer, with a lovely, soft, velvety voice who performed as 'Shusha', the name of an ancient Persian queen, singing in concerts around the country and recording singles and albums. For more than a decade, she had a cult following in both Britain and her native Iran. In the evenings I would fall asleep upstairs while she practised down below, playing her guitar and singing her songs.

However, while I never wished to cause her suffering, there was one particular piece of mischief that I found exhilarating but that my mother considered highly dangerous. And, despite her threats and pleas to stop, I would continue.

From my bedroom window it was possible to climb out on to a small ledge and walk along the length of Shawfield Street, jumping from house to house. I would go to the back of a neighbour's house and shin the forty feet down the drain pipe into the garden, trying never to be caught and it gave me a thrill to return to my bedroom unnoticed. On a number of occasions my mother caught me and remonstrated with me, pointing out the dangers of such escapades. But there was something exciting about those dare-devil antics that compelled me to them. I believe these were the only times I continually disobeyed my mother's orders.

From the age of seven or eight I began to understand and be proud of the fact that I was not a true-blooded Englishman. My introduction to the family history began when my mother showed me photograph albums with mostly sepia and black-and-white pictures of my grandfather and his family wearing their Islamic dress, with robes and turbans, in Iran. My mother would also take me for lunch and tea at the London homes of her Iranian relatives. Always, there would be a houseful of guests laughing and eating and enjoying themselves, and often cuddling me, making me feel loved and generally wanted. I relished the Persian delicacies I was given to eat: golden rice, lamb kebabs, nan bread and exquisite sweets, often honeyed and scented with rose water.

Once I asked my mother to tell me the story of Darius the Great, the man after whom I had been named. Darius, a noble Persian governor who lived in the 5th century BC, conspired with six other noblemen to assassinate Smerdis who had usurped the throne. After killing him, the seven conspirators agreed that he whose horse neighed first the following morning would be accepted as King. On Darius' instructions, his groom took his horse to a field where a mare was in season. The following day when all the noblemen passed the field, Darius' horse, recollecting the mare, neighed in anticipation. At the same time a clap of thunder was heard and all the noblemen took this as a sign of God's approval. As King, Darius the First achieved many military conquests and is considered by historians to be one of Persia's greatest leaders.

Iran became almost my second home, for my mother enjoyed taking my brother and me there to visit her parents and relatives during the school holidays. I loved the smell of the kebabs being cooked at night on a spit over a wood fire in the garden of my grandparents' home, which was located near the Iranian Parliament and Tehran University. Some evenings my grandparents would invite a holy man to come and recite poems, which he did sitting on a stool in the middle of the room surrounded by the womenfolk who had gathered in a circle on the floor to delight in his moving and melancholic tales. Although I could never understand what he was saying, I would stay for hours transfixed by the passion of his remarkable voice, watching the veiled women as they took part in the dervish's ritual, weeping at the saddest moments of his recitation.

Apart from Tehran, my mother would take my brother and me to the Caspian Sea in the north and south to Isfahan, a beautiful ancient city that lies on the edge of the central desert in the middle of Iran, where I visited the magnificent mosques for which it is famous. There, I also took delight in watching the traders and shopkeepers of the bazaars as they haggled and yelled at each other before reaching an agreement, at which point they would smile and embrace, the best of friends.

It was about this time, when I began to go to Iran for my summer holidays, that I met the boy who would become my best pal and, some twenty years later, would stand in the dock beside me at Snaresbrook Crown Court, near Epping, in Essex.

Ben Marsh had a mass of blond, wavy hair that fell below his shoulders in the style of a 1970s pop star. He was the son of Peter Marsh, a self-made advertising tycoon who had started life as a working-class boy in Hull and had become a dominant figure in the world of British advertising.

From our first meeting, we became almost inseparable. We would sit next to each other in class, spend break-time together and often stay at each other's homes during weekends and holidays.

Only months before, my beloved father had called me into the sitting-room, having just received my school report. 'I want you to listen to your report,' he said, before reading it out to me. The report stated that I wasn't doing very well and certainly not as well as my teachers expected. 'I'm disappointed in you,' is all he said.

That remark saddened and embarrassed me and I went away feeling that I had let my father down. It kindled in me a determination to work harder and do better so that he would never have to be disappointed in me again.

I discussed the matter with my mother, seeking her advice. She told me that I had to learn to work hard and, more importantly, to concentrate. I replied that I found it difficult to concentrate at home because of the music she often played.

'That is something you will have to overcome,' she told me. 'When you are really concentrating on your work, you will not hear my music or my singing. You hear my voice precisely because you are not concentrating enough. Do you understand?'

At first, I wasn't sure that I did understand. However, she would be proved right and I soon found myself working harder at school and the results began to show. Within a few months I also managed to study at home and found that by practising concentrating I was able to block out all sounds, including my mother's singing. That piece of advice would stay with me throughout my education, including my days at Oxford. And she would give me more advice, telling me that understanding one's work was, in fact, far more important than simply learning it off 'parrot fashion' for hours on end.

Ben and I developed a fascination not only for science fiction and the adventures of Dr Who but also for science itself, particularly for theories about the origins of the Universe. We would spend whole afternoons discussing various hypotheses that we had come across in magazines designed to interest young people in scientific matters. We became so absorbed in science that, by the age of ten, we had studied and, I believe, understood the basics of Einstein's theory of relativity.

A film that captured our imagination was H G Wells' *The Time Machine*, starring Rod Taylor. We saw the film three times and would discuss everything we could remember about it. Also, Ben showed his generosity by spending his pocket money buying me a copy of H G Wells' *The War of The Worlds*. I treasured that book and read it many times over the years.

It was at about this time that my parents reached the decision to live apart. At the time I sometimes heard raised voices, but had no idea that they were planning to separate. From then on, my brother and I would spend weekdays with my mother in Chelsea and most weekends with my father in the country. While we were reasonably well-off, we were by no means super-rich and my mother had to work hard to support her two children. She toured the country with her group, singing and playing her guitar, writing magazine and newspaper articles and making documentaries for television. Sometimes I thought she worked herself too hard.

Often in the evenings when my brother and I returned from school, my mother would have to leave us eating our supper and spend several hours in the nearby recording studio. I loved to go and pass the time there listening to her recording and I quickly became friends with a number of her musicians. In the summer, if they had finished work when it was still light, we would go to the nearby park and play football.

At the time that my parents decided to live apart, my grandmother, who had been living in a house directly opposite our home in Shawfield Street, died and my father decided to live alone in his mother's former home. In those days, my father was working as an art dealer and he set up his office in the basement of his new house. This meant that, in effect, all that separated the family was thirty feet of concrete road.

My brother and I would spend time in both our parents' homes, sometimes watching a television programme at my father's place and then moving across the road for tea with my mother. Except for the fact that they occupied different houses, their separation made very little difference to our lives and to this day, especially having witnessed the acrimony involved in the divorce of so many of my friends' parents, I am truly grateful for the utterly civilised way in which my mother and father managed their split, placing the highest priority on not hurting my brother and me. They have remained the best of friends.

Ben and I loved our weekends at my father's house in the village of Haddenham, near Ely in the Fen country.

My father had bought The Pond, a small three-bedroom house, before I was born. In the early 1970s, the lady who lived in the house next door to The Pond died and my father decided to buy her property and join the two houses together by constructing a conservatory between them. In that fifty-foot long conservatory, he kept the mementoes and treasures of his days as an explorer in the jungles and islands of the South Seas. Huge tropical plants and large wood carvings, statues some ten feet high, dominated the all-glass conservatory. Inside the house, on bamboo rods, hung exotic-coloured sarongs from the South Sea islands, which my father used as curtains. The work of the Wai Wai Indians of the Amazon, with whom my father had lived in the 1950s — bows and arrows, eight-foot-long blow pipes, paddles with ornate carvings, sculptures to ward off evil spirits — adorned the walls.

Around the second house my father dug a mini-moat where two swans eventually settled. So tame did they become that they would swim around to the back of the conservatory while we were eating our meals, clamber up the grass bank and waddle up to our table where we would feed them by hand.

But it was the garden that fascinated Ben and me, for it extended over several acres and had a large lake. Moreover, we were free to wander across the extensive farmland that surrounded it. For two ten-year-old boys, used to living in the centre of London, the experience of so much land and the total freedom to roam and explore seemed almost magical.

Ben, Constantine and I would go fishing on the lake, hoping to catch pike. We would set off, going out early in the mornings and returning ravenous for lunch and again for tea in the evening. And it was at The Pond that I learned to cook, mainly fry-ups that I would prepare for the three of us when we came home. At night, in the summer, we would camp in tents in the large garden near the edge of the lake, looking at the moon and the stars through my father's binoculars.

I came to see my father's home, which I loved dearly, not as something exotic or extraordinary but as an extension of my father's character, as well as a testament to his earlier life.

My father would capture our imagination with his tales of life in the Amazonian rain forests. He would tell us of the two years he spent there, at night sleeping in a hammock slung between two trees, with the Wai Wai tribes of the northern Amazon; of swimming each morning in deep pools where caymans (a type of alligator) lived; of his long and arduous journeys by canoe into the interior. He would captivate us with the extraordinary colour slide-shows he put on at home showing us the animals, birds, flowers and fauna he had photographed on his expeditions. For young boys, it seemed like an enchanting and adventurous life, and one that I wanted to emulate.

During his slide-shows, I noticed that there was never any sign of a gun or rifle in his photographs. Similarly, at home, although our garden was teeming with rabbits, it seemed strange that my father never shot them. There were no guns in the house and one day I asked him why.

He explained that he did not approve of guns. During his early expeditions to the Amazon when in his twenties, only a single rifle would be taken for the purpose of shooting animals for food. Previously, adventurers had gone armed to the hilt with hand-guns, rifles and shotguns, and had upset and unnerved the Indian population who felt threatened. This had ended in tragedy on a few occasions.

His philosophy had always been to offer only friendship to the Indians and he believed that the way of earning their respect and trust was to go unarmed at all times. And it worked.

'But didn't you ever shoot, Daddy?' I asked him.

'Yes, I did,' he replied, and he went on to recount the last occasion that he had ever fired a gun.

During one of his expeditions to the jungles of the Amazon, my father had shot a curassow, a long-tailed black bird with a large, colourful crest that rather resembled a turkey. The bird's mate became so distraught during the next few hours, shrieking in distress and refusing to be parted from the carcass of its partner, that my father finally decided to put the bird out of its misery and killed it as well.

He told me, 'I think people generally underestimate just how capable of emotions the great majority of animals are. From that moment I decided never to shoot a living creature again.'

He explained that other birds, such as the albatross, were considered to be monogamous and I imagined in my young mind that my parents, too, should perhaps have been a little more like the albatross and the curassow and stayed together.

Although I was perhaps a little wild as a young boy, there was also a serious side to my nature and it was principally through the inspiration of my father that I developed, during my early years, a passion for learning. I would sit at the dining-room table in my father's conservatory and listen to him recounting his adventures while admiring his profound knowledge of the natural world. Even at that young age I realised that, while at times a little eccentric, my father possessed a truly enlightened and original mind, a view I still hold. I gauged the originality of his thought by one simple fact: never once did I hear him offer a second-hand opinion or utter a cliché. Every one of his ideas was his own. Whenever he read or heard something he would consider it for himself, never accepting it as the truth without having first pondered the matter or verified the facts for himself. And when we talked, he seemed genuinely interested in my views. I felt that he treated me like an equal and I loved him for it.

My father recognised in me the same spirit of adventure that had fired him as a young man. One day he told me: 'Darius, I worry for your generation because at least for me there were still one or two unexplored regions in the world where men could test themselves. Large tracts of the northern Amazon where I travelled, for example, were still uncharted territory in the early 1950s. But the world is becoming smaller and smaller, more and more dominated by states and large corporations, "civilised" and "developed for the benefit of man", we are told; in fact, tamed and ruined. Now there are no more mountains left to climb, no oceans to cross or rivers to ford, no dark interiors to explore. Soon, there will not even remain a square foot on the globe where so much as a rabbit will be able to pop his head out of his hole without in some way being photographed, measured, recorded. I wonder how those with free spirits will fit into such a world.'

Another quality that I admired in my father and that sprang from his rare ability to think for himself was his complete lack of any form of prejudice. Whenever he spoke, for example, of the Indians with whom he had lived for several years in the jungles of the Amazon, it was in terms not of 'natives' or 'savages', as they had been called by many of the white men he had met in Brazil or British Guinea where he had travelled, nor in the rather patronising manner of the missionaries with whom he had become acquainted and who had been sent to 'civilise' the indigenous population. Instead he talked of the Indians as his friends and equals. This was no affectation on his part, for our conversations were always private and he had no one to impress. Rather, he genuinely respected all his fellow men and creatures.

It was when I was about ten that I first fell in love. Tall and slim, with long fair hair that fell half-way down her back, Janine was a lovely Yugoslav girl who tantalised all the boys in her class. She seemed older and more streetwise than any of us and we saw in her the quintessential 'wild child' of the 1970s, smoking in the playground, kissing the boys, dancing to rock and pop music. Until that time I had always felt confident with the opposite sex, but Janine made me feel intimidated. I was not sure how I should approach her, wondering if such a girl would ever take any notice of me.

One winter's day, as I walked into the classroom after break, I noticed her at the window standing with her back to me. That morning I had written my name in the condensation on the window pane and I stood back as she drew a heart above my name and wrote the letter 'I' above that. She stopped, looked at what she had written and then quickly rubbed it all out. I was excited and very happy for I knew that my wildest hopes had been realised.

The following Wednesday, as usual, Ben and I went skating with others from the school at the Queensway ice rink. Janine and her best friend, Christina, came too.

As we skated around I noticed that the two girls were missing and saw them walking off the rink to a small alcove. After a couple more tours of the ice, I decided to go and see what they were doing. They were smoking out of sight of the teacher who always accompanied us. I realised that this was the opportunity I had been waiting for. I hobbled over to Janine on my skates, took away her cigarette and kissed her full on the lips. She responded, taking my breath away. It was the start of an exciting relationship that involved kissing and petting every Wednesday afternoon at the Queensway rink. I was in love.

For the next couple of years, Janine and I would enjoy a great time together but my relationship with Ben was also important and we remained close friends. Thankfully, he encouraged me to work hard and the three of us made sure that we studied diligently enough to pass all our examinations.

In order to enjoy my life with Ben and Janine, smoking cigarettes, going to the movies and reading scientific magazines, I decided to find a way of earning some extra money. Couscous and I came up with the idea of asking one of my mother's friends to teach us how to make biscuits, which we planned to sell to the neighbours. We would take over our mother's kitchen and make raisin-type biscuits that ended up looking decidedly home-made and probably didn't taste very nice either. Then we would go from house to house, asking our neighbours to buy some of them. No doubt we were able to sell so many becase we were very cheeky and because most of the adults who answered the door didn't have the heart to turn us away without buying a few.

Another ruse to raise money was to sell small Union Jack stickers, which we bought for 10p each and sold on to shoppers on the King's Road for the exorbitant sum of £1. We would walk along the road stopping people at random and, as with the biscuits, would rely more on sheer cheek than anything else.

'Please buy one of our stickers.'

If, however, our pleas were ignored we would shout, 'Don't you love your country, then?'

Usually, that did the trick and we would get our £1.

In this way we quickly became two of the richest boys at school. On the first evening we earned the remarkable sum of £20. We felt like millionaires and it also meant that I had money to spend on my Janine.

I was eleven years old and had learned a valuable lesson. It seemed to me that quite often boldness and cheek were essential ingredients for success.

Around my twelfth birthday, my parents told me that they wanted me to go to Eton. I had no knowledge of Eton except that it was England's most famous public school and, up until then, my only impression of boarding-schools had been acquired from watching the television series *Tom Brown's Schooldays*. I felt a mixture of apprehension and excitement.

One day my parents took me to the small town of Eton, across the River Thames from Windsor, and showed me around. I remember being impressed by the beauty of the buildings, the magnificent sports fields and the boys in their tail-coats which, even at that young age, I thought looked very smart. I realised though that my shoulder-length hair, of which I was rather proud, would have to go.

My parents explained to me that the primary reason they wanted me to attend Eton was because of its first-class academic record. I liked that. I had just finished reading both *War and Peace* and Charles Darwin's *Origin of Species*. My father had told me that he had read Darwin's book when he was twelve years old and I had been determined to equal his achievement.

For five years Ben and I had been best friends, almost brothers; and for two years Janine had been the most wonderful fun. But I knew I would soon have to leave and start life all over again.

There would be no passionate farewell with Janine because we both understood. When it came to saying goodbye, we kissed each other on the lips and said 'Good luck'. I never saw her again.

Ben and I had always wanted to go to Cambridge University together and we swore that we would see each other there when we were eighteen. It was a lovely summer's afternoon in July, 1977, when we said farewell to each other. It would be seven years before our paths crossed again.

II

According to genealogists who have examined all manner of documents including wills, trusts, records of births, marriages, deaths and so on, the Guppy family can be traced back with near certainty to 1253. Before that date, the name 'Guppy', originally 'de Guppy', seems to have derived from a Saxon called 'Gupa' whose house in the country outside Exeter was called 'Gupehegh', which means 'Gupa's Manor'.

Gupa was a lay monk who, from 1040 to 1070 was minister to the famous Bishop Leofric of Exeter. Bishop Leofric was renowned as a powerful man and a great scholar who, at his death, left a collection of over sixty books, considered in those days a remarkably large library. Oxford's Bodleian Library contains a work, *The Leofric Missal*, written in all likelihood by the Bishop himself, which opens with a description of how Godrich Gupa manumitted a group of slaves belonging to some Vikings. The name 'Gupa' meant 'Bright in Battle'.

The records show that in 1350 one of the wealthiest of the de Guppys, Walter, married an Isabella d'Aubigny and that they kept large homes in Westminster, London, and in the West Country, dropping the 'de' from the family name. Thereafter, from 1450 to 1830, the Guppy family and their descendants lived at Farway House in Farway-in-Chardstock, Dorset.

While some members of the Guppy family made fortunes, others lost them. One of those who fell into the former category was Samuel Guppy of Bristol, who lived from 1755 to 1830. Samuel invented the 'Patent Sheathing Nail', made of pure copper. The mild electrolytic effect created between the pure copper of the nail and the impure copper of the sheathing plates attached to the bottoms of ships in those days, meant that the hulls of British warships were kept free of barnacles and other marine growth. This, in turn, made these vessels travel faster through the seas and also meant that they were forced to spend far less time in dry dock having their hulls cleaned than their enemy counterparts. As a consequence, the British Admiralty viewed this ingenious invention as one of its secret weapons and considered it so valuable in its fight against the French and Spanish fleets during the Napoleonic wars that it paid Samuel Guppy the enormous sum of £40,000 for the rights to the design.

Samuel Guppy's second son, Thomas Richard, who lived from 1797 to 1882, became one of the most renowned engineers of his generation and was the man who originally employed and subsequently encouraged his childhood friend, Isambard Kingdom Brunel, in his many endeavours. Thomas designed and constructed the world's first modern iron steamship, the famous *SS Great Britain*, launched in 1843. With a group of friends from Bristol, he also founded the Great Western Railway and put up the money to launch it. In addition, he and his friend Brunel founded the Great Western Steamship Company.

Thomas's brilliance and foresight, however, were eventually lost to the nation for he suffered from tuberculosis and was advised to live in a sunnier climate. He, therefore, moved to Italy where he built ships for the Italian navy and designed and constructed the famous Iron Market in Florence.

Thomas's brother, Robert, a barrister who lived from 1808 to 1894, travelled as a young man to Trinidad to advise some relatives on various legal matters and fell so in love with the place that he settled there, becoming Mayor of San Fernando eleven times and a member of Trinidad's Legislative Council. He also founded the San Fernando–Port of Spain Railway.

Robert's wife, Amelia, was a brilliant and highly talented woman. A gifted painter, she had a tree-house built for herself in the forests outside San Fernando, where she would stay in order to be close to her subject matter — mainly insects and flowers. Her curiosity and natural sense of adventure led her, at the age of sixty-three, to navigate the Orinoco river in Venezuela in search of particularly beautiful breeds of orchids, accompanied by only a few Indians to paddle her canoe. Her various exploits earned for her the nickname 'Mad Amelia Guppy'. In fact she was not remotely mad, simply a woman ahead of her time who had the ability to think for herself. As history has repeatedly shown, those who possess such qualities, especially women, are often considered eccentric.

Robert and Amelia's son, Lechmere, my great-grandfather, lived from 1836 to 1916 and was a palaeontologist who discovered a new breed of fish in Trinidad which bears the family name, the Guppy fish. He married Alice Rostant, from a rich and famous French family that had moved to Trinidad in the eighteenth century. Alice bore Lechmere nine children.

My father, Nicholas Gareth Lechmere Guppy, was Lechmere and Alice's grandson and was born in Trinidad in 1925. He was educated there before leaving for England in 1938. He attended Trinity College, Cambridge, gaining an Honours degree in Botany and then Magdalen College, in Oxford, where he also studied at the Imperial Forestry Institute.

From 1948 to 1953 my father travelled widely throughout South America, conducting botanical and ecological expeditions and surveying the jungles of the Amazon. He returned to live in England in 1955 and worked as an adviser to *Life* magazine and Granada Television's Natural History Film Unit. His book about his travels in the Amazon and his life with the South American Indians, *Wai Wai*, was published in 1958 and is considered by many to be a classic of its genre.

Throughout the 1950s and 1960s, my father also became involved in buying and selling works of art and, in 1969, was invited to become Executive Vice-President and then Chairman of the Sovereign American Arts Corporation, a publicly quoted American company that dealt in works of art. It was during those years that he laid the foundations of his wealth. However, as my father would explain to me later, after a few years he felt that he could no longer continue working for Sovereign American Arts. 'I was interested in art and antiques but, perhaps understandably, the other directors of the company were more concerned with the bottom line, with making profits year in, year out. And the art market doesn't work like that. One must invest and wait patiently. So I left to continue my life's work.'

My father's passions were his botanical and ecological work, writing books, lecturing, organising and leading expeditions to exotic locations, and travelling widely. There were hardly any remote areas of the world, save for China and the former Soviet Union, that he did not visit. In 1969 he founded and became the first Chairman of 'Survival International', or 'The Primitive People's Fund', as it was originally known, a charity concerned with safeguarding the rights of the world's tribal peoples. At about this time he also edited *Animals* magazine, now the BBC's *Wildlife* magazine.

My father's life changed for the worse after he was persuaded by a friend to invest in Lloyds during the spring of 1981. He believed it would be a safe investment, persuaded that the professionals who ran Lloyds were utterly scrupulous and honest individuals.

However, within a few short years as his losses mounted, he rapidly began to lose faith in the institution of which he had become a 'name'. During the following decade he received only three small payments from Lloyds, as a number of syndicates into which he been placed recorded profits. However, these token payments were swamped by a deluge of demands that, in the end, he simply could not pay. In one year alone, he received a demand for more than £1.3 million, and that was after he had already paid out several hundreds of thousands of pounds to Lloyds.

Eventually, to pay the growing debt, he was forced to sell his house in Shawfield Street off the King's Road in Chelsea, the home his mother had left him in her will, as well as another house that he owned in the same street. This certainly dampened his spirit, but he really did feel cheated when he was forced to sell his house, The Pond, in Haddenham, the lovely nine-bedroom home of my youth set in several acres of lakes and gardens. That had been the place he truly loved, where he would relax and feel at ease with the world.

My mother, Shusha, was born in Tehran, into a family of distinguished and traditional Islamic scholars and administrators that, on her father's side, was directly descended from Muhammad, the Holy Prophet of Islam.

The Iran of my mother's youth, in the years that followed World War II, was a rapidly changing society, with the Shah pushing through a variety of Western-style reforms.

From the age of about five, when her teachers realised that she had a very distinctive singing voice, my mother would frequently be invited to sing at various school functions, invariably unaccompanied by musicians. She studied hard at the Lycée Princesse in Tehran and gained a first-class baccalaureat. At the age of fifteen, although she was considered something of a blue stocking, she also had a rebellious streak and joined the Communist Youth movement of Iran. A year later, she persuaded her parents to allow her to study in Paris where she quickly became captivated by the ideas of Sartre, Camus and Simone de Beauvoir and mixed with *rive gauche* intellectuals and artists.

In Paris, she read classical Persian and Arabic at the Sorbonne and, at the same time, attended numerous philosophy courses. Her father, a philosopher, would have been proud of his independently-minded daughter but she would never return to live in Tehran.

It was during her years in Paris that my mother's voice was trained and that she learned to play the classical guitar. In 1958, she produced her first record, a collection of traditional Persian folk songs. Having gained a good degree in Persian and Arabic, she set about earning a living, acting and modelling as she strove to launch a career as a singer.

In 1960, my mother moved to London to live with her beautiful elder sister who was married to an Iranian diplomat. As she would recount to me when I was a young boy: 'I was asked by a friend whether I would like to meet an Englishman, an explorer, a man described to me as romantic, eccentric, charming, amusing and highly intelligent. His name was Nicholas Guppy, your father. We met one evening in 1960 and the moment I saw him, I knew that he was the man for me. Two months later, we were married.'

Sadly, after ten years of marriage, when my parents found that they could no longer live together, they separated but on the friendliest possible terms.

In 1970, my mother began singing again in earnest as well as writing travel features for *Vogue* magazine and various national newspapers. In the early 1970s in Britain, folk singing became the rage and my mother's beautiful voice was in demand. She began by producing an LP of Persian love songs and over the years made a dozen or so further LPs of French, English and Persian songs. As her reputation grew, she became something of a cult figure. A number of her songs even became number-one sellers in her native Iran. Somehow, she was also able to be a devoted mother to her two growing sons.

When I was very young, my mother would tell me stories of her family and of my Persian ancestors and her childhood in Tehran.

One of my more famous forebears, my mother's maternal grandfather Haji Ali-Baba Alem, a High Court judge, was invited to produce a new Civil Code for Iran after Reza Shah had created a modern independent judiciary. He, in turn, enlisted his philosopher son-in-law, my mother's father, Mohammad Kazem, a prominent 'Mujtahed' (senior theologian), whose task it was to ensure that the new code did not conflict with the country's Islamic tradition. So successful was my great-grandfather's endeavour that even today the Code remains unchanged in its essential elements.

I also learned from my mother how my grandfather, Mohammad Kazem, had become Professor of Philosophy at Tehran University, the first Western-style University in Iran, where the cultural élite of the country had been gathered. He was considered by those who knew him, including many of the clergy, to be a saint-like figure in the great tradition of Islamic mystics whose admirers and devoted students would visit him in his home and talk to him late into the night about all manner of philosophical and spiritual matters.

My mother's elder brother Nassir, became the Deputy Prime Minister of Iran in the Government of Amir Abbas Hoveyda, the Shah's longest-serving Prime Minister. Nasser, my mother's younger brother, left Iran in his twenties and moved to Paris where he settled and became a successful and highly respected painter with an international reputation.

In 1988 and 1991, my mother wrote about her childhood in Iran and her student days in Paris in two books: *The Blindfold Horse* and *A Girl in Paris*. The former won a number of literary prizes, including the *Yorkshire Post* prize for best non-fiction work and was recently awarded France's prestigious *Le grand prix literaire des lectrices d'Elle*.

III

I settled down reasonably well in my first term at Eton, but there was no denying that I missed my parents, my brother and my friends at the Lycée. Although I respected and admired the traditions of Eton, I was surprised that, despite being totally different to my previous school, the aura of the place did not particularly phase me.

I soon became used to the distinctive school uniform of tail-coat, white shirt with stiff, detachable collar, waistcoat and dark pin-striped trousers and conventions such as 'capping' to the masters — the Eton form of salute — as well as the routine of chapel in the morning followed by classes and then games on the playing fields after lunch. The discipline, although contrasting with the more anarchic atmosphere of the Lycée, appealed to me.

However, customs such as the 'colours test' left me cold.

The colours test is conducted at the end of a new boy's first term when he and all his peers are gathered together in the 'library', the mess room of the senior pupils. During that first term, every new boy is expected to master the different colours of all the various Eton sports teams, both at school and at house level. This includes not only the major sports like rugby and cricket but also the minor, more obscure games such as beagling, racquets and 'Eton fives'. In short, there are literally hundreds of different colours that have to be learned.

Towards the end of my first Michaelmas term, or 'Half' as it is known in Eton parlance, the new boys in my house, The Hop Garden, were called into the library and told to stand in a semi-circle at the back of the large, dimly lit square room, while the senior boys who would interrogate us sat on raised tiers at the other end of the room.

They looked menacing, but I could tell that most of them treated the whole affair as a bit of a joke.

The senior boys would throw various shirts, caps and socks representing the different sports teams into the middle of the room. They would then quiz the new boys at random, demanding an instant answer as to what team or house the item of clothing represented. Failure to answer the question correctly would result in howls of derision and condemnation from the prefects. The wretched new boy would be made to feel ignorant and useless and would have a cross put against his name for future reference.

Occasionally, one of the prefects would walk along the line of new boys, waving a cane menacingly. In the old days, he might have thrashed a boy for making the slightest error. But those times had gone and although in some respects a deliberate atmosphere of intimidation was fostered, I could tell that the whole event was now only half serious.

One particular boy, however, who was short and slim with dark hair and buck teeth, committed the cardinal sin of failing to recognise our own house colours when a pair of socks — red with a black skull and crossbones — was thrown in front of him. At first there was a hushed silence as the senior boys drew in their breath, unable to believe the commission of such an outrageous blasphemy but then, a few seconds later, bellows of fury filled the room and half a dozen prefects charged towards the poor boy dragging him off for an embarrassing 'bog wash'.

This punishment was administered by the victim being held upside down by his ankles and having his head dipped into the lavatory while it was flushed. Having been subjected to this humiliation, the boy concerned returned with a brave face, grinning at his ordeal. He had learned a very important Eton code: to whinge is unacceptable and that whenever one has been embarrassed or made to look a fool, the only response is to laugh at oneself. Had he cried, his standing among his peers would have been severely diminished.

I knew that had I been asked the same question as that unfortunate boy, I, too, would have been the victim of a bog wash as I hadn't bothered to learn any of the colours.

However, I had deliberately positioned myself next to the house swot who I was aware had spent hours memorising every single colour. It was accepted that whenever possible all the new boys would help each other. So, whenever I was asked a question the swot, thankfully, was able to whisper the answer to me without being noticed. Unfortunately for the boy who had failed to recognise our own house colours, he had been targeted with such laser-like intensity by the prefects that no other boy had been able to give him the assistance he had so desperately needed.

Any unpleasant preconceptions about English boarding-schools that I may have had before going to Eton — of bullying being rife, for example — quickly disappeared once I got there. For the majority of my time there I found the masters, prefects, and 'fagmasters', who all boys serve in their junior days, to be kind and considerate. 'Fagging' had been an institution at Eton for centuries and many were the tales of boys having been flogged, abused and bullied. There was never any suggestion of such behaviour in my time there, although, as new boys, we still had to perform certain chores for the prefects, such as shoe-cleaning, making beds and preparing cups of tea and coffee.

My fagmaster, Jeremy Harley, would become something of a hero to me. Handsome, fair-haired and athletic, Harley was Captain of the House, a school prefect, a brilliant all-round sportsman and academically gifted. A few weeks into my first term, I was feeling particularly homesick and needed someone to talk to. Having run some errands for him one afternoon I returned to his room where he could see that I appeared upset.

'What's the matter?' he asked.

'Nothing,' I lied.

'Come on,' he said, 'sit down and have a cup of tea. I can see something's bothering you.'

I had been missing my family. I would lie awake at night remembering the warmth and affection of my parents and my brother and wishing I was at home. Most of the time I could cope very easily with my homesickness but, occasionally, it got the better of me.

At that moment I was close to tears, but I was determined not to appear a sissy by crying.

'You're homesick, aren't you?'

'You could say that,' I admitted.

He patted me on the shoulder and said, 'Don't worry, I was just like you. Enjoy yourself here; it'll soon pass, I promise you.'

Those few kind words meant a great deal to me. And he was right. Within a short time, my homesickness had indeed passed.

On my second day at Eton, I met the young man with whom I would share many exciting moments during the next fifteen years. We would forge a friendship that would endure through a roller-coaster ride of adventures. Charles Spencer, then Viscount Althorp, was in the same Classics class as me and sat a few seats away. He appeared easy-going, natural and unaffected. He was tall for his age with a mop of reddish-blond hair, fair skin and an engaging smile.

We would often meet up in our respective houses for a chat or go on runs together along the Thames towpath. Although Charlie had a fun nature, he was predominantly a serious teenager who studied hard and would obtain three 'A's in his 'A'-levels. He also became a prefect and Captain of his House.

When he was fourteen, his father, Lord Spencer, suffered a severe stroke and was close to death. This had a considerable effect on Charlie, for although his father survived, the realisation had dawned on him that, in the not too-distant future, he would have the daunting responsibility of running a large country estate.

At fifteen I became rebellious, resenting all authority. The prospect of masters and older boys ordering me about truly grated. Some of the boys who rebelled wanted to get caught in order to appear heroic to their contemporaries. In this respect, I was different. For me, the most important thing was not to be caught. I felt that avoiding detection and punishment was actually more subversive because, in doing so, I was beating the system devised by the authorities.

I adopted a James Dean haircut and a number of other boys in my house followed suit. Although it was only a small gesture, we felt that we were challenging the system for the great majority of boys at Eton were then sporting what we considered to be boring short-back-and-sides.

My acts of rebellion took the usual teenage expressions, smoking on the roof of the House at night, sneaking off through the fields to the cinemas in Slough and drinking in various pubs in Windsor and Datchet. Some of us must have looked far too young to be drinking alcohol, but the publicans simply turned a blind eye so long as we didn't become too rowdy.

In the Easter term of 1979, I and three friends decided to liven up a dull Saturday evening. One of us went into Windsor and bought a bottle of Scotch from an off-licence. A major difficulty involved in drinking at Eton would be to find a safe place to relax and have a party, as well as somewhere to hide the booze. Some weeks before, I had noticed a trapdoor in the ceiling of one of the passages on the second floor where the four of us had our rooms.

With my great friend, Juan Marquez, we decided to investigate. Equipped with a torch, Juan gave me a leg up to the trapdoor and, after scrambling inside, I pulled him up as well. Inside the enormous loft, which contained a multitude of wooden beams and extended above the entire house, there was plenty of room for us to sit and drink in secret. Disappointingly, we found a number of old whisky bottles, which rather annoyed me because it meant that we hadn't been the first to discover this hideaway.

That night the four of us clambered up into the roof and, within twenty minutes, the bottle was empty. One of the boys, cruelly nicknamed 'Rat', because of his two protruding front teeth, had taken enormous swigs and had all but passed out. Uncontrollable and unable to co-ordinate his arms and legs, to our alarm he began to shout and sing very loudly.

Every night prefects would patrol the corridors checking that all the boys were in their rooms. It was difficult enough getting down from the attic without detection when sober because the drop was more than ten feet, but with Rat singing 'Roll Out the Barrel' and unable to keep upright, it seemed certain we would be caught.

Somehow no one heard the commotion but once we had got him into his room, Rat's condition deteriorated and we began to panic. We knew that the Housemaster would be making his nightly rounds within the next ten minutes and if, as was likely, he came into Rat's room it would spell disaster for us all. One of us made strong black coffee and we poured it into him, desperately trying to sober him up. The rest of us undressed him and managed, after great efforts, to put him in his pyjamas as he thrashed around singing and shouting.

While one of the boys went to keep guard, I tried to force more coffee into him. But he kept mumbling, 'It's all Guppy's fault, it's all Guppy's fault.' I realised that if caught drunk, we would be taken to the Headmaster and receive a beating. More seriously, if after that we were ever caught drinking again, we could be expelled.

I grabbed Rat by the scruff of the neck, shaking him and slapping his face, infuriated that he had singled me out as being responsible for his condition. 'Pull yourself together, for God's sake, pull yourself together!'

The boy who was standing guard ran back to inform us that the Housemaster would be in our corridor within minutes. At this point Rat threw up everywhere, all over the floor and his bed. Realising that we were all about to get into the most serious trouble, I threw caution to the wind and sought the help of a House prefect whose room was at the end of the passage. I gambled that this older boy, Andrew Pickthorn, who had a reputation for being fair, might come to our rescue.

'Andy, we need your help. We're in real trouble,' I explained to him, out of breath from the exertions of trying to control my inebriated friend.

I explained everything that had happened and he came with me to Rat's room straight away. Rat was lying unconscious on his bed dressed in his pyjamas. A pool of vomit covered the floor.

In all the boys' rooms the single iron beds were screwed to the floor in such a way that, during the day, they could be pushed up against the wall, allowing far greater space in the room. Curtains would be drawn around the upright bed and straps would ensure that the mattress didn't fall down.

Pickthorn acted with great speed and intelligence. He decided that the only possible escape lay in pushing the bed up against the wall with Rat strapped unconscious inside it, his head near the floor and his legs pointing towards the ceiling. Having completed this manoeuvre, Pickthorn ran back to his room and picked up a can of deodorant spray and his very smart grey overcoat. He quickly returned and, without hesitating, threw the coat over the pool of sick, opened the window and sprayed the room with the deodorant.

'Get to your rooms and keep quiet,' he ordered as we fled from Rat's room, praying that by some miracle we would escape detection.

The Housemaster tapped on Rat's door and, hearing no reply, walked into the room. He saw that the window was open and that no one appeared to be in, closed the door and walked on down the corridor. He must have known that something was amiss because Rat should have been in his room at that hour of the night in a horizontal position on his bed. Afterwards, we wondered whether he had deliberately let us off the hook but we would never know.

Juan Marquez became one of my closest friends at Eton. Dark-haired, well-groomed, athletic and charismatic, Juan also had the most explosive temper. He came from a wealthy Spanish family, which had homes in Madrid and in Santander. Being a foreigner, Juan at first felt a stranger at Eton but because of his strength of character, as well as his physical build, he would soon win the respect of the House.

During the first few weeks, some of the English boys would tease and pick on him but not for long. Juan had a magically simple solution. Whenever an insult was thrown at him, he would offer the offender three seconds in which to apologise. If no apology was forthcoming, he would then lay into him until the boy recanted. Within a very short time the entire House had got the message, including the older boys.

From our first day at Eton, Juan and I gravitated towards each other. Like him, I knew that I had a slightly different outlook on life from most of the other boys at school because I was only half English. In addition, Juan and I were the only boys in our year who had been educated at co-educational day-schools before going to Eton. In particular, I admired Juan's exceptionally proud manner. The emphasis that he placed on personal honour was a quality that I found very attractive and, I also noticed, was not nearly so prevalent in many of those boys who came from conventional English backgrounds.

For our time at Eton, Juan and I were inseparable and would remain close friends long after our school days. On occasions we would take care of each other, especially when fights broke out. Some of our peers criticised us for being a little too ready to use our fists but in fact, at Eton, fights were not that common and Juan and I would challenge others only if we felt we had been deeply insulted, treated unjustly or wronged in some other way.

On one occasion, when I was fifteen, a rather foppish boy who had been goading me all Lent term, made a comment just as we were about to start a Mathematics class. 'Your mother looks like the back end of a bus,' he said.

As I sat down, Juan, who was sitting next to me whispered, 'You can't let him get away with that, Darius.'

I knew he was right. I looked across to check that the master wasn't about to walk in, stood up and threw myself across the room at him. I was in a fury. I smashed my fist into his face five or six times as he cowered at his desk. When I saw my hands covered in blood, I realised I had done enough. Some other boys shouted that the teacher was on his way so I straightened my tail-coat and went back to my seat.

Calling me by my Eton nickname, Juan patted me on the back and laughed, 'Well done, Darry, soon you'll be as tough as me!'

The fop would never insult me again and, strangely enough, we later became friends.

During my 'O'-level year, at the age of sixteen, I formed a club with a handful of my close friends. One of the great dangers that the more adventurous Etonians had to face was being caught drinking in the Windsor pubs. The penalty for this offence would be a beating; for a second offence, it could mean expulsion. And yet many of us would frequently take the risk.

Determined not to be caught, I would cycle around the back streets of Windsor searching out a secluded pub that was not patrolled by the masters or prefects, members of 'Pop', Eton's prefectorial body, whose duty it was to check that no Etonians were in Windsor out of bounds. From talking to one of the House prefects, I discovered which pubs were checked and eventually I found a picturesque little place, The Alma, which was tucked away in a quiet residential area of the town.

With two friends, Nick Matterson and Bruce Moore, who I knew to be absolutely trustworthy, I would visit The Alma nearly every Saturday night, playing pool, watching television, chatting and downing perhaps five or six pints of lager. Our secret drinking den, which we visited once a week for two years, would never be discovered.

Many of the boys who were on similar escapades were caught as they returned to Eton with alcohol on their breath. We realised, therefore, that we had to find a safe route to and from The Alma. There were only three ways to cross the Thames to reach Windsor and the motorway bridge and the Windsor to Eton pedestrian bridge were constantly patrolled. The third alternative, namely the railway bridge, which was a rather grand, Victorian, iron structure, was never checked.

My friends and I would meet under one of the arches on the Eton side of the railway bridge, which was in the shadow of a small beech tree. Climbing twenty feet or so up the tree, we could then swing from an upper branch and grab a metal railing that ran along the side of the bridge, hauling ourselves on to the bridge itself. Then, we would run as fast as we could along the track and across the Thames, trying to avoid being spotted. Sometimes a train would surprise us and we would attempt to look as nonchalant as possible, hoping that the driver would not report what he had seen.

During the summer term we developed a ritual that involved leaping into the river from the very top of the bridge, a height of perhaps sixty feet, when we returned tipsy after four hours or more in The Alma. On one occasion Bruce was just about to jump when I noticed a Thames pleasure boat passing directly beneath him. I yelled at him to stop. 'Jesus,' he said later, 'I would have been killed if you hadn't shouted.'

Surprisingly, I did also work. In particular, after taking my 'O'-levels, I applied myself to my studies, determined to get into Oxford or Cambridge.

In the summer term of 1981 I was walking down Eton's High Street, dressed in casual clothes, when three girls in a BMW whistled and called me over. They were all eighteen and the driver had only recently passed her driving test.

'Fancy a drive?' one of them asked.

I checked to see that no masters were around and climbed into the back. We drove around Slough and Windsor, laughing and joking. They dropped me off at Eton two hours later. The girls called themselves 'The Parachute Club' because they were all learning to sky-dive. Over the next two weeks I received a number of notes from them, asking for a meeting.

A couple of weeks later, they arrived at my House and we went out for another spin in the car. This time, however, the trip ended in a cul-de-sac in Slough and each girl took it in turns to clamber into the back for a kiss and a cuddle. We laughed, joked, kissed and petted and I felt the luckiest man in the world as these gorgeous, wild young girls drove me back to Eton.

Throughout the following year, my three sky-divers would visit three or four times a term.

One night during my final term at Eton, I awoke to a tapping at my window. It was 1am. I looked outside to see my three friends, who had been throwing pebbles to attract my attention. I was worried because my Housemaster, Tim Card, was in the next room. I felt sure he must have heard the noise. The girls beckoned me to come down and join them and I quickly threw on a shirt and a pair of trousers and made my way down the fire escape.

They all threw their arms round my neck, embraced me and said they were taking me for a drive. They had parked their car near the 'Burning Bush', one of Eton's famous landmarks and a stone's throw from my House. In fact, we never drove anywhere but all four of us stayed there for forty minutes kissing goodbye. I would never see them again.

The following morning Mr Card gave me a look, which I suspected meant that he had a very good idea what I had been up to the previous night. It was an unwritten code at Eton that as long as the older boys were discreet in their misdemeanours and, in particular, never led on the younger boys, then the more liberal masters would usually turn a blind eye.

An example of this practice occurred when an older boy in another house had been sitting by the open window of his room smoking a cigarette late at night. Suddenly, he heard his Housemaster approaching along the corridor outside, followed quickly by the inevitable knock. As the door opened, he threw his cigarette out of the window, fearing his Housemaster would smell the tobacco smoke. Thinking on his feet and in a desperate bid to stop his Housemaster entering the room, he shouted, 'Wanking! Wanking!'

There was a pause and the boy waited, wondering whether his ruse had been successful. Relieved, he watched as his Housemaster's silhouette withdrew quietly, closing the door discreetly behind him.

The following afternoon, his Housemaster called the boy into his study and with a smile put it to him tactfully, 'I have no objection to your masturbating, but in future would you kindly refrain from doing it out of the window?'

Other boys were not so fortunate. A friend of mine was expelled when he was caught *in flagrante delicto* with an admiral's beautiful daughter. Then eighteen, he was a popular chap and many boys considered that he had been unfairly treated in view of the fact that, sometime before, two boys had been caught in bed together and had been dealt with far more leniently.

I was always fairly treated by my housemaster, Tim Card. A bachelor in his late forties, Mr Card was 6ft 2ins tall, powerfully built and had thick, black curly hair swept back from his forehead. Card was popular with the boys, highly intelligent, very fair, rather shy and a first-rate teacher. He also had a sense of humour.

Every evening at 8.30pm, he would summon all the members of the House to the dining-room for evening prayers. Once, on the occasion of his birthday, he announced after prayers, 'Thank you all very much for your kind present. You may like to know that today I am forty-nine.' Pausing, he smiled and added, 'You could now say that I'm a perfect square!'

Throughout my five years at Eton, I had a good relationship with Mr Card. He was by no means a soft touch; indeed, whenever I was out of line or misbehaved he would punish me, usually ordering me to assist him for several hours in his beloved garden of which he was very proud and which he had turned into one of Eton's finest.

I also developed an understanding friendship with the House Dame, Anne Froggatt, the matron assigned to look after the boys' domestic needs. A former nun in her sixties, 'M Dame', as she was known, would become popular with all the boys. During our 'A'-level exams she would invite us to her apartment in the House and give us hot drinks because she believed these would help us relax and sleep well before our exams.

One night I stayed behind and we had a chat. We had been talking of the years she had spent in a convent and about religion in general. Out of the blue, she said, 'Did you realise, Darius, that you have very monastic qualities?'

Surprised, I asked, 'What makes you say that?'

I had never seen myself as particularly monk-like, especially in view of my rebellious attitude to many of the school rules, my interest in girls and the fact that I had spent most Saturday nights during the past few years secretly drinking with my friends in The Alma.

She went on, 'I must tell you, Darius, that consistently, in fact every term, you are the boy who spends least money on himself.'

It was the Dame's responsibility at the end of term to collate each boy's bills for items such as clothing, stationery, medicines, books, sports equipment and tuck.

I had no idea until that moment that I enjoyed quite a spartan life and I told her, 'Believe me, it's not deliberate. I have whatever I need but I suppose I'm just not a very extravagant person.'

I would leave Eton with three 'A's in English, History and French 'A'-levels, but those first-class results had not been achieved without work and application. I had played both the Eton 'Field game', a hybrid of rugby and soccer, and football but had never found the inclination to excel at them. The sports I preferred were boxing, which had been banned at Eton before I arrived, and kick-boxing which had never been an Eton sport. Another passion of mine had been for long-distance running and I also enjoyed another lonely sport, single sculls. I loved to row alone and would spend hours during the summer term rowing down the Thames from the Eton boat-house to Queens Eyot, an island some miles away. I relished the intense physical exercise, timing myself against the clock, and discovered that the solitary sports encouraged a great concentration of body and mind.

Throughout my years at Eton, Charlie Spencer and I had become friendly but because we were in different Houses our paths had not crossed that often. Whenever we found ourselves together, however, we would often gently tease each other, as we did with everyone we were friendly with, but not in a vicious way. It was our way of showing affection towards those we liked.

During school holidays we would also see each other occasionally. Once, I remember asking Charlie what must have seemed a slightly naïve question — was the Diana Spencer I was reading about in the newspapers his sister?

He replied, in a quiet voice, 'Yes, it is actually,' and I sensed he didn't wish to discuss the matter any further.

The next time Charlie spoke to me of his sister was on a cold, sunny February morning in 1981. We bumped into each other on the way to early morning assembly.

'Good morning, Darry,' he said.

We talked about school matters and just before we parted he said, 'By the way, Diana's announcing her engagement to Prince Charles this morning.'

'Really?' I replied. 'When is it being officially announced?'

'In a few hours' time.'

As we parted I felt happy for Charlie on the one hand, but I also had misgivings that his life would never be the same again. People would want to know every tiny detail of his private life and the Press would never leave him alone.

During my final year at Eton, I applied myself to achieving good 'A'-levels and getting a place at Oxford University and at the end of the Michaelmas term of 1982, I learned that I had been accepted by Magdalen College to read History and French.

Leaving Eton was a more emotional experience than I had imagined it would be. I had forged marvellous friendships, many of which I have maintained to the present day. Some of my friends, such as Juan, had been like brothers to me. It is this sense of camaraderie that is, without doubt, the single aspect of my school days that I miss the most.

Many people consider it trendy or politically correct to criticise Eton, a trend which is quite common, strangely enough, among Old Etonians. While I believe passionately in greater social equality, I do not believe that the route to achieving it requires an envious attack on excellence, and there is no denying that Eton is an excellent school.

On my final day, I packed and said tearful farewells to my friends. As I walked down Common Lane, I bumped into Charlie outside his House. He was loading his belongings into his car.

'Well done, Darry,' he said to me. 'I hear you got into Magdalen.'

'Thanks, Charlie. I hear you did likewise. Congratulations,' I replied. 'I look forward to reading History with you. Good luck and I'll see you there next September.'

'Good luck, Darry,' he said, shaking my hand. 'I'm sure we'll have a lot of fun together at Oxford.'

IV

I was enjoying a cup of afternoon tea in a New York apartment on the Upper East side when my mother took a phone call. She had come over from London to help an old friend of hers, Edwina Sandys, stage a major trade exhibition entitled 'Britain Salutes New York' and I had flown from Los Angeles, where I had been taking a working holiday before going up to Oxford, to join her.

My mother's face appeared to pale as she handed me the phone. 'It's your father.'

'Darius, I have some bad news,' my father told me. Then he hesitated.

'Look Dad, don't beat about the bush. Please explain. What is it?'

'You must listen carefully, Darius, because it's terribly serious.'

'Please just tell me.'

'You remember my informing you that I was a member of Lloyds?'

'Yes, of course I do. Why?'

'Well,' he continued, 'they've just sent me a massive demand for money and all the forecasts are that they might have lost me everything.'

'What?' I exclaimed.

'It means we could be wiped out, everything we own may have to go — the house in the country, the paintings, everything I've worked for and hoped one day to hand on to you and your brother.'

My mind was spinning, hardly able to take in what my father was telling me.

'But Dad,' I said, 'how could you have got yourself into such a position?'

I had some idea of how Lloyds of London worked, but had never bothered to find out the precise mechanics of its underwriting and syndication system. In that instant, I promised myself to make it my business to study and learn everything I could about Lloyds simply to discover how such a situation could have arisen.

He replied, 'It's more complicated than you think. I'll explain everything to you when you return home. But it's not only me in such trouble; there are literally thousands of people in the same situation. Judging from the facts that are beginning to emerge, Lloyds are going to have a hell of a battle on their hands.'

The shock of my father's potential ruin hit me hard. I desperately wanted to get back home to talk with him at length and learn all I could about the débâcle that was threatening him with financial disaster. Perhaps unfairly, I kept on castigating him in my mind for having gambled all his money, no matter how safe and apparently respectable Lloyds had seemed.

The news ruined my exciting working holiday. I had flown to America four months earlier with just $200 in my pocket, determined not to be a burden on my parents. I had found work in Los Angeles painting a beautiful sailing yacht and had been given permission to sleep in the crew's quarters. I had been forced to work not only to feed myself, but also because I had only asked my father for a one-way ticket to the States, determined to earn my living and use any money left over for my return fare. Eventually, I had earned enough to buy a 500cc Honda trails motorbike on which I would bomb around LA, driving like a maniac and never wearing a helmet. I must have been mad.

In Los Angeles, I had met a group of Englishmen of my age who lived together in a Culver City apartment and survived working as waiters. I had moved in with them and had soon found myself playing Jeeves at various Hollywood bashes.

At one particular party I can remember chatting to Kirk Douglas, Gregory Peck, Liza Minnelli, Frank Sinatra and some other celebrities. It was all great fun.

In my spare time, I had learned how to strip and repair motor bikes and at night, I would ride down to Venice beach and walk along the sands mixing with the young locals, roller-skating, working-out or jogging. And I had met and fallen for a beautiful, older Californian girl, tall, blonde and long-legged who took me under her wing and introduced me to all her friends as 'my Englishman'. We enjoyed our times together and she had shown me every aspect of LA life.

The day after my father's devastating phone call, I visited a library to consult back issues of *The Financial Times* and *The Wall Street Journal* and read any article I could find about Lloyds of London, but by the end of the day I was still no wiser about exactly how Lloyds operated.

Later that day I spoke again to my father on the phone, trying to glean as much information as possible. Slowly I would come to realise as I investigated the facts for myself over the next few months and years, that he had not, in fact, been as foolish as I had originally assumed, nor had he gambled the family's money in a reckless way. Instead, in many respects he had been duped and, like thousands of victims ruined at the hands of unscrupulous and dishonest Lloyds' professionals, had been the victim of incompetence, negligence and perhaps even fraud.

On the flight back to London, I became more and more angry. I was convinced we would lose The Pond, our cherished home of twenty years. I remembered all the magical times, fishing from a boat on the lake, camping out in the garden with my brother, playing in the woods and sitting round a log fire on winter evenings. The thought of everything that had made those memories possible being snatched away made me burn with anger.

By the time I landed at Heathrow I had vowed that, whatever the cost, those who were responsible would pay.

*　　　*　　　*

America had been a new experience for me and I had enjoyed a society that seemed genuinely less class-obssessed than the one I had been used to in England. There, nothing seemed impossible no matter how lowly one's background and beginnings in life. I had seen how America's culture encouraged free thinking and the pioneer spirit and wondered if Britain would ever achieve such goals. At the same time, the puritanical side of my nature had made me appreciate that such a spirit unchecked can rapidly degenerate into a culture of hedonism and the creation of vast gaps between the hugely wealthy and those on the breadline.

I had done well for myself in America. I had enjoyed working hard and back in Britain I got off the plane with £2,000 in my pocket.

A few weeks later I was walking down the King's Road on a warm

May day when I saw a D-registration British Racing Green MGB roadster with wire wheels being driven slowly with the roof down, by a forty-year-old, slightly balding, former hippie.

I walked towards his car and called out to him, 'How much do you want for the car?'

'Sorry, it's not for sale,' he shouted back.

'Are you sure?' I asked, taking a wad of notes from my back pocket.

He pulled to the side and stopped. 'Are you serious?' he asked.

'Yes, of course I am,' I said, 'otherwise I wouldn't have stopped you.'

'Straight up?'

'Yes,' I replied. 'Let me have a look at it.'

I knew absolutely nothing about cars and relied instead on what I had learned about motor bikes in LA. The man opened the bonnet and I pretended to understand what I was looking at. Examining the car, I checked to see if there was any rust, reckoning that the vehicle was almost twenty years old.

After a few minutes, I asked him again, 'Tell me, how much will you sell it for?'

We haggled for about five minutes. He wanted £1,200 but I was only prepared to offer a maximum of £950. I refused to budge and it soon became clear he was interested in my offer. I showed him that I had cash to prove that I wasn't bluffing and eventually he accepted my offer. I agreed to meet him later that day at his Fulham flat and a few hours later I drove away, the proud owner of an MGB sports car.

Four months later, I drove up to Magdalen College, Oxford, to start some of the most exciting years of my life. I had been fortunate in finding accommodation in the beautiful eighteenth-century New Buildings, rather than in the modern Waynfleet building over the Cherwell River, which had been built in the 1960s and was where the great majority of Magdalen 'freshers' began their university life. Throughout my years at Oxford, I never tired of the architectural splendour of Magdalen with its cloistered quadrangle, its beautiful chapel and its spectacular bell-tower, Oxford's most famous landmark.

I even managed to persuade the college porters, one of whom was a former policeman and another a champion onion grower, to let me park my car outside New Buildings, an unheard-of privilege. It would remain there for the time I spent in college.

I met up with Charlie Spencer on Freshers' Night, the formal dinner for the new undergraduates held in the college dining-hall. He and I sat near each other and spent most of the dinner chatting together. At the end of the meal Charlie poured me a large goblet of vintage port, rather than the tiny glass everyone else was using for their after-dinner drinks.

'Down in one, Darry,' he challenged me.

I downed it in one. It was the start of a drinking bout that went on until the early hours of the morning. After three or four goblets of port, each holding perhaps half a pint, I was feeling distinctly drunk.

'Man or mouse?' Charlie would say in a loud voice, holding a fresh decanter and ready to pour me another huge goblet. He knew that I would never back down.

'Man, of course!' I shouted back at him. And, with a yell, he would pour two more goblets that we would both empty in one. The dinner was over shortly after 10pm but we finished drinking sometime after 3am. I could never remember how the evening ended or how I managed to find my way back to my rooms.

The next day we all had to be on parade for the official Magdalen College freshers' photograph. I felt like death. Charlie did the decent thing, however, and came round to my rooms to see if I was still alive and capable of appearing for the photograph. Somehow I managed to make the photo call, but I would never drink port again during my three years at Oxford.

'Man or mouse' became the phrase we would employ to spur each other on to tackle whatever challenge had been laid down by the other. Neither of us ever said the word 'mouse', for that would have been an admission of spinelessness. Such challenges were to cover an array of incidents involving women, drinking bouts or foolish, dare-devil antics.

During my second year at Oxford I co-edited with another friend, Boris Johnson, the satirical university magazine *Tributary*, which specialised in poking fun at fellow students in a friendly, non-malicious way.

On one occasion, *Tributary* decided to make a promotional offer in the way that many women's magazines often do with samples of products, such as perfume, shampoo and so on. We dreamt up the idea of offering students a 'love potion' to spice up their sex lives. Not having the slightest idea what to use for such a potion, I contacted Max Factor, the cosmetics firm, asking whether we could have two thousand sample phials of their latest scent, Le Jardin, for a promotion.

Four of us spent the best part of a night sticking these phials on to the front of each copy of the magazine, advertising them as 'love philtre'. That particular issue sold out almost immediately. We never knew what Max Factor thought of the promotion because, after providing the samples and seeing the magazine, they did not contact us again.

My first two years at Oxford were a round of parties, womanising and long nights of serious drinking. Social life revolved around various dining societies, the most renowned of these being 'The Bullingdon', referred to in Evelyn Waugh's satirical novel *Decline and Fall* as the Bollinger Club. Although The Bullingdon had the reputation of being Oxford's most distinguished dining-club, many undergradutes rather frowned on its flamboyance and ostentation.

While membership of The Bullingdon brought with it much riotous fun, inevitably there were also certain drawbacks, the most obvious being the severe strain on members' cash flow that resulted from the very expensive dinners, which always included champagne and the best French wines. These dinners were invariably held at the most expensive restaurants in Oxford and The Bullingdon 'uniform' of a navy-blue tail-coat with white silk lapels and gold buttons, coupled with a canary yellow waistcoat, cost nearly £1,000.

Since the club was restricted in number to only two dozen undergraduates at any one time, the election process for membership was always a very intense and rowdy affair. It was usual for the voting procedure to take place in a member's rooms at three in the morning after a night of high living and heavy drinking.

Elections, at which members would put forward their candidates, were held at the end of every term. On one such occasion Charles Spencer was elected, but declined the invitation. Perhaps understandably, he did not want to be associated with what were perceived as raffish societies. At the end of one term I put forward a great friend of mine, Radek Sikorski, a Pole and a supporter of Solidarity who had agitated against the ruling Communist junta in his home country. Radek was striking-looking, with short, straight blond hair, broad, high cheek-bones and rather Slav features. I liked him because he was different and more adventurous, it struck me, than many of the other undergraduates. He had lived under the yoke of an oppressive regime in Poland and had shown the courage and imagination to rebel against the system. His natural sense of adventure would demonstrate itself when, after leaving Oxford, he travelled to Afghanistan to write a book about the Mujaheddin's resistance to the Soviet invasion of 1979. The work, *Dust of the Saints*, was a gripping account of the heroic lives of a group of resistance fighters.

Radek's election took place in the rooms of Toby Mansell-Pleydell, the President of 'The Buller', as we affectionately called it, in University College. Toby was one of The Buller's members who I admired most because, although he had had a conventional upbringing, he also possessed a very romantic nature with which I identified. His love of adventure would take him to Hungary after going down from Oxford, where he would set up his own business. I suspect that, like me, deep down he considered the twin sister of individualism to be the spirit of anarchy.

It was 4am at the end of a summer term, when we were all in particularly aggressive moods, shouting and screaming abuse at each other. Some of us had to be parted repeatedly by the more sober members, like boxers in a clinch being separated by the referee.

I suspected that the opposition didn't want Radek as a member because he was a foreigner, a Pole, who they believed might diminish the 'tone' of the club and whose image simply wasn't right for The Buller.

'Not suitable material' was the phrase many used that night in an effort to comdemn Radek.

'Just because he's not some fucking English poof!' I yelled. 'That's the truth of why you won't elect him! We want people with balls in this club, not just a load of Hooray-Henry wimps like you!'

One member leapt to his feet, 'If he's voted in, Darry, then I'll bloody resign!'

'Go on then, bugger off!' I shouted. 'This club needs new blood otherwise it'll become like the English upper class, inbred and effete.'

After several more hours of argument the Radek supporters, including Toby, the President of the Club, finally forced the issue and he was voted in. It gave me great pleasure to drive immediately to his rooms in a private house in Oxford, bang at his door and be the first to congratulate him. From his face it was clear that he was speechless, and indeed positively alarmed when all twenty-three members crashed into his rooms, turning the place upside down in the traditional manner of welcoming new members to Oxford's most exclusive dining society.

Shortly after our arrival, a bemused and wary landlady came downstairs in her dressing-gown. Taking in the scene of devastation, she sought an explanation.

'It's his birthday, baby,' I said, rather sheepishly. It was the best I could come up with. Still, the answer seemed to satisfy her, because she shrugged her shoulders and walked back upstairs.

My own election had, likewise, been a tightly fought issue. Boris Johnson, my co-editor at *Tributary*, a friend from Eton and now a prospective Tory candidate for Parliament, had put my name forward. As I learned from him later, the Club had been sharply divided. But I would never discover the issues they had fought over.

Despite the outrageous cost of the dinners, which usually amounted to £400 a head at 1984 prices, members of the dining society had found an expedient solution to the problem of how to subsidise those who were less well-off and could not afford the exorbitant bills — a few undergraduates from very wealthy backgrounds were invited to become members and were left in no doubt when they joined that their generosity would be much appreciated.

During those elections in which such pragmatism was called upon, opposition to candidates on the grounds of their backgrounds or their ethnic origin would evaporate instantly when it was learned that they were suitably wealthy. On one particular occasion, an Indian undergraduate was keen to join the club. When his name was initially put forward, certain of the society's members appeared a little startled.

'Doesn't that gentleman hail from the sub-continent?' one of them sniffed.

Before anything further was said another, more tolerant, member spoke up, 'Quiet please, gentlemen. Listen to me. I think you should all know that this candidate is from a very wealthy Indian family and, as I understand it, he has the reputation of being a most generous young man.'

There was silence as everyone looked at each other, quietly nodding approval. A vote was taken and the Indian undergraduate was voted in, overwhelmingly. Throughout the next few terms he would happily pay four to five thousand pounds for the Bullingdon dinners, enabling the less solvent members to contribute perhaps only two hundred pounds a time. Minding not one iota, he was happy to demonstrate his munificence.

As I left that meeting I shook my head in resignation and smiled to myself. 'How typical of the English establishment,' I thought. 'They take exception to peoples' backgrounds yet will happily grovel before them if they happen to be rich.' I was reminded of British politicians bowing before the every whim of Arab oil sheiks.

As well as the expensive dinners for which it was famous, the Bullingdon also threw champagne breakfasts once a term, usually taking over a well-known hotel like The Bear in nearby Woodstock, close to Blenheim Palace. Invariably two or three top-class strippers from London would be invited to attend and would be heralded into the dining-room when the champagne had been flowing for some time.

One or two of the more inebriated members would be selected by the strippers who, having divested themselves of their clothes, would make sure they were given special attention. Sitting on their knees, the strippers would bury the faces of these barely conscious individuals in their ample bosoms and excite others to take whatever liberties they wanted. The shouts and cheers from the dining-room would be evidence of how well the strippers were doing their job. They would always be well-paid for their services and would never become annoyed, even when the more drunken undergraduates went too far.

In my second year at Oxford, I was elected to the notorious 'Piers Gaveston Society', another Oxford dining-club with a reputation for depravity and throwing parties which, so legend had it, would inevitably degenerate into orgies.

One of the most infamous men in English history, Piers Gaveston, had been the lover of King Edward II (1284–1327). The King had showered gifts, Royal estates and treasures on his young favourite, who rapidly became the most powerful man in the realm. In 1312, the jealous Barons rebelled, seized the luckless Gaveston and executed him. An even worse fate would befall Edward II for, having deposed him in favour of his son Edward III, the barons had first imprisoned Edward and had then put him to a grizzly death in Berkeley Castle by forcing a red-hot poker into his rectum.

Although the Society itself consisted of only a dozen members, the parties thrown by The Piers Gaveston at the end of each term were certainly extravagant affairs. In my Oxford years, the leading luminary of the club was Gottfried von Bismark, the great-grandson of the famous

19th-century German Chancellor. Tall, slim with a huge forehead and swept-back hair, he appeared the quintessential German aristocrat. Charming, amusing and intelligent, Bismark became close friends with Olivia Channon, the daughter of the Tory Minister Paul Channon, who had arrived at Oxford at the same time as me.

I had first met Olivia at a party at Tiffany's in New York during the 'Britain Salutes New York' festival. We had got on exceptionally well and I found her amusing, attractive and, although she could appear haughty to some people, wonderfully self-deprecating. At Oxford, we would often chat into the early hours of the morning and Olivia soon became 'one of the boys', a popular figure, especially with the male undergraduates.

At most Piers Gaveston parties members and their guests, both male and female, would be asked to attend in outrageous fancy-dress costumes. Some would arrive in military uniform, others dressed as knights in suits of armour while others wore flamboyant, long evening gowns, made up with lipstick and eye-liner. Many of the girls would arrive in 1920s Charleston-style evening dresses, with beads and black boas. However, despite the historical Gaveston's homosexuality, the great majority of the club's members were healthily heterosexual and enjoyed any opportunity to prove their virility.

Typically, the guests would arrive at ten o'clock in the evening and the party would rage on through the night. Drink and occasional drugs dominated the proceedings and, as people became more relaxed, they would also lose their inhibitions. Couples would move off into bedrooms in the early hours and sometimes three or four groups would disappear into a bedroom together.

In fact, although these parties had a reputation within the University for utter debauchery, I suspect that a lot of the flamboyant goings-on were more the product of a desperate attempt by certain undergraduates to out-bid each other in depravity, as it were, than of any genuine wildness of spirit. I am sure that in the company of their parents or in the presence of polite society, these same young irrepressible souls became the very models of sobriety and respectability. The fact that so many of them are now merchant bankers, advertising executives, civil servants and prospective MPs seems to illustrate my point.

Understandably, the activities of these various societies caused consternation among the more serious undergraduates, who viewed our excesses as offensive and a little too much like Waugh's *Brideshead*

Revisited. But I always suspected that such moral posturing may in fact have been a cloak for pure and simple envy.

In my final year a number of Magdalen women undergraduates decided to take action and to single me out for censure. A body of them, calling itself the Magdalen Women's Group, had been formed with the aim of debating its members' grievances against a number of the college's male, and sometimes even female, students.

Its initial meeting was a much publicised event in which the first motion to be discussed and voted upon was billed as: 'Henceforth, Magdalen women will not pander to the whim of Darius Guppy.' Needless to say, the motion was carried overwhelmingly. However, much to the annoyance of those who had engineered this public relations exercise, far from having the desired effect of humiliating me and causing me to be ostracised, the entire episode achieved the very opposite and secured my reputation for the rest of my time at Oxford and beyond!

Despite my rakish image among some at Magdalen, I did, in fact, have some wonderful relationships with a number of undergraduates, although many of these relationships were based on friendship rather than purely physical attraction. Of course, like the majority of my peers, I enjoyed the fun times and the outrageous parties and joined in with enthusiasm, but my fonder memories are of taking my girlfriends for long walks by the Cherwell, listening to classical music in their rooms long into the night, and enjoying romantic candle-lit suppers. I don't know if I ever actually fell in love during my days at Oxford but I did always enjoy these relationships which, generally, were based on mutual trust and a determination to enjoy our days at Oxford to the full, not wanting to waste a single moment of our time there. There were, however, the occasional tears, which I couldn't stand and would shy away from mainly because I feared that too deep an involvement might impede my determination to play hard and work hard. And, throughout my three years at Oxford, I realised above all else that I had to leave with a good degree.

When I arrived at Magdalen in September 1983, my immediate task was to pass my History 'Prelims', or Preliminary Exams, which would be held three months later at the end of the Michaelmas term. This meant that I had to get down to hard work straight away. It was vital to pass these Prelims because those who failed would be 'sent down' (expelled) from the University. I was fortunate to have as my History tutor the famous Professor Karl Leyser and in that first term he taught me in my chosen subject, 'The Barbarian Invasions of the Roman Empire'.

Like me, Professor Leyser had rooms in New Buildings. On my first day back after the Christmas holidays I was walking up the wooden stairs that led to my room with a girl friend on my arm when we met the Professor.

The charismatic Karl Leyser, took off his felt Austrian hat, bowed low to my friend, and said in his deep German voice, 'Mr Guppy, you have covered yourself in distinction.'

'That's a rather nice way of putting it,' I thought to myself.

Up until that moment I had had no idea whether I had passed my History Prelims, but the Professor seemed to be telling me that I had. He went on, 'You have achieved a *bene*,' meaning that I had gained a distinction. I smiled at him and thanked him because I had genuinely enjoyed all the tutorials he had given me in his private rooms and I knew he had been the inspiration that had helped me achieve this result.

Before going up to Oxford I had always had a keen interest in History, and had concentrated on the nineteenth and twentieth centuries. At Oxford, I would become passionate about the subject in general, but in particular about the French Revolution. Dr Laurence Brockliss, a tall, slim young man with great personal magnetism, who I admired for his egalitarian and enlightened attitude regarding all political matters, would be responsible for encouraging my enthusiasm for the subject. Both Charlie Spencer and I had decided, after only a few tutorials, that we wanted to specialise in the French Revolution because we had found in Dr Brockliss a man who could inspire us.

Many tutorials, scheduled for one hour, would last far longer while Dr Brockliss and I debated, sometimes heatedly, various aspects of the French Revolution. I appreciated the way that Dr Brockliss, as well as my other tutors, seemed genuinely interested in their students' views. They treated their pupils as equals and I came to understand that the crux of Oxford's teaching method is the unique relationship that is fostered between master and disciple. It seemed a far better method of encouraging enthusiasm for a given subject than simply giving lectures to large groups of students.

Instinctively, both Charlie and I sided with the Revolutionaries, as did Dr Brockliss. I admired the fact that despite Charlie's background he, too, should want to identify with those who had sought to overthrow the established regime. Our heroes were men like Robespierre, Danton and the young Bonaparte. I became so inspired by these historical figures that I would learn by heart long tracts of the speeches they had delivered to the National Assembly.

From my Oxford studies, and in particular my learning about the French Revolution, I formed a view of history that led me to believe that the development of mankind had always been a matter of the 'haves' exploiting and oppressing the 'have nots'. I was no Marxist and yet I found myself adopting distinctly left-wing views.

After weekly lectures given at Balliol College by Dr Colin Lucas, an authority on the French Revolution, Charlie and I would walk the half mile back to Magdalen along Broad Street in the frosty winter evenings, arguing passionately about the lecture we had just heard and I was happy that his views were very similar to mine.

These men, Professor Leyser, Doctors Brockliss and Lucas, as well as my other tutors such as Dr Angus MacIntyre, who taught me Political Theory including Aristotle and Hobbes, Dr John Stoye who tutored me in the eighteenth-century Enlightenment, Dr Gerald 'Bomber' Harris with whom I studied the English Reformation, and Doctors Toby Garfitt and Alan Raith, my French tutors — all commanded my respect more than virtually anyone I have met since.

My relationship with my various tutors at Oxford crystallized my attitude towards authority in general. Since those days, many have seen me as anti-authority, no doubt because of my crime and my subsequent defiance towards the system, but I believe that the relationships I built up with these men gave me a basis on which to judge others later. I happily accepted the authority of my tutors because they inspired it by their intelligence, their manners, their grace and their attitude towards everyone, not simply their students. I have never been able to stomach being ordered about by people who believe that their position in society is sufficient to demand and command the respect of others. For me, the person in a position of power should earn it rather than expect it by right. After leaving Oxford, however, I would find that far too many people in positions of authority would assume that I should respect them as if my respect was theirs by right. This facet of my personality would cause me certain problems later in life, irritating to the point of distraction many of those with whom I would come into contact, in particular the police, the prosecution lawyers, Lloyds' lawyers, the judge at my trial, the prison service and also certain sections of the Press.

Besides our tutors, Charlie and I also became great friends with the Magdalen porters, those men who, in effect, were responsible for both the running and the policing of the College. The Porter's Lodge was the hub of college life where everyone would check the notice-boards and collect their mail each day. It was also a meeting place for many students.

There were many porters but Charlie and I became great friends with three in particular: Mike Strutt, the ex-policeman; Tony Wickson, the champion onion-grower; and a man called Bill Cox. When they were on night-duty we would spend hours chatting with them over cups of tea while they talked about the history of the college, recounting Magdalen lore and describing in great detail the accounts of ghost sightings that had punctuated the college's history.

From the first day that Charlie arrived at Magdalen, journalists and photographers from most of the national newspapers tried their utmost to interview and photograph him. His sister, Diana, had been married only two years before we arrived at Oxford and the Press were eager to print any stories about the Spencer family, especially the young heir to the title. Journalists tried many tricks to gain access to the college, posing as students, tourists and even, on one occasion, as a Rastafarian. I do not know how the porters managed to keep the Press away but somehow they made sure that no member of the *paparazzi* ever gained access to Charlie. Not one picture of him in college ever appeared in a newspaper, something he greatly appreciated.

It was during our time at Oxford that Charlie and I cemented the friendship that would continue through all my future troubles. Oxford has a 'cliquish' reputation but in his selection of friends Charles confounded such a notion, deliberately avoiding those Old Etonians and other Public School boys and Sloane Ranger types who he believed behaved in a pompous and snobbish way. This did not mean that he abandoned his former Etonian friends, but that he wanted to form new friendships with a wider group of people from different backgrounds.

His behaviour was in sharp contrast to some other privileged and titled students, such as Alexander Fitzalan-Howard, nephew of the Duke of Norfolk, and master of the University beagles, and considered by Charlie and me as the archetypal Hooray Henry.

Both Charlie and Alexander would became romantically involved with the highly intelligent, blonde Janna Vernon, who turned a number of heads at Oxford with her engaging personality and exciting demeanour. Although Charlie and Janna became lovers in their first term, that was all it would ever be and Janna, sensing this, opted instead for the safe 'Fitzi' — as Alexander was known — eventually marrying him after leaving Oxford.

One event in particular sealed my friendship with Charles. In the summer of 1985 his girlfriend, Rachel Kelly, an attractive, bubbly and clever girl, threw an end-of-term party at the house she rented in Oxford. I was chatting with friends in the garden at the back of the house when Charlie came up to me. 'There are five gate-crashers,' he said, 'and they won't leave. Come and give me a hand and we'll get rid of them.'

Standing in the hall I saw the group of gate-crashers looking around as though they wanted to steal something. They were dressed in leather jackets and jeans. Two of them ran up the stairs and I followed them with Charles.

'Come on,' I said, 'you're leaving.'

They looked at each other and walked down the stairs to their mates.

Then I told them all to get out. As they were walking out, however, one of them snatched a bottle of white wine that was on a side-table in the hall. I saw red and hit him in the solar plexus with my left fist followed by a right to his jaw.

Immediately, one of his friends leapt on my back while the others piled in, throwing punches and kicking me. At that point Charlie joined the fray, trying to get them off my back. At this stage, I went berserk and felt no pain as the blows rained down on me. I lashed out and hit as many of them as I could. Together, Charlie and I continued fighting them until they backed out of the house.

But it didn't finish there. Outside, in the courtyard, one of them had another go at me, kicking me in the stomach. I followed him outside, grabbed him by the head and hit him three times in the face. At that, they left. I walked back into the house and noticed that the hall, which had been crowded with guests, had emptied. Charlie had been the only one to come to my assistance. A few minutes later, when it was obvious that the coast was clear, the hall began to fill up again, some of the male guests protesting their loyalty and bemoaning the fact that they had happened, somehow, to be in a different part of the house when the fight had broken out.

Charles and I would spend many weekends together with our friends at his seven-bedroomed home on the Althorp Estate, a gabled Gothic-style house called The Falconry, adorned with fox masks, marble busts and stuffed birds. Often, we would go shooting on the estate, taking pot-shots at the hundreds of rabbits from a jeep and, in the season, joining the organised shoots with beaters and gun dogs. Winters were particular fun. Enjoying excellent dinners, sitting by log fires, swapping stories while listening to classical music, my mind inevitably turned to my father and the awful predicament into which he had been thrown by the so-called 'professionals' who had run Lloyds and brought him to the edge of ruin.

In our second year at Oxford Charlie and I shared a house with four other undergraduates, two men and two women. Sometimes we would take dinner in the college hall, but more often than not we would have our meals in the far less glamorous surroundings of our living-room, eating Chinese and Indian takeaways on our laps while watching television or listening to music.

During the summer term of 1984, I became acquainted with the beautiful young woman who would eventually marry Charlie. Victoria was the younger sister of Christopher Lockwood, one of my friends at Magdalen who was two years above me. We met at a country house party in Wiltshire and instantly became friends. I found Victoria a gentle, shy, vulnerable girl, refreshingly unlike many of the Sloane Ranger types one generally meets at such parties. It would, however, be five years before she met Charlie.

It was at the start of my second year at Oxford that I renewed my childhood friendship with Ben Marsh, the man who would risk everything with me and, eight years later, would stand beside me in the dock and be sent to jail for five years.

We had met again when he had telephoned during the summer holidays of 1984. We hadn't even spoken to each other for seven years but the moment we saw each other again, the strong bond that we had shared all those years ago was re-established. At the age of twelve we had said farewell, promising to meet again at Cambridge. Now we would be together at Oxford, Ben reading PPE (Politics, Philosophy and Economics) at St Peter's College.

We would spend a lot of time together, in each other's college rooms, eating at The Trout restaurant on the river and always talking about our respective subjects or current issues. It was marvellous to see him again after so long and I realised how much I had missed him.

One day, out of the blue, Ben said to me, 'Darry, I'm sure that in the future we'll go into business together.'

'And what are we going to do, exactly?' I asked him.

'I don't know,' he replied, 'but whatever it is, let's make it something interesting and exciting.'

During my last days at Oxford, I met another man who would play a critical role in my adventures. I had secured a job in the City as a Eurobond dealer with a well-known American investment bank, which I would take up in September 1986 after coming down from Oxford. Another undergraduate, an Indian named Ishan Dutta from St Edmund's Hall, had been offered a job with the same firm.

One day in the summer term of 1986, when I was having a lunchtime sandwich in a delicatessen on the High Street, I noticed a slim, handsome, clean-shaven Indian of average height and assumed that it was Ishan Dutta. I introduced myself and after a chat we shook hands agreeing to have lunch together when we started work in the City.

Throughout my time at Oxford I became absorbed in religious music and would spend hours in Magdalen's small and beautiful chapel listening to the fine Magdalen Choir, sitting alone and contemplating in the candle-lit church while the brilliant organist rehearsed his music.

I had never been given formal religious instruction other than attending morning chapel services at Eton. Nevertheless, from an early age I had been fascinated by all religious subjects and had studied both the Bible and the Koran in some detail. I had always been aware of my Islamic heritage, but at that stage had not decided which path to follow. What I did know, however, was that religion would play an increasingly important role in my life.

The Chaplain, Father Jefferey John, with whom I would become close friends and who would later visit me in jail, had noted that I frequently attended church where I would sit alone in meditation. On occasions, we would talk in his rooms and I came to admire his combination of deep spiritual insight and worldly knowledge. Above all, however, Father Jefferey had a sense of fun. He would gently tease me about one particularly innocent woman undergraduate who appeared terrified whenever I entered the chapel to pray. Apparently, on seeing me enter, she would instantly make the sign of the Cross as though to protect herself on account of my reputation for wild living.

There were others who lived the wild life at Oxford and one was Olivia Channon, the vivacious daughter of former Tory Minister Paul Channon who died of a drugs and alcohol overdose just hours after completing her Finals. Olivia had been a good friend of mine and many others at Oxford. She had a tremendous zest for life, and was a girl who enjoyed partying and being surrounded by her friends.

I sat my last Finals paper twenty-four hours after Olivia's death. As I walked into the main lecture hall on Oxford High Street, I felt forlorn. I had hardly slept the previous night thinking about my tragic friend and I wondered whether I would have the strength of mind to address the examination paper that would dictate my future. I had done everything I could to prepare myself for my Finals, trying to condition myself physically as well as mentally by going on five-mile runs every day, but that day I felt a wreck. Throughout the exam, I couldn't get Olivia out of my mind. I kept wishing that I had been celebrating with her the night she died, convinced, no doubt like the rest of her friends, that had I been there I would perhaps have been able to help her.

One of Olivia's best friends, another student, Rosie Johnstone, would eventually become the scapegoat. In time, she would be sentenced to nine months in jail for supplying the heroin that had killed her friend. We all felt that Rosie, a lively and attractive girl, had been the victim of a system that dictated that someone had to pay for what was in essence a tragic accident. It appeared that the authorities were determined to apportion blame and, in this case, Rosie was made to carry the can. Everyone knew that, at worst, she had simply agreed to pick up some drugs for Olivia as a favour, but to suggest that she had somehow been directly responsible for her death was absurd.

The exciting and romantic days of Oxford and all that it had meant to me were now over and, like everyone else, I had to wait two months for the results of my Finals. When they arrived and I discovered that I had achieved a first-class degree I was naturally pleased, for my passionate interest in my studies had borne fruit. However, at the back of my mind, one concern dominated all my thoughts — how to restore the family fortune and avenge my father's financial downfall.

V

In October 1986, I drove down to Oxford for my Graduation ceremony. Charlie and I had agreed to meet at Magdalen that morning to collect our BA certificates. He had told me that his sister, Princess Diana, would accompany him, along with their mother, The Honourable Mrs Frances Shand Kydd, my own mother and our history tutor, Dr Angus MacIntyre. I met Charlie outside the Porter's Lodge at Magdalen from where we walked down the High Street in our black gowns to the Sorbonne, a French restaurant.

It was there that I met Diana and her mother. 'Your Royal Highness,' I said, bowing to Diana. We shook hands and she replied, 'Nice to meet you, Darius.'

Mrs Shand Kydd smiled and said, 'I've heard a lot about you, Darius.'

Charlie's mother and I hit it off instantly. As I have often found when meeting people in the public eye, what I had read about her in the Press proved to be untrue. She was a wonderful conversationalist and highly attractive. Grand without being snobbish, proud without being haughty, she was also fun and vivacious.

Diana was quiet throughout the lunch, but became genuinely interested when my mother talked about her travels in the mountains with the nomadic tribes of her native Iran. Describing the simple, harmonious lives of these nomads, unchanged from the time of their forefathers, she recounted her journeys with them as they migrated with their flocks during the spring months from the plains of Khuzestan near the Persian Gulf through the Zagros mountains to high pastures near Isfahan, living in tents woven of goat hair, fording torrential rivers, walking the hundreds of miles along narrow precipitous paths until they reached their destination.

It was a life totally foreign to Diana, yet she was obviously captivated by my mother's recollections. She said little, but listened intently.

I was surprised that she appeared so natural and unassuming, not remotely arrogant or presumptious, and by the end of that lunch I thought of her not as the young goddess adored by the British public, but rather as a very pleasant, well-spoken, pretty young woman with an enchanting smile — Charlie's sister, who happened to be the Princess of Wales.

Later that afternoon, Charlie and I attended the formal ceremony for collecting our degrees and, having said goodbye to our guests, I drove back to London. It was on that drive that I realised my Oxford days were gone for ever. The ceremony had conveyed a sense of finality to my time there and I was filled with nostalgia as I remembered my friends, my tutors, the buildings, the whole place. I knew I would miss them all very much.

Within two hours of arriving at my very first job, working as a bond dealer in Bishopsgate, in the City of London, I realised I had made a dreadful error. I phoned a friend and told him, 'I think I've made a big mistake. This place is just not me.'

'My advice is to stick it out, Darry,' he said. 'Give it a few months. You can always leave if you really can't stand it.'

I could see from that first morning that the image of the City as an incredibly exciting place was bogus. Once upon a time it may indeed have been very stimulating, with merchants trading tangible commodities — coffee, tea, whatever, which had been shipped from exotic, far-off lands through tempestuous seas and off-loaded from tall ships on to the docks. But the modern-day equivalents of these merchants, the bond dealers and stockbrokers, who reckon only with neon blips on a flashing computer screen — exciting perhaps by virtue of the quantity of money they represent but unreal nevertheless — lead depressing lives by comparison, at least as I saw it.

On that first day, the seasoned dealers were already talking to each other about their potential Christmas bonuses — despite the fact that it was only September. I was quickly to learn that their own pay-packets, and even more so, other people's pay-packets, constituted their favourite, sometimes it seemed their only, topic of conversation.

That first afternoon I was taken under the wing of a rather matronly ex-Magdalen graduate who had worked for the company for two years. She pointed out the offices of the senior managers and directors and advised me in hushed tones, 'Darius, it's very important that you stay until midnight as often as possible. As you may know, bonus time is coming up.'

'But supposing I've finished my work,' I asked rather naïvely, 'do I still have to stay late?'

'That doesn't matter,' she replied, almost tut-tutting, 'the important thing is to be seen to be occupied. Just mill around looking busy even if you've got nothing to do — it works wonders.'

She went on, 'Take Jeremy in the corporate finance department. Did you know that last year his bonus cheque was for £22,000 and he's only been out of Oxford three years? At New Year, he turned up at my cocktail party in a brand-new black Porsche.'

In a whisper, she added pointedly, 'He's a big hit with my girlfriends.'

I lowered my voice and asked her, 'Are you really suggesting that such a cheap, bourgeois trophy as a mere motor car would arouse such amorous feelings in your girlfriends? Don't you think the fact that he is the heir to a banking fortune might play some part in their calculations?'

She looked puzzled at my cynicism. 'Of course not. Don't be so silly! He's just very charming.'

That first evening I did stay late, but would never do so again. From then on, I decided to leave the office when I had finished my work, irrespective of what effect this might have on my Christmas bonus. I would often notice my matronly adviser walking around the office with large bundles of paper — always within view of the directors and managers — and generally looking busy and I knew that I wouldn't last very long.

A man who shared my cynicism about the City was a director of another bank, whom I shall call Henri de Riencourt. De Riencourt was a suave, well-dressed man in his forties whose distinctly unromantic views about the world of high finance I found refreshing in the City. One day, when he invited me to his office for lunch and was trying to get the measure of me, he said, 'Do you know, Darius, generally speaking we don't like taking people who get first-class degrees because they can be intellectually arrogant at times. We prefer graduates with second-class degrees because we find that they tend to know their place and make better corporate men.'

He puffed on his large cigar and sat back in his leather-bound chair, smiling and waiting for a reaction.

'If you ever employ me, I'm sure you will find me very humble,' I replied sarcastically.

He laughed.

We would occasionally talk about the current world economic situation. At that time, the Western banking system was over-exposed to Third World debt and there was considerable concern among many in the financial markets. De Riencourt's view was that the entire banking system would collapse one day. 'It's not a question of if,' he said, 'it's a question of when. All this debt building up; banks having to merge and become bigger and bigger, seeking protection in size for their weak balance sheets; this crazy economic concept of growth, growth at all costs, for ever and ever. Sooner or later, the whole edifice will collapse.'

'So what do you suggest we do, Henri?' I asked, a little concerned.

'Take what you can and run while the going's still good. Do you understand? The whole thing is bullshit,' he replied. Then he added, 'I like you, Darius.'

I smiled at him. 'I'm sure you do. I'm a very likeable person, Henri — just like all the people in your bank who make the directors a lot of money. I wonder what would happen if I worked for you and I underperformed, though?'

'I'd sack you. Instantly!' he answered, rocking back in his chair and laughing heartily.

I laughed with him. At least he was honest.

Others, indeed, the great majority, developed convoluted and specious arguments to justify their almost obscene salaries. Trading bonds was hardly intellectually challenging, but many of the dealers and senior bank staff pretended, even to each other, that it was a highly specialised and complex science.

To a novice entering this frenzied world of instant action and reaction, the task of mastering the skill of dealing in bonds did, indeed, seem overwhelming at first. The huge open-plan office, the battleship of flashing lights and pulsating computer screens that accommodated several hundred screaming traders and salesmen, all bellowing obscure phrases, was bound to stun the outsider entering the room for

Left: Photofit of lead armed robber as described to the New York police by Darius and Ben Marsh.

Below: Lloyds' cheque made payable to Darius' company after the successful completion of the sting.

Top: Police exhibit of synthetic diamond, in excess of 230 carats in weight, used by Risdon in his attempted insurance fraud.

Below: Ben Marsh relaxing just before his diving trip to Jordan with Darius, Summer 1990.

Opposite: Peter Risdon, posing with a revolver after selling his story to a national newspaper.

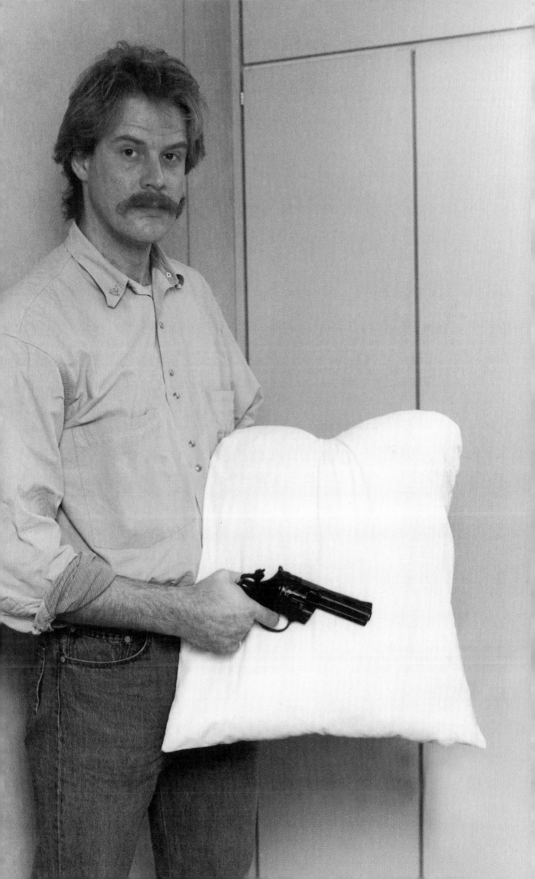

Top left: Room safe in cupboard in Room 1207 of the Halloran House Hotel.

Top right: The remains of the twine used to tie up Darius and Ben is on the floor.

Below: The bed nearest the camera is where Risdon fired the single shot. The knife was used by hotel security staff to cut Darius and Ben free.

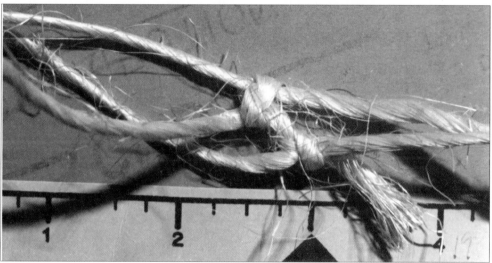

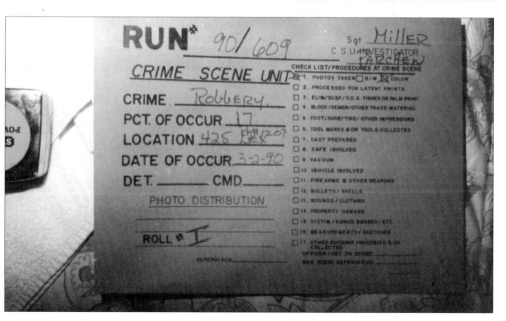

Top: Muzzle flash on the bed and pillow from gunshot.
Centre: Twine used to tie up Darius and Ben Marsh during the robbery.
Below: Scene of crime photos, NYPD – Room 1207, Halloran House Hotel.

Right: Headline in the *Daily Star* two days after Darius' conviction.

Below: Letter from Lord Spencer to Darius confiscated by the South East Regional Crime Squad officers when they searched Darius' home and sold subsequently to the *Daily Star*.

DAILY STAR special on

CHARLIE CHUM IS A ROYAL INSIDER!

The Falconry
Althorp
Northampton NN7 4HF

Dear Dino,

If you're not inside, please come and shoot here on Dec. 15th. Stay the weekend — Patricia's welcome — or else make a daytrip of it. I'll warn Ivor that you are returning...

Love,

C.

Darius and Patricia outside the Court of Appeal, April 1994.

Above: Lord Spencer emerging victorious from the High Court after successfully suing Express newspapers for defamation over libellous allegations of his financial involvement in Darius' sting, 1996.

Opposite: Ben and Darius being driven away to HM Prison Brixton from Snaresbrook Crown Court after the guilty verdict, February 1993.

the first time. In fact, the basic concepts were simple and most new recruits learned them within a few weeks.

It appeared to me that this relatively staightforward operation — trading in what amounted to pledges by corporations and governments to pay interest and repay capital to lenders at some future date — was really no different from the street stall-holder shouting the price of cabbages all day. What was different, however, was the money these dealers were taking home each week, in comparison with their less illustrious counterparts in Petticoat Lane. It seemed clear that even something as unattractive as usury could be made to look glamorous if enough money was involved.

Perhaps the single event that stamped the most indelible impression of the City on my mind occurred when, on a Monday a few weeks after arriving at the bank, I overheard a telephone conversation during lunch break between a dealer on a nearby desk and one of his counterparts in another City firm.

The individual concerned had left Oxford some five years before me and had worked in the bank ever since. He had carved out a niche for himself in the exciting world of domestic corporate floating rate bonds and had clearly prospered.

I could only hear one side of the conversation:

'Nice weekend, then?' A pause. 'Yeah, fine thanks. Must tell you something very funny though. On Sunday I drove down to Oxford — just for a laugh, really — and also to show off the new Ferrari, it has to be said.' Another pause. 'Red. Beautiful. Goes like a bomb. Anyway, I was driving back to London on the M40, doing about a hundred and twenty when I saw a clapped-out old Volkswagen Beetle that had broken down on the hard shoulder. I slowed down and could see that it had black smoke belching from the bonnet. It was in a right state. Two students were next to it looking miserable and drenched through from the rain. It was really pissing, I can tell you. They were obviously freezing and were thumbing a lift. So I decided to stop. As I drew up to them, you should have seen their faces — the look of absolute relief. Anyway, I pressed the button for my electric window and down it went. Do you know what I told them? "Serves you right for having such a common car!" And then I drove off! They must have been livid!'

At this, he hooted with laughter, almost choking on his bacon and avocado sandwich.

One of the bosses on the Money Markets desk was a tall, overweight, brash American whom I shall call Matt Sheldon. His desire to stamp his authority on all new recruits to his little world was obvious. For the first few weeks I, and the other freshers, tolerated his manner but after a while it began to grate.

Our tricky relationship came to an uncomfortable head when Sheldon took a week's holiday. Having no work to do, I decided to consult the *Eurobond Directory*, a large, blue paperback with the names, addresses and telephone numbers of the various banks and other financial institutions that had offices in the City of London. On my own initiative, I had decided to try to put together some deals for the bank while Sheldon was away. The best accounts were of course closely guarded by those dealers, like Sheldon, who were the bank's longest-serving traders. Understandably, as a new boy, I had been given the less important ones.

I managed to put together a few deals that made the bank a decent profit, in particular with one client, a US bank. The bond dealer with whom I struck the deals invited me to dinner at Blake's Hotel one night and offered me a job with his firm. However, because I knew that my future would not lie anywhere within the Square Mile, I politely declined.

When Sheldon returned and looked through the weekly audit of all the transactions conducted by his desk, he realised immediately that it was me who had been making the deals with the US bank.

It took him half a second to explode: 'Darius!' he screamed, picking up a telephone handset.

I looked up instantly, as did everyone else around the desk, startled by Sheldon's yelling.

'Do you see what this is?' he shouted. 'This is dynamite! Don't you ever pick up this phone again without my permission.'

Already perspiring, he took a breath and continued his tirade against me so that most of the vast room could hear him bellowing, 'It takes years of experience to learn how to deal in bonds. I've been at this job ten years and it still frightens me. It's dynamite, I tell you, it's dynamite!'

He stopped for another instant, then, with his head ducking and weaving like some manic boxer's, he resumed, 'You fuck up and you could lose the bank millions of dollars in just one call!'

He paused, out of breath. I focused on his eyes, an exercise requiring not a little skill considering that they were spinning like a gyroscope. Once they had settled down, he asked, a little more calmly:

'Well, what do you say to that?'

'Matt, calm down!' I replied. 'You look like some sort of psychotic Mohawk.'

Sheldon glared at me and returned to his seat. He did not speak to me for the rest of the day. The following morning, he informed me that the account was his and from that moment on, he relegated me to carrying out menial, administrative tasks. I knew that my days were numbered.

Five months later, I would leave the bank after another row with Sheldon. At that time I was still not allowed to deal in bonds without obtaining his prior authorisation. I was bored and frustrated and decided to tackle him about my future.

I asked him when I would be allowed to trade again.

'When I think you're ready for it,' he replied.

'Well, I think I'm ready now.'

'Well, I don't, Buster.'

'In that case, there's not much point in my staying any longer, is there?'

'Yeah. I think maybe you should leave,' he said, without looking at me.

'Good, I agree with you,' came my reply. 'So long.'

I cleared my desk immediately and left. I took the tube back home to Chelsea and drove up to Oxford to see Ben Marsh. I had seen how so many graduates who had joined the bank, once young and idealistic, had become wired into an unhappy world of quick money — usually blown as soon as it was earned — of long, empty hours mesmerised by flashing lights and screaming down a telephone, hooked into a life that they knew was bad for them, like once-beautiful, doomed junkies. A burden had been lifted from me; as though I had been released from prison.

Quite often during those nine months at the bank, I would drive up to Oxford and stay the weekend at Ben's house. As I was earning good money, I would often take him out to dinner in town and to lunches in the countryside. During those months our friendship became even more important than usual to us and we had decided that, if possible, we would start a business and work together after he came down from Oxford the following year.

My new friendship with Ishan Dutta, who also worked at the bank, flourished mainly because, like me, he looked on the City with a certain cynicism. Unlike me, however, he was prepared to bite his lip and go along with the system.

I also got on well with the Money Markets Desk's secretary, Debbie. We would often flirt harmlessly and she would ask my advice about the problems she always appeared to be having with her boyfriends. After informing her that I had been called Darius because my mother came from Iran, she remarked, 'If you're Iranian, then why don't you come to work on your flying carpet instead of by tube?'

One person I did admire at the bank was Omar, a slim, young Algerian who visited the office most days of the week to clean shoes. I would watch Omar kneeling at the feet of some of the bank's directors, polishing their shoes for perhaps ten minutes or more, as they puffed on their Havana cigars while conducting multimillion dollar deals on the phone. When Omar had finished he would look up at them, immaculate in their expensive pin-striped suits and hand-made cotton shirts, to take the one pound coin left on the side of their desk. Such a sight might have made even the odd Tory voter think of embracing Bolshevism.

Omar, who had learned English in just six months, and I would often have a coffee together at the desk during the lunch breaks. The fact that he was a Muslim interested me greatly. We would talk about religion and I was truly impressed by his commitment to his faith and by how he spoke with such passion about the heroes of Islamic history, men who had repeatedly risked their lives and fought with such intensity to establish God's will on earth.

In the spring of 1987, just before leaving the City, I — and a girl from Yorkshire who had also obtained an Honours degree in French — were chosen to represent the youth of Britain at celebrations in Paris marking the thirtieth anniversary of the Treaty of Rome. Young graduates from the other EU nations were also there. We spent five days in Paris, visiting the French capital's historical landmarks and art galleries. I particularly enjoyed going to those places that I had read about during my Oxford studies of the Revolution. We also attended a ceremony at the Arc de Triomphe, where we laid wreaths at the Tomb of the Unknown Soldier. It was there that we met the late President François Mitterand and his Prime Minister, Jacques Chirac.

One lunch time we were all invited to dine at the Prime Minister's headquarters and Monsieur Chirac asked me what I did for a living.

'I'm a banker,' I replied.

'A banker,' he repeated. Laughing, he went on, 'Can you tell me why every Englishman I meet nowadays is a banker?'

I sensed he was being gently sarcastic and said, 'Don't worry Monsieur Chirac, it won't be for long.'

'Good!' he replied.

From Paris, I flew to South Africa and after landing at Johannesburg travelled to the Afrikaner town of George on the Cape. Since my childhood I had always had an ambition to learn to fly and I knew that if I went to a flying school in South Africa, there would be little chance of my training being interrupted by bad weather. I had taken my annual holiday allowance from the bank — an entire month — in the hope that I would obtain my Private Pilots' Licence in one go.

I was fortunate that my flying instructor, Jim, a young, fair-haired Englishman who had emigrated to South Africa, was an excellent pilot and a dare-devil with it. He not only taught me to fly in the conventional manner, but also to put the aircraft into crazy spins and rolls. At the end of each lesson, we would fly out over the ocean, climb to 5,000 feet, raise the nose high, pull back the stick as hard as possible, allow the Piper Cherokee to stall and then force the plane into a spin by pressing down on one of the rudders. Spinning like this was an exhilarating experience, seeing the world revolving around the aircraft as we plunged towards the sea. At about a thousand feet, I would push hard on the opposite rudder until the plane stopped spinning and then apply more power, pulling the stick back and starting to climb again.

Jim wasn't supposed to teach students these types of stunts, but he felt that I would be capable of learning such tricks without panicking. The first time I tried a spin I must admit that, when the aircraft went into a rotating free fall, twisting as it plunged towards the emerald sea, my heart certainly beat a little faster than normal but, when it was all over, and the plane was flying straight and level once more, I felt a keen sense of achievement and exhilaration.

Despite the fun of aerobatics, however, my favourite pursuit was to navigate across the sensational South African landscape, landing at deserted air strips in the middle of nowhere, featureless but for a wooden shack and a wind-sock. On those occasions I felt truly free.

Shortly after leaving the bank, I spent a weekend with my father at his home near Ely, in Cambridgeshire. Four years after taking that fateful telephone call in New York, my father was still holding on to his home after taking out various mortgages in order to pay the debts he owed to Lloyds. He showed me some sapphires he had bought during a holiday in Sri Lanka and casually suggested that I might think of importing and selling gemstones to earn some money.

I discussed the possibility with Ben Marsh and we decided to give it a go. We went to see a friend of my father's, a gem dealer working in Hatton Garden, who advised us about the best countries then producing top-quality gemstones. The dealer also gave us a brief introduction to the basics of buying and selling precious stones. We learned that the highest quality rubies came from Burma, Thailand and Cambodia; the best sapphires from Burma, Sri Lanka and Kashmir and that Colombia, Zimbabwe and Zambia were where the best emeralds were mined.

We decided to visit Colombia.

During the following month Ben and I dedicated ourselves to learning all we could about emeralds, as well as reading up on other gemstones. We knocked on doors in Hatton Garden and Bond Street, cheekily introducing ourselves to top dealers. We attended jewellery auctions at Christie's and Sotheby's, visited libraries and read all we could about precious gems and their potential markets.

We soon learned that the precious stones market is to a great extent an artificial one. In many countries such stones can serve not only as a means of avoiding taxes and foreign exchange controls, but also as a way of avoiding the expropriation of an individual's wealth by unscrupulous governments. For centuries, valuable jewels have provided the perfect means of concentrating wealth in a small, transportable and easily concealed form.

In the modern world, these gems can also provide an efficient means of laundering money. In Colombia, for example, the emerald and cocaine trades are to a certain extent interrelated, cocaine dealers often preferring to be paid in emeralds rather than cash.

Our arrival in Bogota, the Colombian capital, in the summer of 1987, could not have been more inauspicious. We stepped off our Avianca flight from London and waited for our luggage to be deposited on the carousel. My bags were among the first to arrive. Then we lingered for more than an hour while the airport emptied, but Ben's luggage did not arrive.

Half an hour after the carousel had stopped turning, Ben looked at me despondently and remarked, 'Darry, I've got a bad feeling about this.'

Later, in our hotel bedroom, we laughed as Ben, two inches shorter than me, tried on my clothes. It would be forty-eight hours before his luggage was finally delivered to the hotel, having been sent to Venezuela by mistake.

Before leaving London we had arranged to meet an American gem dealer, Fred Pertsch, in Bogatoa — a relaxed young man in his thirties who didn't seem at all phased by the violence there, although he would always coolly carry a loaded hand-gun in his hip-holster. Only two days before we arrived, Fred had arranged to see some prospective gem dealers at his home, a heavily fortified bungalow in the suburbs that also doubled as his office. There were ten-feet-high walls around the perimeter, closed-circuit TV cameras and armed security guards on duty twenty-four hours a day.

As though describing a banal afternoon walk in the park, Fred explained to us, 'There were three of them.' After a pause, he smiled and added, 'I got two of them; out there in the street.'

He went on, 'In this country, shooting and being shot at is a fact of life. You just learn to live with it. Besides, there's a pile of money to be made out here.'

I had brought $10,000 in cash, my entire savings, to Bogota, hoping to establish our planned venture of buying gems around the world and selling them back in London at a decent profit.

We had learned from our studies in England a basic rule of thumb employed by gemmologists called 'the four Cs'. These four Cs represent the colour, clarity, cut and carat of any given stone and it is always a combination of these factors which determines its value.

That day, Fred Pertsch taught us an important lesson: it is better to invest in a few, top-quality stones than in an abundance of poor-quality ones.

After chatting for half an hour, Fred opened a drawer in his desk and took out a small white envelope about the size of a cigarette paper, which gem dealers call a 'brifka'. He opened it carefully on the desk and asked us to take a look at the emerald inside, saying, 'Now this is a real bute.'

It was a 4.3-carat emerald worth perhaps $20,000. As we took it in turns to examine the magnificent jewel with our small magnifying glasses, or 'loupes', we began to appreciate the beauty of top-quality Colombian emeralds, noticing how the flaws, called 'inclusions', formed unique patterns known as 'gardens'. The emerald in question had also been particularly well cut and polished, thereby maximising the brilliance and, in the process, the value of the stone.

Ben and I looked at each other, realising that investing our $10,000 in emeralds would take a long time to make us millionaires.

But Fred turned out to be a kind man. He had quickly worked out that he was dealing with two 'rookies' fresh out of university who wanted to earn some money. Realising that we could not afford his wares, he nevertheless showed us his large collection of top-quality emeralds. After an afternoon of his expert tuition we left, empty-handed.

During our two-week stay we saw a number of other dealers. On occasions, these dealers would arrange for us to be collected from our hotel in bullet-proof limousines; at other times we would find beat-up old American-style taxis waiting to take us to our appointment. But, almost invariably, we would be escorted by armed police outriders with the more sinister dealers sending their own armed heavies to assist.

At nearly every meeting we attended, guns would be on open display, on the tables, on desks and in rifle cases on the walls. And most of the staff carried sub-machine guns slung lazily over one shoulder. I grew to like Bogota, the vibrancy of the place, the local colour, the beautiful people, but there was also a permanent undercurrent of menace with every newspaper stall displaying pictures of the previous night's grizzly gang warfare, showing the bodies of victims, blood congealing on their gunshot wounds.

Within a fortnight, we flew out of Bogota having purchased just three emeralds and having spent virtually all of our $10,000. We had no idea of the regulations governing the export of these stones from Colombia but we decided to take a gamble, smuggling them out of the country, rather than having to go through the tedious process of filling out endless forms.

Ben simply put the three emeralds in his wallet behind a credit card. As we passed through Customs, an officer stopped us and searched all our belongings, ordering us to turn out our pockets. He picked up Ben's wallet and examined it, but, fortunately for us, he didn't take out the credit card and look behind it to see if anything had been concealed there.

When we returned to London we had no intention of declaring the emeralds in case the Customs officials demanded we pay VAT or import duty on them. Once again, we took a chance and walked casually through Customs. No one stopped us.

The following morning we took a tube from our two-bedroom apartment in Stockwell, south London, to Hatton Garden. We called on a few dealers and to our amazement found that, on average, the profit we achieved worked out at more than 60 per cent. We sold the gems over the next two weeks, for a total of $16,000. We had made $6,000, before expenses, from our first venture.

During the four months since leaving the City, I had often wondered whether I had been sensible in abandoning a well-paid job to risk all on striking out on my own. The moment we sold those gems, and had the money in our pockets, I knew that I had taken the right decision. But it would not all be that easy.

A month later we decided to make a return trip to Bogota, but realised that it would be pointless for both of us to go there, doubling our expenditure. We tossed a coin and Ben won. While he was away making us another $5,000, I was busy in London studying the Government's Business Expansion Scheme, or BES, a scheme introduced to encourage wealthy people to invest their excess income in high-risk business proposals in return for beneficial tax breaks.

Despite the initial success of our venture, we had a problem. We could make a living buying and selling gems, but we would be unable to generate the critical mass of money required to develop a thriving business without a further injection of capital. After reading through the BES fine print I discovered that there was a loop-hole, which permitted investment in jewellery and gems, while disallowing other commodities and assets such as gold and real estate.

In December 1987, our business plan was accepted by a firm specialising in raising money for BES projects. Four months later our company, Inca Gemstones PLC, with Ben and me as directors, began trading with capital of £1,150,000. Ben's father, Peter Marsh, the advertising tycoon, put up £50,000 and became non-executive chairman.

While waiting to see whether our scheme would be sponsored, I spent Christmas 1987 on the Isle of Seill, near Oban, on the West Coast of Scotland at the home of Frances and Peter Shand Kydd with Charlie and his girlfriend, Katie Braine. During those ten days Frances and Peter were exceptionally warm and hospitable, making their guests feel very much at home.

During the day Charles and I would go off shooting duck, snipe and pheasant all over the countryside, and at dusk would make our way to a small lake near the sea to wait for the duck, teal and widgeon to return from their feeding grounds. Having covered our faces and hands with thick mud to camouflage ourselves, we would then sit with our guns on rocks above the lake, our hands numbed by the bitter cold, waiting patiently to spot the returning birds, silhouetted against the rain clouds and darkening evening sky. At night we might bring home half a dozen or so birds, which we would hang, pluck and cook.

In the evening after dinner, we would usually play scrabble or charades and Frances taught me Scottish dancing. We would practise dancing to tapes in the house and, in the New Year, went to the Oban New Year Ball. The following year we all returned to Scotland and enjoyed another fine Christmas on the Isle of Seill.

Throughout 1988, Ben and I, accompanied by our gemmological consultant, went on a number of overseas trips to India, Thailand, Sri Lanka and Switzerland where we bought rubies, emeralds and sapphires, building up our stock of gems as required by the BES rules, which stipulated that the capital raised by the company had to be turned over and not simply banked.

During the same year, I produced a business plan for the setting up of a fund to purchase dry-cargo bulk carriers for chartering out to shipping companies and took it to Merrill Lynch, the American investment bank. I raised $50,000,000 in equity and a further $30,000,000 in debt and earned a handsome six figure sum from the deal. This money enabled me to help out my father to some extent by renting his Chelsea home. The remainder of the money would eventually be used towards a gold-smuggling operation that I was to set up with Ishan Dutta.

Peter Marsh had rented a part of his large offices in Tavistock

Square to Inca, from where we conducted our gem-dealing business. One of Peter Marsh's secretaries was a tall, beautiful 19-year-old redhead with long, pre-Raphaelite hair, named Kim. Kim was innocent, kind, and natural. Brought up in south London, she often teased me about my Eton and Oxford education.

One of our favourite summer pastimes was to climb over the iron railings into Kew Gardens at midnight with a bottle of champagne and wander through the beautiful moonlit park, passionately involved in each other, before going back to my house. On one or two occasions we were almost caught by the Park's patrol, but would lie still under a tree waiting for the patrol vehicle to pass.

One evening, Kim had to work late and the offices were empty when I came to see her. She was waiting for an overseas call and I started to kiss her neck. Within minutes, we were on the huge brown leather sofa in Peter Marsh's office when we heard the noise of the cleaners making their way along the corridor to the office. We had no time to dress and it would have been quite obvious what had been going on if they had walked in. I leapt to my feet and ran to the door, grabbing the handle. There was no lock on the door so I had to hold the handle in the closed position while the cleaners outside tried to get in, unable to understand why the door handle wouldn't turn.

I could hear their comments and was hardly able to stop myself laughing out loud. Kim rapidly dressed and eventually the cleaners left. I managed to dress while Kim checked that the corridor was clear. Before they returned, we had fled via the fire escape.

Kim and I went out together for about a year and I much preferred her delightful humour, her sense of fun and her honesty to so many of the Sloane Ranger girls who would invite me to their dinner parties and summer fêtes. Rather than attend such uninspiring functions, I much preferred to spend the night at the cinema with Kim or stay home with her in my Stockwell flat.

In the summer of 1988, I took Kim to the Magdalen Commemoration Ball. It was a truly nostalgic event for me. I had only left the college two years before and throughout the evening I bumped into a number of my former tutors and their wives. I took Kim to New Buildings and showed her my old rooms. The furniture was still the same and the haunting memories of Mozart echoing down the stairwells came back to me. Kim looked beautiful that night and I was proud of her. As the evening drew on, it became cold so I lent her my black tail-coat to keep her warm. She enchanted everyone she met and, although she had felt shy at first, she became more confident as people, young and old, came to chat, asking to be introduced and commenting on how lovely she looked.

Later that year, my father was finally forced to sell The Pond owing to his crippling bills from Lloyds. He sold the house to a property developer and one night I persuaded Ben to drive up to Ely to see my old home, where we had spent so many childhood weekends together, one last time.

The old rowing boat was still moored under the tree where we always used to leave it, next to the two concrete steps my father had laid back in 1964. Even the paddles were still in the boat. We got in, untied it and rowed to the middle of lake in the clear moonlight. It had been ten years before that Ben and I had last done this and I was filled with sadness. I knew that I had lost the home of my youth for ever.

VI

Three days after I arrived in Bombay, the meeting was arranged. Shortly after lunch, as I lay by the pool of the President Hotel, Ishan Dutta walked over to me.

'It's all been fixed,' he said. 'We have an appointment in one hour.'

I went to my room on the fourteenth floor and quickly put on a pair of white cotton trousers, a sleeveless shirt, a linen jacket and my dark glasses. Downstairs, amid the sound of squawking crows and the honking of car horns, we hailed a cab.

'The gold district,' Ishan said to our driver. We climbed into the car, a standard black Indian taxi with a yellow roof, a replica of the British Morris Oxford of the early 1970s and one of the most common sights in Bombay.

On the way to the gold district we were slowed down by one of Bombay's habitual traffic jams. Eventually, we passed a water lorry that had crashed and was lying on its side in the middle of the road. Around the truck, dogs lapped at the water that had spilled on to the road while on top of it a family of six, a father and mother and their children, had managed to make a picnic and, having laid out plates and glasses, were quietly eating their meal. It was surreal. There were no police, no ambulance and no one seemed to take the slightest notice of what had happened as they slowly filed past in their cars.

While we were stuck in the traffic, I heard a tap at the window. Outside was a tiny, emaciated sixty-year-old man, dressed in rags and sitting on a skateboard. He had no legs, just tiny stumps. He had one good arm, but the other was withered and twisted, with no fingers. He put the gnarled stump of his hand through the window and I gave him

200 rupees, which was then worth about £5. The man's eyes opened wide in astonishment at my generosity and as soon as I had put the money into his palm, he raced away without a second look. Somehow he managed to propel and guide himself, darting at speed through the busy traffic on his skateboard, his head no higher than the wheels of the cars.

The gold dealer's offices were located in a congested side street, packed with pedestrians, cattle, taxis and hundreds of cyclists all ringing their bells at the same time, or so it seemed. His personal office was at the top of a small five-storey building, a sign of considerable prestige in that area of Bombay. Ishan and I were escorted into the lift by one of the dealer's henchmen. The lift, with old-fashioned iron gates, jolted noisily upwards when the button was pushed and somehow managed to inch its way very slowly to the top. Such obvious opulence was an indication of the exalted status of our gold dealer, Mr Goutti, who was awaiting our arrival.

Before meeting Mr Goutti, Ishan had told me:

'Don't be deceived by appearances. The man is very wealthy and is one of the biggest and most powerful merchants in the community.'

The office was a spacious, sparsely furnished room. At one end of it stood a 1960s metal and formica desk, on top of which lay a number of out-of-date gemmological magazines. A few posters of diamonds in dilapidated frames decorated the walls and an old fan whirred from the ceiling. Two black plastic chairs awaited us.

Mr Goutti was a major diamond merchant. He was also one of the few government-authorised bullion dealers in Bombay. He was just over five feet five tall, rotund, and about forty years of age. The left side of his face seemed to be paralysed, the eye half-closed, the lip stretched upwards. He smiled at us from behind his desk and we walked over to him.

He got up, shook hands, introduced himself in his pidgin English and invited us to take tea with him. As we talked and sipped tea, this wealthy and powerful man, shabbily dressed and operating out of these run-down premises seemed to me as cunning as a fox, a fox that never stopped smiling.

Throughout the conversation Goutti spoke to us in ambiguous terms, indicating that he would be prepared to help us, but without committing himself in any way. For all he knew, we could have been

Government agents investigating possible black market dealings just as easily as genuine traders.

Occasionally we would be interrupted by a light tapping on the door after which a dishevelled local gem dealer would enter the room and show Goutti a stone of some description. After a cursory look at the gem, Goutti would dismiss the dealer with a flick of his hand.

Once such dealer, however, a short man of advanced years, barefoot and dressed in a dirty loincloth and who could have been mistaken for a beggar, took out a brifka and put it on Goutti's desk. Goutti opened the package and smiled even more broadly than usual.

Ishan told him, 'Mr Goutti, do you know that Mr Guppy comes from London and deals in gems himself?'

Goutti nodded, smiled again and handed over the package and a loupe. 'Perhaps you like to see?'

As I examined the gem, I quickly realised that I was holding an outstanding Kashmir sapphire, ten carats in weight and of breathtaking beauty. It must have been worth several hundred thousand dollars. I looked at Goutti and the bedraggled dealer.

'Not a bad stone,' I said as I handed back the package to Goutti, who seemed amused at the surprise I had tried to disguise.

A few words of Hindi were exchanged between the two men whereupon the dealer took back the gem, bowed to Goutti, then to Ishan and me and shuffled out of the room, concealing the sapphire in his grimy loincloth as he left.

*   *   *

I had found myself in the bustle of Bombay's gold market thanks to the Inland Revenue.

In the autumn of 1988, after Inca Gemstones Plc had been trading for only a few months, Ben and I had had a meeting with Revenue inspectors at our accountants' offices near Lincoln's Inn Fields. We did not realise at the time that this meeting would set in motion the train of events that would lead to the destruction of our company.

The inspectors had informed us that, as a BES enterprise, we were required to turn over our capital and trade in our stock of gemstones on a regular basis. They made it clear that if we held on to the company's stock for a year or more they would interpret such action as investing for the purposes of the BES rules rather than trading. This, in turn, would mean that our BES status would be withdrawn by the Revenue and our shareholders would lose the tax relief on their investments as a consequence.

The Revenue's stance would effectively cripple Inca's business from that moment on, because the essence of a successful gem-dealing company requires it to be able to hold on to the stones it purchases until such time as a buyer offers the price required to secure a good profit. By insisting that Inca should continually turn over its stock of gems, the Revenue was effectively signalling to the rest of the market that the company was a seller and, as a result, the prices that Inca could have achieved, had it been allowed to hold on to its stock like any other gem-dealing company, were never realised.

In short, in order to keep its advantageous tax status for the shareholders, Inca was nearly always forced to sell its stones at a loss. In time, this would create a hole that somehow had to be plugged.

Back at our offices that evening, Ben and I had felt depressed and disappointed.

'What a stupid rule to impose,' Ben had said angrily. 'We can't possibly make the business work like that.'

He had gone on: 'These bloody bureaucrats haven't got a clue about how the gem market actually operates. Now, every Tom, Dick and Harry in Hatton Garden will be queuing up to buy our stones at knock-down prices.'

I had replied: 'That's one interpretation. The other is that they have a definite clue what they're doing. Maybe this ruling of theirs is deliberate. Perhaps they just think we're a couple of smart-arse youngsters who found a loophole in the BES rules and they're determined to make us pay for it.'

'We mustn't let them beat us,' I had continued. 'Somehow, we must find a way round this.'

'Too right, Darry. We've got my Dad into this company and I can't disappoint him. We've also borrowed a hundred grand to buy shares in the company.'

It had become very clear that we needed to find another source of income to preserve the company's capital.

*   *   *

Initially, in December 1988, I had travelled to Bombay in the hope of finding a source of gemstones so cheap that we would be able to mark them up and make a profit, despite the Revenue's stipulation about how we should trade our stock.

At that time Ishan was working for a bank in Bombay. I had telephoned him from London and briefly explained to him that I would be travelling to Bombay shortly and would like to meet him. I suggested that there was a possibility we could do business together, especially if he could introduce me to some gem dealers with whom I could trade.

It was while reading the *Bombay Times* and waiting for Ishan in the reception area of my hotel that I had noted the bullion prices in the paper's business section. Borrowing a calculator from one of the waiters, I had calculated that the price of bullion in India fluctuated to between 35 and 55 per cent higher than in London.

When Ishan had turned up for our meeting I had asked him why the price of gold in India was so much higher than in London.

He had explained about the huge demand among Indian families for gold jewellery. For many Hindus gold has an almost sacred value, being used for dowries and religious purposes as well as constituting the traditional method of preserving wealth. It is generally estimated that, in India, there is billions of pounds' worth of undeclared gold, the vast majority of which is smuggled into the country and sold on the black market.

Ishan had remarked: 'Do you know that people have made absolute fortunes in this country from smuggling gold?'

Suddenly I had realised that this could be a way of saving Inca.

I had asked Ishan: 'Well, why don't we do it?'

'Are you serious, Darry?'

'You know me, Ishan,' I had answered. 'Of course I am. The question is, are you serious?'

Now, a couple of months or so later, Ishan had decided to take a few days' holiday from his banking job and spend some time with me investigating the bullion market. Together, we had gone through the Bombay *Yellow Pages* searching out possible gold dealers to help us in our enterprise.

Before our meeting with Goutti, we had met with a number of other dealers and, from our enquiries, the picture that had emerged revealed a close relationship between the gem, bullion and currency black markets.

At that time, there were strict laws in India forbidding the transfer of Indian currency out of the country. Permission for all such transactions had to be given by the Indian Central Bank. As a result, black market currency dealers became a very important element of the Indian business culture. In particular, gem and bullion traders found that they had to seek the help of these currency dealers, or 'Havala brokers' as they are known locally, to carry on overseas business and, as a result, many of their business dealings were outside the law.

A typical transaction would involve the Havala brokers arranging payment — say, in London — of a hard currency, such as pounds sterling or American dollars in return for which they would take the rupee equivalent, plus a hefty commission, from the Indian trader in Bombay. The gems and bullion traders in London and Bombay were happy, as was the currency dealer. No individual lost out and in this way, Havala transactions became an accepted and indeed essential business practice in India. And, while such transactions were technically against Indian law, the Indian authorities tended to turn a blind eye, especially if the odd financial inducement was forthcoming.

By this time we had set up the meeting with Goutti, and after much research, Ishan and I had resolved to test the scheme. To me the idea seemed not in the least immoral, because there would be no victim and no fraud. We would be dealing in a perfectly legitimate substance, namely gold, and selling to willing buyers at the fair market price. The Indian legislation regarding bullion and foreign exchange had been designed, in large part it seemed, to give the Government control over private individuals' resources and not for any higher purpose.

Having completed our meeting with Goutti, Ishan and I went out on to the street where I saw my faithful Indian taxi driver, waiting for me in his usual manner — lying on the bonnet of his car playing cards with his taxi driver friends.

'Tree, tree, tree!' I called. Instantly, he jumped up, rushed over to me, stood to attention and saluted, shouting, 'Yes, Sah!'

When I had first arrived at the President Hotel in Bombay, 'Tree, tree, tree', as I called my driver, had taken hold of me and pushed me towards his taxi while fending off the other drivers who were trying to pull at my bags, eager for business.

At the end of my first hectic journey in his taxi in which we had miraculously weaved and nudged our way through the chaotic traffic of Bombay, he had thumped his chest, proud of his car-dodging skills, shouting 'Tree, tree, tree!', as though it were his name. It was, in fact, the licence number of his taxi, '333'. Whether it was the result of expert surveillance techniques or simply an uncanny ability to anticipate where I could be found, every time I emerged from a hotel or some other location I would be greeted by his habitual scream of 'Tree, tree, tree!' and he would push his way through the throng of people and grab hold of me, pulling me towards his vehicle.

I liked 'Tree, tree, tree' enormously. He was 5ft 9ins tall, thin, with a black moustache, dark hair and gleaming white teeth. He had the cheekiest smile imaginable and an impish personality that combined to make him the most lovable rogue. At the end of every taxi ride, which I knew should have cost about thirty rupees, he would ask for a mere four hundred rupees. After remonstrating with him playfully, I would invariably end up handing over the full amount.

Thinking, correctly, that he had conned me, he would then remark, 'You are very hard man, Mr Guppy,' at which point he would run off to his colleagues and gamble his earnings, playing cards on the bonnet of his taxi.

Having read between the lines and deduced that Goutti would be happy to liquidate our gold for us, the major problem that Ishan and I now had to address was how to smuggle the bullion into India. We had been informed that most of the contraband bullion brought into India originated in the United Arab Emirates, usually Dubai, from where it was ferried across the sea by dhow to Bombay.

We investigated the possibility of smuggling the gold across the Arabian Sea in a light aircraft, which I would fly with Ben Marsh as my co-pilot. For quite some time, our plan was for Ben and I to take off from Abu Dhabi, route over Muscat in Oman and from there make our way across the Arabian Sea to a spot north of Bombay, where Ishan would be waiting for the drop. Such an operation, especially if carried out at night, would require the use of homing devices for Ishan to keep track of the gold. It would be while making enquiries in London as to the best possible form of tracking device that Ben and I would come into contact with Peter Risdon, the man who would help us over a year later in the execution of the New York gems sting and who would eventually betray us to the police.

From Bombay I travelled to Abu Dhabi and found a six-seater, twin-engined Cessna 421, otherwise known as a 'Golden Eagle', which was available for hire. With extra fuel tanks, it would be possible to fly to Bombay direct without needing to refuel.

Everything seemed to be falling into place. Fate even appeared to take a hand in the plan. When I returned from Abu Dhabi, as I climbed into a black cab at Heathrow for the ride into London, I noticed an advertisement on the folded seat in front of me for the 'Counter Spy Shop' in South Audley Street, Mayfair. This seemed a likely place to buy the homing device required to carry out our smuggling plan.

Over coffee in our office the following day, I talked Ben Marsh through the whole project, telling him about my friend Ishan Dutta, the profits that could be made from smuggling gold into India and the plan we had devised to fly the gold from the UAE into Bombay. I also told him about the advertisement I had seen in the taxi for the Counter Spy Shop.

At this stage, it was suggested that I should put my own private money into the plan for we did not want to risk Inca's funds in a venture that might fail. At a later stage, if the smuggling became profitable, Inca could then liquidate its stock of gems and invest some money in the gold project.

Under the BES rules, we were not permitted to deal in gold, so we planned to disguise our gold purchases as gem deals, by persuading a friendly overseas company to issue dummy invoices to Inca. We estimated that if all went according to plan, Inca would make about a 50 per cent gross return on its capital for every shipment that successfully evaded detection and, after all expenses were taken into account, perhaps as much as 40 per cent net. If the project worked as we hoped, then Inca would become a profitable concern despite the stipulations regarding the company's methods of trading, which the Inland Revenue had insisted upon and which we knew would eventually ruin the company.

Two days later, Ben and I visited the Counter Spy Shop. The expensive gadgets on display ranged from radio scramblers, body armour and lie detectors, to direction-finding equipment, eavesdropping devices and stun guns.

Ben and I could hardly stop ourselves laughing out loud at the sight of a rather expensive pair of sunglasses that were fitted with rear-view mirrors, apparently enabling the wearer to ascertain whether he was being followed. As a joke, we tried them on. Having experimented with different positions for the rear-view mirrors, we concluded that they were hopelessly ineffective.

'Can I help you gentlemen?' said a tall, rather gawky-looking man in an apologetic voice who appeared from the back of the shop. He was wearing an ill-fitting, light-grey suit.

'Are you gentlemen interested in purchasing a pair of these sunglasses?' he enquired.

Ben chuckled and said, 'Don't you think they're a bit of a joke?'

'No Sir, I don't,' the man replied, obviously a little hurt. 'I can assure you, Sir, that these glasses are made to the highest specifications and are considered an invaluable asset by the world's major security services.'

He paused, lowered his voice, looked furtively around and added, 'Including Mossad.'

Ben and I looked at each other, unable to believe that the man was being serious.

Ben quipped, 'Shouldn't they be fitted with wipers for when it rains?'

Stumped, the man replied, 'Quite, Sir,' took them off Ben without a smile and replaced them on the counter.

I told the man that we were interested in homing devices and he beckoned us to follow him downstairs.

We entered a windowless, carpeted conference room with a large table in the middle and half a dozen chairs around it. Apart from this, the room was bare.

'Don't worry, gentlemen,' he said, 'you have nothing to fear. This room has been swept for bugs. Everything we say in here is entirely confidential.'

He added, 'By the way, the name is Risdon.'

Not wishing to reveal the true use to which we intended to put the homing devices, I explained to Risdon that the equipment we required had to be tough and durable because we were making an expedition to the Himalayas and supplies were to be dropped out of a plane, which we would subsequently have to locate.

Risdon explained to us that there were two devices he would recommend. The first was a small transmitter, to be attached to the supplies, that direction-finding equipment on the ground could home in on. The second was a flashing infra-red device, invisible to the naked eye, but which could be picked up with night-vision binoculars.

We told him that we would need to consider the matter further and perhaps shop around. In a loud whisper, Risdon reassured us, 'Gentlemen, you have my assurance of utter discretion and complete professionalism. After all, I deal with law enforcement agencies and extremely wealthy clients all the time. My reputation would suffer irreparably if ever I was indiscreet.'

As we were leaving, I saw one of the shop's specialities, a briefcase with a false bottom. I noticed, however, that when the briefcase was open it was obvious that it had a hidden compartment. The idea, however, of such a compartment would later prove invaluable.

Before leaving, I handed Risdon my business card. It was the worst mistake I ever made in my life but, at that moment, I believed we would never meet the man again. We shook hands, and his palm was sweaty. I wondered why.

Three months later, in the spring of 1989, I took a phone call at our new offices in Jermyn Street.

'Mr Guppy?'

'Yes, speaking,' I replied, trying to recollect the voice.

'This is Peter Risdon here. We met some time ago when you visited the Counter Spy Shop in South Audley Street. I wondered if you would care to visit me in my new shop that I have just set up. It's called Electronic Techniques and Services, ETS for short.'

A few days later, Ben and I went to visit him. His new offices, situated in south London, were not as plush as the Mayfair set-up, but the place buzzed with activity.

Risdon introduced Ben and me to his partner, Tom McLaine, a squat, tough, athletic man in his fifties, who spoke in a deep, gruff voice and wore sovereign rings on all his fingers.

''Ello, Mr Guppy, 'ello, Mr Marsh,' he growled in a slow, deliberate voice.

Ben and I would grow to like Tom McLaine very much. As a child, he had been frequently maltreated and beaten by his father. In his youth, he had turned to crime and violence had become a habit. He had served two prison terms, the second had been ten years for armed robbery. He had been released in 1982 and had since gone straight. To us, Tom McLaine seemed the epitome of the honest rogue.

Later, Risdon would tell us that while McLaine had put up the capital for the new partnership, ETS, he had brought in the clients. He added with a guilty chuckle, 'You can guess where they came from. I came across most of them in South Audley Street.'

On nearly every occasion that we met Risdon and McLaine together, Peter Risdon would do virtually all the talking while Tom McLaine looked on in silence. It soon became obvious to us, however, that Risdon was intimidated by McLaine, who exuded an aura of strength and menace.

We stayed chatting to Risdon for a couple of hours that day. He became very friendly, boasting that his company would become a major force in the security business within two years, with profits of several million pounds. He even offered us a stake in the company, saying he could bring us in at a rock-bottom price. We replied that we would consider his suggestion.

I asked Risdon if he had ever worked on behalf of the police or HM Customs.

'What kind of work do you mean — legitimate or illegitimate?'

'Do you mean you do both?' I asked, rather incredulously.

He winked knowingly and replied, 'This is 1989, Mr Guppy. What do you think?'

He continued, 'You have no idea how many times we're asked by the police to bug peoples' phones illegally because they can't get a court order to tap them.'

'Really?' I asked.

'All the time. Listen,' he said, 'we anticipate the police being one of our principal sources of revenue.'

I asked Risdon how long he would need to obtain the direction-finding equipment we had discussed three months earlier in the Counter Spy Shop.

'Two weeks would be sufficient,' he replied.

Dutta and I had calculated that we would be dropping perhaps forty to fifty kilos of gold at a time in two rucksacks. In each of the rucksacks we planned to put two transmitters in case one broke or malfunctioned, so we estimated that we would need six of them for good measure. We would also need two direction-finding units on the ground, in case one failed. Risdon anticipated the total cost to be in the region of £3,000.

We told Risdon that we planned our expedition for sometime in the summer, but had no firm dates. I emphasised, however, that we would need the equipment by the end of June. We would confirm the order at a later date.

Throughout those first few months of 1989, I had been spending most weekends flying a variety of light aircraft from Elstree and Cambridge airports. I had obtained my Instrument Rating and Multi-engine Rating, which enabled me to fly in poor weather conditions and to fly aircraft with more than one engine, all of which meant that I now had the full qualifications required to fly the 'Golden Eagle' from Abu Dhabi to Bombay.

Ben and I would practise dummy-runs, dropping rucksacks full of lead ingots over the flat Essex countryside. One morning, in the spring of 1989, Ben was on the ground near Earl's Colne aerodrome, a tiny airfield with a grass runway and a tower manned by an old, rather doddery airtraffic controller, while I was attempting to locate him from my aircraft above. He was equipped with a hand-held transceiver and I was communicating with him using the aircraft's radio.

As I flew over the area, Ben came up on the radio, 'Darry, I can see you. Steer twenty degrees west and you'll be straight in line with me.'

'Wilco,' I replied.

'You're too far to the left, turn five degrees east and then you'll be spot on line.'

After a pause he said, 'Perfect. You're bang on.'

A minute later, I saw Ben standing in a field by a hedge about one hundred feet below. What I was doing was strictly illegal — aviation law stipulates that all aircraft have to maintain a minimum height of five hundred feet above ground level or the nearest tall object. It also forbids the unauthorised throwing out of any object from an aircraft. Ben was waving frantically at me. I circled once and then dropped the left wing as I pushed two socks filled with lead ingots out of the port window.

'Ben, have you found it?'

'Yes, I can see it. Great!' he replied. 'See you later.'

As I turned towards the airfield, I changed frequencies and immediately heard the voice of the Earl's Colne controller screaming excitedly, 'Attention! Attention all Earl's Colne air traffic! This is Earl's Colne tower. Attention please! There is a madman in an AA5.' (The type of aircraft I was flying that day.) 'He has been buzzing the tower and is flying just above the trees at fifty feet. Steer clear of the airport! I repeat, the man is mad!'

After a brief pause he screamed again, 'Here he comes again! I can see him! He's coming straight for me!'

I suddenly realised that my aircraft's call sign, written on the side of the fuselage, could be easily seen at anything under five hundred feet and I could face severe disciplinary action for such dangerous flying, which in all probability would cost me my licence. So I applied full power and climbed as fast as possible above the regulation five hundred feet.

Over the radio I heard another voice ask the controller, 'Did you get the registration?'

'No,'came the reply. 'Missed him.'

While our experiment had worked, it had been obvious for some time that although a couple of runs in the 'Golden Eagle' from Abu Dhabi to Bombay might constitute an acceptable risk, in the longer term the repeated reliance on such a method of smuggling would be unrealistic. Sooner or later, the Indian air-traffic controller's suspicions would be aroused by regular trips being made by the same pilots in the same aircraft along the same flight path. We needed to re-think the strategy.

The false-bottom briefcases I had seen in the Counter Spy shop in South Audley Street gave me the clue I needed. I decided to experiment with the help of Risdon.

I knew that, between the exportation of goods from the UK and their importation into India, a British or Indian Customs Officer could at any stage of the process conduct a thorough search of the goods in question. I considered that most smugglers would either describe their contraband on the paperwork as legitimate goods of some description and hope that it would slip through the net, or else conceal the contraband within the goods themselves — gold bars in garden gnomes, for example. Perhaps a more subtle approach would be to hide the contraband in the goods' packaging — the cases or boxes or crates in which the goods were being transported. To this end, I decided to commission the construction of a prototype metal crate with a false bottom in which we could experiment with concealing our gold bars.

The bars that we intended to export to India from England would weigh one kilogram each, be approximately one-third of an inch thick and the size and shape of a spectacles case. The room required to be left by the false bottom need be, therefore, quite small.

I telephoned Dutta in Bombay and he agreed with me that the new plan might be preferable to the original idea of dropping the gold out of an aircraft. We resolved that once I had designed and arranged the construction of a prototype crate, we would experiment with importing lead ingots into India of the same size and shape as the gold bars before trying the real thing. Dutta's responsibility would be to find a suitable product for importation into India, which we could put into the crates once the gold had been concealed in them. Due to the huge tariffs that India placed on the majority of its imported goods, that product would have to be included on India's 'Open General Licence', a list of essential goods not produced in India and exempt from any importation duties. This was fundamental — if we were required to pay a duty of 200–300% on the goods being imported, any profit we made on smuggling the gold would be virtually wiped out.

I designed an aluminium box three-feet long, two-feet wide and three feet high with a false bottom only half an inch deep. All the edges were riveted to make the crate secure and also to help conceal the secret compartment.

As I discussed the construction of this design with Risdon at his offices, he would ask probing questions that I felt were none of his business, such as where exactly the gold was going, how much gold we were intending to smuggle, how much profit we anticipated making, and so on.

McLaine, like me, thought that Risdon was becoming too nosy.

'Shut up, Peter!' he snapped. 'Stop asking our clients stupid questions. The man wants a box made and it's none of our business. All right?'

In the meantime, Dutta had found the ideal product to import into India. Exhaust gas analysers, which measured the exhaust emissions of motor cars, were included on the 'Open General Licence' list. Since Bombay suffered from an enormous pollution problem caused primarily by older motor vehicles with outdated exhaust systems, we considered that there might be a demand for such a product .

We decided that I should purchase two such analysers in London and fly with them to Bombay. There, we would try to secure an order with a taxi firm.

A few weeks later, Ishan and I went to visit a prospective purchaser in Bombay. The exhaust gas analysers, made primarily of plastic, had cost about £25 each. Having investigated the market for such items back in London, I had chosen the cheapest version. A good-quality analyser would have cost £400 and a very sophisticated machine over £4,000.

The demonstration of our product would prove a disaster.

We arrived at the taxi firm's headquarters in the heat of the midday sun. Under my arm I was carrying a cardboard box that contained the very light, yellow plastic exhaust gas analyser with a couple of black knobs and a dial, that Ishan had sold so convincingly to the company's general manager on the telephone.

The rotund general manager of the taxi firm came out into the square where a hundred or so taxi drivers were lounging around, having been told to attend the demonstration.

Ishan introduced me to the manager, Mr Patel, and, taking the pathetic analyser out of the cardboard box, informed him that the product had been manufactured to the highest possible specifications and was a fine example of British technology. He then addressed the drivers and told them that garages all over Britain used the excellent product, which had been on the market for a number of years. Mr Patel and the drivers seemed impressed.

'I will now demonstrate how the machine works,' Ishan announced.

Mr Patel immediately took command, calling over two drivers and telling them to bring their vehicles to be tested. Within a few minutes two taxis were in the middle of the square, their engines running, and their exhausts belching out thick black smoke.

Ishan bent down and fitted the analyser's plastic tube on to one of the exhausts.

'If you will all kindly stand back so that everyone can see, please,' he said in a tone of authority.

'This needle on the dial here will shoot up the moment I switch the machine on, indicating the level of pollution that is being pumped into the air.'

'Mr Patel,' he asked, 'would you like to turn the switch, please?'

Looking important in his best suit, Mr Patel stepped forward and turned the appropriate black knob. Nothing happened. The needle on the dial hadn't moved a millimetre. Meanwhile, the taxi's exhaust continued to cough out clouds of black smoke.

The crowd of taxi drivers gathered closer to look at the dial while Ishan desperately twiddled the knobs in an effort to extract some sign of life from the machine. Still nothing happened. He looked up at me despairingly, so I sprang forward and tried to make the wretched gadget work.

'I think there's been a slight technical hitch,' I explained to Mr Patel, trying to gain time as I picked the analyser up and shook it vigorously. I then placed it back on the ground, reconnected it and tried again. Once more, the needle didn't register. I looked at Ishan whose face had been blackened by the fumes and began to laugh. Ishan soon joined in, but Mr Patel looked distinctly unamused.

Embarrassed, we promised to return with another machine at a later date and beat a hasty retreat, taking the useless analyser with us. Later that day, we tested the reserve machine on another vehicle and this time it worked. We did not, however, return to the original taxi firm but made an appointment for the following day with another one. On this occasion the demonstration went without a hitch.

After securing an order from this second taxi company, we returned to the new offices that Ishan had taken after quitting his banking job, so sure had he become that our venture would be successful.

From his offices in a tower block high above the bay, we celebrated with a drink as the red sun dipped below the waves. We watched the small cargo boats ferrying back and forth to the large ships anchored out at sea, and wondered whether any gold was being smuggled that day.

We now had a firm order for our exhaust gas analysers from a large Bombay taxi firm; in Goutti, a Government-authorised bullion dealer ready, we were convinced, to distribute and launder our smuggled gold; in the aluminium crates, a method of transporting the gold bars, and sufficient funds to carry out our enterprise.

Back in England, I had one or two loose ends to tie up before the scheme could finally be put into operation. First, I needed to create a front company. I came up with the name 'Regent Motor Accessories' for the firm that would export the gas analysers and had several hundred invoices and letterheads printed. Then I set up an accommodation address in Jacob's Well Mews, in London's West End, in the name of the company. I adopted the alias of Tim Marshall and in

Bombay, Ishan Dutta took the name Aklak Addewala and opened an account with the State Bank of India for 'Indian Gas Analysers', the importing company. He also set up an accommodation address in Bombay's Nariman Point.

There was one final hurdle. We did not want the authorities to know that we were exporting gold from the UK to India so it became necessary to produce fake airway bills, which we could use to show that the gold we were purchasing in London was, in fact, being exported to Switzerland. These airway bills would also enable us to claim back the VAT we had paid on the gold and that we were entitled to have refunded to us in the event of the gold being exported from the country.

Peter Risdon became our forger as well as the supplier of the false-bottomed crates, and a friendly jeweller in London agreed to put the gold we purchased through his books because, due to the BES restrictions, Inca was not allowed to trade in bullion.

By August 1989, we were ready to commence our smuggling operation. First, however, we would experiment with a trial run in which lead bars would be used in place of gold, just in case we had forgotten something in our planning.

One day, Risdon delivered a single aluminium crate to my late grandmother's house in Shawfield Street where I was living at the time. I closed the curtains of the ground-floor sitting-room and found that I could pack thirty-six gas analysers into the crate. The false compartment had room for at least twenty one-kilo gold bars, but I decided to restrict the number to four bars so that, in the event of a Customs officer, either in England or Bombay, deciding to unpack the crate and weigh it, the empty container would not be so disproportionately heavy as to arouse his suspicions.

First, I wrapped each lead bar in cling film and then glued the cling film to the bottom of the crate with Araldite, a particularly strong epoxy resin. I then further secured the four ingots with masking tape so that, however roughly the crate was handled, even if it was dropped, the lead bars would not move or rattle around at the bottom of the crate.

In the spaces between the lead bars we packed polystyrene chippings for yet further security. I put the false bottom into place and attached individually every one of the fifty rivets required to secure it

85

with a rivet-gun I had purchased especially for the purpose. Having completed this exercise, I stepped back and examined the empty crate, imagining that I was a Customs Officer who had emptied the crate of its contents and was looking around inside it. For more than fifteen minutes, I inspected it from every angle and, to me, the false compartment seemed completely undetectable.

Next, I packed the thirty-six cardboard boxes that contained the analysers into the crate and filled the gaps between the boxes with polysterene chippings. Again I stepped back to examine the finished item and, finally, I secured the top. I picked up the crate and estimated that it weighed about fifty kilos, meaning that the four lead ingots constituted only a small proportion of the overall weight.

The following morning, I hired a van and drove it to a freight-forwarding company near Heathrow. I introduced myself as Mr Marshall and explained that I was sending a few samples of a new product to Bombay in the hope of future orders. I handed over the requisite paperwork including the certificate of origin, various invoices and a copy of the letter of credit that Ishan had opened with the State Bank of India to make his order for the gas analysers.

In the event of the lead ingots being discovered, I made certain that no one, including HM Customs or the police, would be able to trace me. I paid the freight charges with a banker's order that I had obtained with cash; the invoices had only the Jacob's Well Mews accommodation address on them, and the rent for that office had been paid in cash. I was convinced that any investigation would draw a blank.

About a fortnight later, the phone rang in my house. It was Ishan Dutta.

'Darry. It worked.'

VII

Weekend parties at Althorp House in the late 1980s were always brilliant and extravagant affairs. Countess Raine Spencer, Barbara Cartland's daughter who married Lord 'Johnny' Spencer in 1975, possessed a definite talent for organising dinners and dances so that the great house pulsated with activity.

Whenever I spent the weekend at Althorp, I would stay at The Falconry, Charlie's Gothic-style house on the estate that conjured up images of Transylvania more than of a typical English country home. Usually, a number of couples were also invited to stay and, from time to time, the high point of such weekends would be one of Raine's spectacular evenings.

Typically, Raine would invite up to two hundred people at a time — perhaps fifty for dinner and another hundred and fifty or so guests who would arrive sometime after 10pm for dancing and drinks. Raine liked to mix her parties and guests would include politicians, writers, businesspeople, and celebrities from the world of theatre, cinema and television, together with a smattering of 'Establishment' figures, a number of peers and their ladies.

Althorp House has been renowned for generations as one of England's finest stately homes. Generations of Charlie's family have spent fortunes amassing a spectacular collection of antiques, silver, porcelain, works of art, carpets and exquisite furniture. At Raine's parties, such opulence was on show for all to enjoy.

Those evenings, Raine was in her element, welcoming people at the top of her voice, acting as the master of ceremonies and generally organising everyone. 'Darius, how lovely to see you!' she would welcome me, flashing a huge smile. On first-name terms with all the guests, she never made an error as to their identity, despite the fact that more than two hundred people might be in attendance, many of whom she had not seen for years.

During one particular party, Charlie asked me to join him for a walk around the house in order to show me how his stepmother had altered the magnificent interior. He took me through the Marlborough suite, the library, the dining-room, the halls, the state rooms and the bedrooms. As we toured, he would point out marble columns that had once been white but were now flourescent green or sweet-wrapper purple; bright satin curtains that had replaced magnificent heavy drapes; exquisite eighteenth-century furniture, restored with an over-zealous use of gilt that would have embarrassed Liberace.

'This place looks like a whore's boudoir,' he remarked, angrily. 'You should have seen how delightful it all was in my grandfather's time. I can remember coming here as a little boy. It was totally different.'

He broke off, went to a shelf and reached for a leather-bound book on Althorp House. Thumbing the pages, and pointing to a number of photographs, he showed me how the house had looked in the 1940s. As he enumerated the changes that had taken place over the past fifteen years or so, he shook his head dejectedly.

'One day, Darry,' he said, 'I promise you I'll restore this house to its former glory. Millions of pounds have been wasted on decorating this place, if you can call it that, and millions more will be required, I'm afraid, to recapture its original beauty.'

Sometimes, at the end of one of these parties Charlie, other guests staying at The Falconry, and I, would slip away after midnight to take a dip in the swimming-pool behind the house. I found this refreshing in more ways than one — although I liked many of the people I had met at those parties, there was a side of me that felt that such evenings were ultimately decadent, in the same way that pre-revolutionary French society had been decadent. Many of the people attending had seemed oblivious to a world beyond the party circuit.

Deep-down I have always despised the world, which, sadly I have too often come into contact with — a world of gossip, chit-chat, minor scandal and social competitiveness. I look with particular scorn on those party-goers whose ambition in life is to have their pictures taken by so-called 'society' magazines as they pose in their party outfits, looking a little too much as though they are having the most wonderful time of their lives. I have witnessed some of the most accomplished gymnastic manoeuvres as social butterflies, desperate to be snapped drinking champagne next to some grandee, navigate through throngs of guests towards a photographer from some glossy magazine. While such comportment is perhaps forgivable in a 20-year-old, it has always surprised me to witness it in older generations.

Whenever I have been approached by photographers on such occasions, after a polite 'no, thank you' if they persist, my social finesse has tended to extend to the only language these people understand — a few sharp words, followed by a threat to push their cameras down their throats.

At first, some photographers thought I was kidding but the regular ones soon realised to keep well away from me. Since my days at Oxford I have considered the society magazines to be vapid and vacuous journals, promoters of snobbery, which bring out my most fanatical instincts.

I would, however, always enjoy weekends at The Falconry, which only a small group of people attended, generally friends with whom I could chat about matters that interested us. I have always preferred the company of a few intimate friends rather than going to large parties and having to endure endless hours of small talk and I suspect that, in this respect, Charlie was very like me.

Sometimes we would take horses and go riding for several hours in the Park. On one occasion, disaster nearly struck. Charlie, his girlfriend Katie Braine, Nick Weslowski, a Polish friend, and I took out four horses on a fresh, sunny day in May.

After a couple of hour's riding, we dropped in to see Jane, Charlie's sister, her husband Sir Robert Fellowes, now the Queen's private secretary, and their two children Laura and Alexander, who were living on the estate in the Garden House, a charming, Georgian *bijou* home with a walled garden. While our horses rested, we had a cool drink and played with the children before setting off again.

On our way to the main house, I began to canter quite fast and Katie, who was riding next to me, suddenly gave a yell as her horse took off into an uncontrolled gallop. 'Stop this horse!' she shouted. 'Stop this horse, please!'

Katie was an experienced rider and she struggled to rein her horse in, but it rapidly became obvious that it was not going to stop and there was nothing Katie could do about it. Charlie and I galloped alongside her trying to grab the reins of her horse, but we couldn't quite get close enough.

'Don't worry, Katie, don't worry!' we shouted. 'Just hang on, keep cool, keep cool!'

While Charlie and I tried at least to look as if we were on top of the situation, I suspect that in reality we had not much more control of our horses than poor Katie.

To her credit Katie did keep her cool and for five minutes, which seemed more like an hour, the three of us galloped headlong down the sweeping lawns towards Althorp House, just missing the over-hanging branches of trees that seemed to be invisible to our runaway horses. Eventually, Charlie and I managed to manoeuvre our horses alongside Katie's and bring it to a stop. Katie dismounted, utterly exhausted. She slapped her horse and burst into tears, overcome by relief. In fact, we had been very fortunate in managing to come to a halt only a few yards short of a wide cattle grid.

On another occasion I took Charlie for a spin in a light, four-seater aircraft around the estate, taking off from Sywell Airfield, near Northampton. We flew over the main house and buzzed the gamekeeper at two hundred feet. Charlie was fascinated to see the layout of the whole estate from an aerial perspective.

Apart from flying, my other great passion was kick-boxing, a sport I first took up properly in early 1989 when I was taken by a friend to a free-style karate club in London's King's Cross. As I watched world-class exponents of the sport that night, I determined that I would practise it myself. The King's Cross *Dojo*, the Japanese term for a karate gymnasium, was run by Sensei Meiji Suzuki, one of the all-time great masters, who had been World Karate Champion on many occasions. Under his leadership his club produced a continuous stream of British, European and World champions and one of them, Dwyer Evelyn, became my personal instructor.

At least three times a week, I would go to the King's Cross Dojo to train on my own and in groups. The high point of the evenings were the sparring classes, in which ten to twenty other boxers would take part. These sessions, sometimes two hours long, would involve fighting one-on-one for three minutes at a time with a minute's rest between each round. After each round, we would change partners in order to experience different fighting styles. We were equipped with protective head-gear, mouth guards, groin protectors, gloves and shin pads, sensible precautions as the sparring could become very physical at times.

During these bouts, in which fists and feet were used to strike the opponent, it was surprising that not only did no one ever suffer serious injury but that afterwards there was a remarkable camaraderie among all the participants. Often, we would go for meals together or meet up at a number of tournaments. The energy and enthusiasm we all displayed inside the club helped to create an atmosphere of trust and friendship that drew everyone together outside it.

The black belt grading sessions, considered by many martial artists from several different clubs to be the toughest in London, were the highlight of the Dojo's activities. Under the club's rules, the prospective black belt would have to fight, in turn, the club's seven senior fighters, all of whom were champions. Throughout these sessions the seven champions would be determined to test him to the ultimate and would aim, if possible, to injure him, even to the extent of hospitalising him.

During one particular black belt grading, my girlfriend and I were both spattered with blood even though we were sitting five yards from the action. The challenger, hardly able to stand up by the seventh round put up a heroic struggle, so much so that Sensei Meiji promoted him not simply to black belt, but to black belt second dan. The following evening, when I returned to the Dojo, I found the successful fighter hardly able to walk. He was limping severely, had two black eyes, a cut lip, his arm in a sling and a wonderful smile of achievement on his face. Truly proud of him, I gave him a hero's embrace.

I came to like and respect many of these fighters who came from a variety of countries and backgrounds. They would become good friends and for more than three years I spent much of my spare time in their company. It was the camaraderie that I enjoyed as much as the actual kick-boxing, although the sparring in particular gave me a phenomenal adrenalin rush that I never found to a similar degree in other sports.

In the summer of 1989, Charlie and I were invited to an evening garden party in Pelham Street thrown by our friend Nick Weslowski. To my surprise Victoria Lockwood, who I hadn't seen since my Oxford days, was also there. She looked painfully thin and fragile, but very beautiful with a sort of medieval serenity about her. During the years since I had last seen her I had followed her career as a successful model, photographed by David Bailey and others, and watched as she had become a well-known face on the pages of fashion magazines.

I knew from looking at her that she had been suffering from some form of eating disorder and she talked to me of her problems, not wishing to dwell on them but rather to skate around them, explaining how she was now recovering but needed more time to sort herself out. She seemed more sensitive than I could remember and I found her gentle and vulnerable. After chatting for about an hour, Charlie came over and I introduced them to each other.

The following day Charlie phoned to ask for Victoria's number. 'I think she's stunning, beautiful,' he told me, and I knew he was smitten.

During the next six weeks, Charlie would phone from time to time, inevitably bringing the subject around to Victoria. I had witnessed Charlie's reaction to previous girlfriends with whom he had become involved, but never before had I found him so romantic as he seemed with Victoria.

At about 8.30am one morning, some weeks after Nick Weslowski's party, the phone rang as I was preparing to leave for the office. It was Charlie. 'Darry,' he said, 'Victoria and I are getting married.'

'That's great, Charlie,' I replied.

'I'm putting her on to you,' he said.

'Darry, I'm so happy,' Victoria told me, her voice trembling with obvious emotion. 'Isn't it wonderful?'

'Great news, Victoria, I'm so happy for you,' I replied.

'Listen Darry, Charlie's got a question he wants to ask you. I'll put him on.'

'Darry, I want you to be my best man.'

'I'd be delighted,' I replied.

'Good, that's one thing sorted out.'

Two or three weeks later, Charlie and Victoria decided that there should be a small supper at Charlie's house in Notting Hill so that the two families could get together before the big day. They invited Charlie's mother Frances, John and Ellie Lockwood, Victoria's brother

Christopher, and me.

During the meal there was only one potentially awkward moment when John Lockwood cracked a joke. Frances mentioned that a few days previously, one of her grandsons, Alexander Fellowes, who had recently started prep school, had bitten her on the arm while they were larking around. John leaned over and said, 'The boy obviously has impeccable taste.'

Frances smiled graciously. The ice had been broken.

I talked for some time with John Lockwood because he worked at the Civil Aviation Authority and we discussed the problems of light aircraft pilots having to fly in Britain's congested airspace. When I discovered that Victoria's mother Ellie was a part-time magistrate, I suspected that she would not exactly appreciate the fact that I was about to start smuggling gold into India and I wondered what her reaction would have been had I mentioned it.

Throughout the dinner party Charlie and Victoria were constantly together, kissing and cuddling, holding hands and looking at each other. When I left that night I felt happy that my best friend had found a girl with whom he had truly fallen in love.

Charlie asked me to organise his stag night, saying that he wanted the arrangements to be a surprise. I booked the dining-hall at Brooks', one of the most famous and certainly the most agreeable of London's gentlemen's clubs, and invited thirty of his closest male friends, many from his Eton and Oxford days.

I collected Charlie from his home and took him to Brooks' in St James's in time for pre-dinner drinks. Expensive wines flowed throughout the five-course meal and many took it in turns to say a few words and recount various hilarious anecdotes about the groom-to-be. There were, however, a number of guests who could hardly string more than a few words together by the end of the main course. The evening had only just begun.

At 11pm we piled into taxis and made for the next rendezvous, the largest suite we could hire on the top floor of the Hilton Hotel in Park Lane. One of the guests had arranged for some strippers to attend and at about midnight, a number of beautiful young girls walked into the suite to cheers from those still standing. They disappeared into one of the bedrooms and came out looking sensational. They had brought along their own tapes and a ghetto blaster and, as we sat around for the following hour, the girls put on a show for us. Some of the guests ended up in various states of undress but Charlie did not indulge, although he seemed to enjoy thoroughly the entertainment that had been organised.

At 3am, Charlie decided to escape while he could still stand but the party would continue until dawn. The girls were great sports, putting up with lots of nonsense and ribald remarks but never once losing their sense of humour. They danced with all the guests, although some could barely put one foot in front of the other, and seemed genuinely to enjoy the party. Eventually, after a full English breakfast, the party finished and we all went our separate ways. During the next few days I received phone calls from most of the guests saying how much they had enjoyed themselves and how pleased they had been to see Charlie relaxed and having fun. They all felt that we had given him a send-off he would never forget.

A few weeks later, more than two hundred people, mainly relatives and close friends, attended Charles and Victoria's wedding at St Mary's Church in Great Brington, in Northamptonshire — an exquisite building, part of it dating back to 1200 and a few miles from Althorp House, where generations of the Spencer family lie buried. Charlie and I arrived in his black Range Rover to find hundreds of well-wishers lining the road to the church, cheering and waving their Union Jacks.

After posing for official photographs for the crowd of over a hundred Press photographers, we went inside to await Victoria.

At eight o'clock that morning I had met Charlie's sister, Diana, at Althorp House where she was staying. I had showered and dressed in my tails and had gone over to the main house to see Charles who was breakfasting with his mother. As I ran up the stairs, I saw Prince William and Prince Harry running around the house with the Fellowes children.

From one of the bedrooms, Diana suddenly appeared barefoot and dressed in a long, white nightgown. Seeing me dashing up the stairs she seemed slightly taken aback.

'Good morning, Darius,' she said.

'Good morning, Ma'am,' I replied, a little embarrassed.

At that moment, we saw William and Harry and a couple of other children rushing headlong down the corridor and we smiled at their rumbustious behaviour.

'Have you seen Charlie?' I asked.

'No, I'm sorry, I haven't. How is he by the way? Nervous?'

'He's fine, very cool.'

'Was that your black Mercedes parked outside The Falconry?' she asked.

'Yes. Why?'

'I like it very much. I was thinking of buying one myself.'

'They're great,' I replied. 'But excuse me, I must find Charlie.'

'Yes, of course,' she replied, 'see you later.'

A few hours later, sitting directly behind me in church were Prince Charles, Diana and William. Understandably, the young Prince was fidgeting and turning round, looking out for Victoria. 'When's she coming?' he must have asked half a dozen times.

I had been given both the bride and the bridegroom's wedding rings for safe-keeping and, like many a best man before me, became convinced that I would drop them, something which would have been calamitous because just where Charlie and I were due to stand throughout the ceremony, was an open heating grill below us in the stone floor. I kept visualising dropping the rings and seeing them disappear into the cellars below the church. Fortunately, all went well.

Victoria arrived at the church with her father in a magnificent nineteenth-century carriage, borrowed from the Spencer family's exceptional collection of carriages and coaches. Pale and beautiful, she looked as though she had stepped from an eighteenth-century portrait in her elegant, antique, cream lace wedding-gown, with Russian sable trimming the end of her veil and the waistline of the dress.

The page boys, Prince Harry, then five, and his cousin Alexander Fellowes, then six, wore biscuit-coloured silk trousers and frilled shirts with burgundy taffeta sashes, as well as broad-rimmed dark green hats so that they looked almost identical to one of the Spencer ancestors as a small boy, whose portrait by Joshua Reynolds in 1779 hung in the main house. The bridesmaids were Emily McCorquodale, then six, and Eleanor Fellowes, also six, both Charlie's nieces, who wore pale chiffon gowns trimmed with burgundy, a design copied from a portrait of Lady Georgiana Spencer by Thomas Gainsborough in 1763, which also hung in the big house.

After the hour-long service, conducted by the Archbishop of

Canterbury, Dr Robert Runcie, Charlie and Victoria, their parents and the bridesmaids retired to the vestry to sign the official register. Outside, there was much celebration and the bride and groom stepped into their horse-drawn carriage, which would take them back to Althorp House where a magnum of champagne that Charlie had left there earlier awaited them.

I had found the entire day rather melancholy, not just because it rained for most of the time, but because for me it spelt the end of so many carefree days of youth. Charlie, my best friend, with whom I had enjoyed so many memorable times, was beginning a new life. In The Falconry visitor's book I had written the comment, 'The end of an era' and although of course I was happy for him, inevitably I also felt a little nostalgic. By the time the wedding ceremony had finished, I just wanted to be on my own.

Immediately before the wedding breakfast, I had chatted with Charles about the speeches. He had indicated to me that he intended to make a short speech, thanking everyone but standing on his feet for as little time as was necessary. When the wedding cake was brought in I realised that I would rather not go ahead with the traditional best man's speech.

'Charlie,' I asked when we were alone, 'do you mind very much if I don't make a speech?'

'No,' he replied, 'no problem at all. I'm keeping mine short.'

'Are you sure?' I pressed.

'Yes, Darry, don't worry. I really don't mind. Promise.'

I felt relieved that he had taken it so well.

After a few hours of mingling with the guests in the big house, I looked at my watch. It was time to make the phone call that had been worrying me all day. I went to the study and dialled the Bombay number where, it had been arranged, Ishan Dutta would be waiting to give me news.

Only days before, having successfully smuggled through a dummy run of lead ingots to Bombay, I had dispatched our first shipment of gold and the call would tell me whether it had arrived safely. I had put the whole of my personal wealth into this consignment. If the authorities had discovered the bullion I would be in real financial trouble, Inca would in all likelihood have to be liquidated and I could face bankruptcy.

The phone rang only twice before Ishan Dutta answered.

'Ishan, since you're not in jail, I presume it went well?'

'Good news, Darry, it cleared.'

'Any problems?' I asked.

'No, it went like a dream.'

After putting the phone down, I realised just how tense I must have been. An intense feeling of elation mixed with triumph swept through me. I sat down in an armchair and looked out of a window at the rain falling peacefully in the Park. Everything I had gambled on for the past ten months had finally succeeded. And, as I drove back to London later that evening, I recalled every move I had made in buying the gold, packing and shipping it, and the agonising wait for it to clear the Bombay Customs.

*   *   *

Ten days before, I had telephoned a Swiss bank in the City, enquiring into the spot price of gold. I had then asked, in as matter of fact a voice as possible, whether the bank would be prepared to accept cash in payment for any bars that they sold me. I had wondered whether this question would cause the bank official on the end of the phone to become suspicious and had hoped that there was not some automatic mechanism whereby when someone made such an enquiry out of the blue, the police were immediately informed. But it was a risk I had had to take.

Having established that what I was asking for was indeed possible, two days before I was due to purchase the bullion I had flown to Switzerland, where I had the sum required to purchase the gold on deposit in a Swiss bank in Geneva. I had collected the money in £50 notes, put it all in a green hold-all and returned the same day. I had travelled business class and had kept the holdall in the locker immediately above my head. At no time did anyone stop me and on returning to Heathrow, I had walked straight through the Customs green channel.

That night I had stayed at home and read, keeping the bag full of money under the bed. The following morning, I had driven to a bank in the city and parked on the double yellow line immediately outside. I had walked into the hall and addressed one of the cashiers: 'I'd like to buy twenty kilos of "four nines" (twenty-four carat) gold and I'd like them in one-kilo bars, please.'

The cashier didn't blink an eye, but asked how I intended to pay for the bullion.

'Cash. How much will it come to?' I asked.

'One minute, Sir.'

She left her position and returned with one of the bank's managers who came out into the main hall.

I had checked the London fixing price of bullion that morning and knew that the gold I had ordered would cost approximately £185,000 including 15 per cent VAT.

'Could I have a word, Sir?' the manager asked, speaking in a quiet, secretive manner.

'Yes, of course.'

He explained: 'Sir, you must understand that due to recent, how can I put it, rather inconvenient drugs legislation, we now have to check the provenance of all large quantities of cash that are deposited with our bank. I am sure you can appreciate that I am duty-bound to ask you where this money has come from.'

I was dressed in a tailored black pin-striped suit and I suspected he thought that, with my dark, almost Latin, looks, I was probably some Colombian drugs baron. For a moment, I felt like putting on a spurious Spanish accent just to tease him a little but in the end thought better of it.

'Of course I understand your position,' I told him.

'From the bank's point of view,' I went on, 'where would it be most convenient for the money to have come from?'

After a moment's thought, he replied, 'I suppose it would be particularly convenient if it was part of an inheritance.'

He chuckled, as though sharing a joke with me.

'Well then,' I told him, 'of course that's where it came from.'

'In that case, Sir, I anticipate no problem with your prospective purchase.'

'That's excellent. We understand each other perfectly.'

'Quite so, Sir.'

He added, 'You will excuse me then, Sir. I had better attend to your needs. Let me recap. You require twenty kilos of "four nines". Is that correct?'

'That's right,' I replied. 'Shall I wait here?'

'That will be fine, Sir. I'll have an invoice drawn up.'

I handed over the satchel full of money. 'While you're having the bullion brought up, perhaps you would ask someone to check the money and let me have the balance?'

'Excellent, Sir. I must add that I do like doing business with gentlemen.'

Twenty minutes later he produced the bullion, the invoice and the balance of my money.

Two bank messengers placed the bullion, all twenty kilos of it, on the leather sofa beside me.

The manager said, 'Everything is in order, Sir. Here is the balance of your money. May I say what a pleasure it has been.'

As I walked out of the bank carrying the twenty kilos of gold in my briefcase and my rather empty holdall, I saw a City of London police officer standing by my car.

'Good morning, Sir. Is this your car?' he asked.

'Yes, it is, Officer,' I replied, walking towards it.

'May I request you to move it immediately, Sir, otherwise I will have to call for it to be towed away.'

'I'm sorry, Officer, but I had an important collection to make from that bank.'

To prove my point I handed him my briefcase containing the bullion.

Surprised by the weight, the officer said, 'What have you got in here — a body?'

'Not quite,' I replied, 'some gold bars.'

I went and opened the boot of the car and the officer placed the briefcase inside.

As I walked towards the driver's door, I quipped, 'Thanks very much. Now if you would like to go into the bank, you can untie the staff.'

He smiled, 'Very funny, Sir.'

I drove home planning my next move, realising that throughout I had to be meticulous in everything I did.

That night I packed five crates with exhaust gas analysers, putting four kilos in the bottom of each crate and making sure, as with the lead ingots before, that the bullion was secure. The following day, I delivered the crates to the freight-forwarding company which I had used in the previous trial run, together with the usual documentation.

It was a few days after this that I had driven to Northamptonshire for Charlie's wedding, hoping that at some point during the celebrations I would be able to speak to Ishan.

*   *   *

A few days after the wedding, I took an Air India flight to Bombay and Ishan met me at the airport.

'Everything OK?' I enquired.

'Fine,' he said. 'The crates are in the warehouse.' Then he smiled and added, 'Let's hope the gold is there as well.'

I knew what he meant. It was of course always possible that the Indian Customs had found the bullion, carefully replaced it, and were waiting for us to pick it up.

The next morning we drove in Ishan's jeep to the fenced compound near the airport, which was permanently patrolled by armed guards and where the crates had been delivered. We had rented an entire warehouse, about thirty yards long by twelve yards across, so that we could dismantle our crates in private.

None of the warehouses had power points, so we had taken along a hand-drill to remove all the rivets individually from each crate. After half an hour's work, we were drenched in sweat owing to the extreme temperatures inside the building. We were working in heat of more than a hundred degrees and had taken off our shirts in an effort to cool down. Outside, buzzards were hopping lazily around in the heat.

'This is stupid, Ishan,' I remarked. 'At this rate, we'll still be here at midnight!'

'I agree,' he said, 'but we have to do it by hand because there's no power for an electric drill.'

'Perhaps,' I said, 'but wait a minute. I'll be back.'

I took the jeep, which had been parked outside the warehouse, and drove to the main entrance gate, a few hundred yards away. I asked a guard if he could let me borrow a sledgehammer from the compound's stores and, in exchange, gave him a few rupees.

Back in the warehouse, we chose a crate at random, took out the gas analysers, turned the crate upside down, whereupon I lifted the sledgehammer above my head and smashed it against the false bottom of the crate. After three or four blows, it dropped down and the bars slid to the ground.

I looked at the door, half expecting Indian Customs Officers to rush in to the warehouse. Then I turned to Ishan. 'We're in business,' I remarked, wiping the sweat from my brow.

Within twenty minutes, we had smashed open the other four crates and had found all the gold intact. We put the bullion in a briefcase and drove off to Ishan's apartment in Colaba Hills in Bombay. We phoned Goutti, the bullion and gems dealer we had approached some months before, and he told us he would send his runner, Bancil, to collect the gold.

During the next few days Bancil would arrive, sometimes accompanied by other runners, and collect just a few bars at a time. He would then go out into the marketplace and sell the bars to the dealers who offered the best price. The transactions would always be for cash, in rupees, and he would then deposit this money with his boss, Goutti. While we waited for the various transactions to be completed, Ishan took me sightseeing around Bombay, including to the remarkable Elephanta Island.

Ten days later, Goutti phoned, telling us that all the transactions had been completed and inviting us to his office. There, he explained in great detail precisely what had happened, informing us how much he had managed to obtain for the gold, the percentage amount of his commission, and the amount the currency dealer had deposited in my bank account in Geneva. The black market currency dealer had charged a massive 20 per cent for changing the rupees into sterling and depositing the money in Switzerland. Later, I would phone my bank and confirm that the figures were exactly as Goutti had explained. We had made a net profit of £40,000 after all expenses.

Later, we would get around the problem of India's currency restrictions by purchasing gemstones for the cash rupees generated from the sale of the gold bars in the market, smuggling them to Geneva, New York and Bangkok and selling them for hard currency. In this way, we would manage to make profits of between 40 and 50 per cent per shipment after all expenses had been paid.

Back in London after that first success, Ben and I were jubilant. I had found a way of making substantial money and of saving Inca. All we had to do was to carry on smuggling the bullion and raking in the profits.

Later, however, during a visit to India, we would hear some bad news that threatened to wreck our money-making venture. Market sources in Bombay were convinced that the Indian Government was planning to legalise the importation of gold bullion. Were this to occur, it would render to nought our smuggling activities. Soon the profit margins on our shipments started to drop as the market began to discount the effects of the proposed legislation. This would mean finding larger amounts of capital to invest in the gold project in order to maintain our current levels of profit.

We had no idea how long it would be before the Indian Government might act, but time was now of the essence. Unfortunately, we still did not have sufficent capital to make massive short-term profits by smuggling tons of gold bullion.

For many years, I had been turning over in my mind how I would get back at Lloyds for bringing my father to the edge of ruin. From all I had read since the Lloyds scandal broke, I felt that certain Lloyds agents were in large measure responsible for what had happened, putting investors' money into dicey syndicates that would one day collapse under massive insurance claims.

I needed capital, and quickly, and so did Inca. I decided that Lloyds would provide it. So I hatched my plan of vengeance.

VIII

For the previous few years, I had seen my father racked with worry over his mounting debts to Lloyds and had made it my business to find out as much as I could about the practices of the Lloyds' professionals, which had ruined so many 'names'.

The picture that emerged was not a pretty one.

In 1978–79 it had been widely known in the insurance market, at least among the professionals, that impending claims, primarily from asbestosis and pollution, were immeasurable. The then Chairman of Lloyds, Murray Lawrence, sent a letter around this time to all agents in Lloyds warning them of the approaching tidal wave and advising them to alert their 'names' accordingly. However, for some reason this letter was ignored.

Indeed, it seems clear that instead a strategy emerged among the Lloyds' professionals to expand their business out of imminent catastrophe by recruiting large numbers of uninformed 'names' and spreading the risk among them. In my view, those agents, who were aware of impending disaster, but who nevertheless enrolled 'names' after this point without warning them were at best guilty of gross negligence.

Now, some have argued that this process, which accounted for the very great expansion of Lloyds in the early 1980s, evolved entirely coincidentally, others that it represented something more sinister. For me, there are simply too many coincidences and give-away signs to make the former view a credible option.

Perhaps the most renowned accusations that have been levelled against Lloyds concern the practice of 'reinsuring to close'.

At the very time that large numbers of 'names' were being lured into Lloyds through a massive recruitment campaign, and while an avalanche of claims was hanging over the market, for some reason, reinsurance — the selling on of risk by syndicates seeking to 'close' (or finish their business) — became remarkably cheap. The big buyers of this risk were the so-called 'dustbin' syndicates into which, typically, the great majority of 'names' were placed by professionals who benefited from healthy commissions irrespective of the performance of their clients — people such as writers, artists, clergymen, retired army personnel and non-business folk — in other words, the type of people least in a position to kick up a fuss when disaster struck. Analyses of the performance and membership profiles of these 'dustbin' syndicates have revealed, however, that certain people associated with Lloyds managed with uncanny consistency to avoid these disastrous syndicates and, indeed, some have fared rather well throughout a period of stupendous losses at Lloyds.

In addition, although a number of agents' businesses have gone bankrupt, many of these agents continue as individuals to live lavish lifestyles. Indeed, at the very time that thousands of names were being reduced to virtual penury, such agents were awarding themselves large bonuses.

In short, from everything that I had read on the subject, and from numerous conversations with those involved in litigation over the Lloyds débâcle, including lawyers and even Lloyds' professionals themselves, there was and remains little doubt in my mind, that exactly the same series of events, had it involved a less important institution, would have landed a lot of people in serious trouble.

One day, in the autumn of 1989, I decided to broach the subject to my partner Ben Marsh, not knowing how he would take to the idea of ripping off Lloyds of London. He had always known of my anger towards Lloyds for what they had done to my father, but he had never quite realised the extent of it or just how far I was prepared to go.

Some weeks after the first successful shipment of gold to India, Ben and I were discussing the problems that faced Inca. We both realised that the company was seriously under-capitalised and could never achieve any substantial profits owing to the crippling restrictions placed on it by the Inland Revenue. Now, the economic recession, which had hit the international gem market hard, had only served to compound matters. We had reached a crisis point and a drastic solution was required.

'You know that it's absolutely vital we make some real capital and pretty quick, don't you?' I said to Ben, bringing up an issue that we had often discussed in the past.

'Yes, I know, but what the hell do we do about it?' he replied.

'I've been thinking a lot about the problem,' I went on, 'but I don't know for sure how we can make enough capital to save the company in the longer term.'

'We know the gold smuggling won't go on for ever,' Ben said, 'so what do we do after that?'

'I might have an idea,' I suggested, thinking aloud.

'What? Rob a bank!'

'No. Rob Lloyds instead,' I replied.

That stirred Ben. 'What do you mean?' he asked.

'Only an idea.'

'No, go on, Darry. Tell me. What's on your mind?'

'Listen,' I said, 'I've been thinking. You know that our insurance policy is with Lloyds under a Jewellers Block Policy. What do you think would happen if we lost all our stock?'

'Like all insurance companies, they'd find some way of getting off the hook, especially bloody Lloyds,' Ben replied, without a hint of irony in his voice. He continued, 'Do you remember those pagers that were stolen from my car about a year ago?'

'Yes, they were only worth a couple of hundred pounds.'

'Well, Darry, when we put in the insurance claim they found some clause written in unreadably tiny print in the terms and conditions of the policy. And they didn't pay.'

'Perhaps,' I said. 'But that was a tiny claim and it wouldn't have been worth taking them to court over it, which is precisely why they didn't pay up. With a much larger claim, provided we did things in a watertight way, their reputations would be on the line. If they tried any hanky-panky we'd take them straight to court and it would look very bad for them indeed if it was clear that they were just trying to wriggle off the hook. Their so-called reputation is the only thing they can hide behind. Strangely enough, I think it's precisely the big claims that they'll think twice about before trying any stunts. Anyway, what do we lose? If they don't pay the company goes bust, but if we don't put in a claim, the company goes bust in any case.'

'Darry,' Ben said, 'are you being serious?'

'Dead serious.'

'Have you got a plan?'

'I think so,' I said. 'I've been thinking how it could be done. And it might just work.'

For a moment or two, Ben said nothing. Then he jumped to his feet. 'Yeah, why not?' he exclaimed. 'Stuff Lloyds! Anyway, it'd be a real challenge.'

Pursuing my idea, I continued, 'How about if we get robbed?'

'What, you and me?' Ben asked.

'Yes,' I said. 'You and me. Of course we'd have to make it totally realistic.'

'You're telling me,' he laughed. 'Otherwise not being paid by Lloyds will be the least of our troubles. Somehow I've never fancied the idea of sharing a cell with a sex-starved six-foot-five armed robber with a penchant for blond men! I don't know about you Eton boys,' he quipped, 'but that's definitely not my scene at all!'

Again, he paused.

Then, in a quiet, unemotional voice, he continued, 'OK, Darry, let's go for it. And let's just hope that armed robber doesn't have bad breath!'

During the next few weeks, Ben and I discussed many possibilities about how we would carry out the sting. Most of the discussions took place at my home in Shawfield Street, where Ben had a room.

So many different motives combined to drive us into action. While the prospect of making some money for ourselves was certainly a factor, it was by no means the only, nor even the most important, one. Ben and I had always had a very practical approach where money was concerned — money was quite simply a means of exchange. There was nothing glamorous or romantic about it. If anything it was distasteful, only useful in so far as it afforded those who had it a certain freedom from economic slavery. Indeed, it would in time become one of our prosecutors' major problems to prove a lavish lifestyle on our parts, for the prospect of such a lavish lifestyle could be, or so they supposed, the only sane motive for having done what we did. When no evidence of extravagance on our parts was discovered, however, any neat little theories about greed had to be abandoned. In fact, from the way in which we structured our sting on Lloyds, while as individuals we certainly benefited financially from our actions, by far the biggest beneficiary was clearly Inca, of which Ben and I owned only some 5 per cent, for it was Inca whose stones would be insured and it was Inca that would, therefore, be the beneficiary of any insurance pay-out.

Other factors were more important to us — a desire for revenge on my part, coupled with a desperate wish to save our company on both our parts. But while it was a combination of motives that had prompted our initial decision to sting Lloyds, there is no denying that sheer bravado took over after that point and carried us through. Many people, I daresay, have fantasised about some daring plan in their lives but it takes something more, some extra ingredient, to actually execute it, to translate a dream into a real event. For us, it was the desire to pit ourselves against the system and win. It was this mélange of motives, therefore, which spurred us into action. Any one of these motives taken on its own would have been insufficient.

At first, we planned to stage the fake robbery at our offices in London, but soon decided that it would be better to be 'robbed' abroad in order to create investigative and judicial difficulties for the authorities. New York seemed the ideal location — it was the world's largest gems centre; Ben and I had been there many times and knew the place well; also, Inca's gemmological consultant had advised us to try selling our stones in the lucrative New York market; and, finally, we knew that robberies were very common in New York.

One of the major problems that we faced at that time was how to carry out the sting without involving anyone else. At first, we agreed we wanted no one else involved for obvious reasons but the more we examined the possibilities of staging the 'robbery' on our own, the more impractical it seemed.

One of us could always rob the other, but we decided against this because we needed each other to corroborate the story. We also felt that it would be unfair that only one of us, namely the 'victim' of the robbery, should have to take all the heat, the police questioning and the psychological pressure.

In addition, we realised that a gun would be needed for a variety of reasons. For one, we understood that the great majority of robberies in New York involved firearms. We also knew that firing a gun would make the robbery appear far more realistic. But if we used one ourselves, then we would need to dispose of it before calling the police.

This would mean one of us leaving the scene of the robbery to throw the weapon into the East River or wherever we decided to get rid of it. Whoever it was would then risk being spotted. Furthermore, if we fired the gun at say 2pm, then left the scene to dispose of it, returned some time later, say 4pm, tied each other up and finally called the police, they would be able to ascertain roughly when the gun had been fired, and our whole story would be fatally compromised.

In short, although neither of us liked the idea, we came to the firm conclusion that we needed a third person to help us carry out the plan.

Ben and I were fully aware that once the robbery had taken place, especially if a firearm had been discharged, we would be subjected to intense grilling by the police and the loss adjustors invesigating the insurance claim. Our stories would have to be consistent in every detail. It was almost certain that we would be separated and cross-questioned about what had happened.

For this reason we concluded that it was essential for us to experience what would be, to all intents and purposes, a genuine armed robbery; to go through the trauma of being tied up, shot at and robbed in order to give a truly convincing account of what we were to claim had happened.

'It's not going to be easy,' I told Ben.

'I know,' he said, 'we can always trust each other but the crucial question remains — who are we going to find as our accomplice?'

We considered flying to New York and hiring some local hoodlum with a gun who we could pay perhaps $500–$1,000. The problem lay, of course, in how to approach the right person in a place where we were strangers. Looking back on it, it would have been decidedly better if we had opted for this course of action, for the one thing I should have changed in our plan was our eventual choice of person to carry out the robbery.

In choosing our accomplice, we clearly had to find someone in whom we had some basic trust, for there was always the possibility that the person we approached might simply agree to everything we suggested and then later reveal our plan to the police. If, however, we put our idea to someone in whom we had a reasonable degree of confidence then, at least if he turned it down, he would not use it against us. In addition, of course, the accomplice also had to be someone who would be prepared to become involved in a conspiracy to cheat Lloyds of London.

We considered asking Tom McLaine for we knew that he had served a prison sentence for armed robbery and we believed we could trust him. Instinctively, Ben and I liked McLaine more than Peter Risdon because he seemed more direct and more honest. McLaine was a man of violence with a hell of a temper, but we also considered that he possessed the criminal's code of not 'grassing'.

We fully realised that in any conspiracy, indeed any campaign of any description — be it military, political, or even something like a business takeover — the one element that no one can ever guarantee entirely against is the possibility that one of your team, is, or might later turn out to be, a traitor.

One day, when McLaine came to our offices to deliver some of the crates that were used in the gold-smuggling operation, Ben and I decided to approach him.

Testing the water, I asked him: 'Tom, we're planning a sales trip to New York and we'll be carrying a lot of gems. We may need a bodyguard. Would you like to come along?'

'Sorry mate,' he replied, 'but I don't have a passport so I can't go anywhere. With my record, I don't think I'd be very welcome in the States, either.'

When he had left the room, we looked at each other. 'Damn!' said Ben. 'That means we'll have to ask Risdon.'

Risdon had often boasted to us about his alleged criminal activities. Crime seemed to fascinate him and he looked up to McLaine because of his past 'form'. Risdon constantly seemed eager to prove himself to McLaine but, while Ben and I felt that he relished the idea of being a successful gangster, we questioned whether he realised fully what this would entail. Nevertheless, although he seemed something of a dreamer, we doubted that he would betray us. Moreover, throughout our relationship of nine months with him, he had proved efficient in providing the crates to smuggle the bullion, as well as the fake airway bills that had been required to show shipments of gold going to Switzerland as opposed to India. We also knew that other people were using his services for a variety of dubious and criminal dealings.

Other points suggested that it was unlikely he would inform on us.

For one, we knew too much about his illegal activities to make it worth his while. And there was something else — he was terrified of McLaine. Although Risdon was a tall man, standing at 6ft 5ins, while McLaine was a short, stocky man of 5ft 8ins, McLaine would have eaten him for breakfast.

On one occasion we had witnessed McLaine lose his temper with him, chasing him round the office. Risdon managed to escape, running out of the building with a look of terror on his face and not returning until he had phoned to see whether McLaine had cooled down. Eventually, Ben and I had been able to prevail on McLaine to leave Risdon alone, telling him that beating him up wasn't really worth his trouble. Reluctantly, McLaine had agreed and let the matter drop. In short, we felt confident that Risdon would never risk earning his hero's displeasure, and a damn good beating, by committing the cardinal sin of grassing his accomplices.

We decided to put the plan to him and arranged to meet in a tapas bar in Clapham. Ben and I arrived separately in our cars on a cool October evening and found Risdon sitting at a quiet corner table.

Briefly, I explained the history of my father's association with Lloyds and how this had made my motives very personal. Ben explained that Inca was in financial difficulties and went on to outline how we planned to fly to New York, stay in a plush hotel, and arrange for someone to rob us at gunpoint so that we could claim the insurance from Lloyds.

'How much will the claim be for?' Risdon asked.

'About two million pounds,' I said.

Playing the man to whom everyone went with such requests, he sat back in his chair and smiled, relaxed, ever the professional.

'And we want you to act as the robber.'

He nodded. Naturally. Of course, of course.

Ben continued, speaking quietly, 'Listen, Peter. We'll be providing all the capital and expenses for this job and we'll be the ones putting our necks on the line. When the police come to interview us, the heat will be on Darry and me. If it goes wrong, we're the ones who go to jail. Basically what we want you to do will take perhaps half an hour. And if you're prepared to go along with the plan, you can rest assured that we'll pay you handsomely for your services.'

'I appreciate all that,' Risdon said, now leaning forward and looking round the room. 'You could probably get some local mug to do it for fifty quid but that would be too risky. To be frank, I need the money so I'll do it for fifteen grand plus all expenses, but no less. At least that way you'll be sure of a professional job.'

Risdon sat back expansively. 'Listen, Darius, you know I've helped you in other matters and you've never had a complaint. Right?'

'That's true,' I agreed.

Risdon could sense that we still weren't entirely convinced.

'Listen,' he said, 'I stood trial in Scotland for an armed robbery when me and two other blokes were supposed to have tried to rob a hotel with a sawn-off shotgun. We got off in the end. I can tell you, when we were charged I kept my cool, totally. No cop would ever crack me now. I've been in this game far too long for that. Seen too much. Know too much.'

I looked him in the eye and said quietly, 'We'll need a gun and you'll have to fire it at us so that the robbery looks realistic.'

'No problem,' he said, 'I can get you one easily from my extensive contacts in the States. I know a lot about weapons and things. Listen,' he continued, not wishing to lose the initiative, 'at the moment I'm negotiating with the Ministry of Defence to supply arms to an African state that must, of course, remain nameless. It's classified information, you understand.'

I looked at Ben to see whether he still had doubts. 'Peter,' I said, 'I have no doubt that your criminal pedigree is second to none. The question is simple. Can you get the gun, preferably with a silencer, and have it in New York within the next few months?'

Risdon whispered his reply: 'Consider it done.'

'So we're all agreed then?' Ben said.

'As far as I'm concerned, it's already been done. You've got a deal. Fifteen grand plus all expenses, including the cost of the gun. And I want it in cash, pounds sterling.'

Risdon paused, took a deep breath and said, 'I want five thousand up front and ten when the job's done. All right?'

'It's a deal,' Ben replied.

As Risdon took a large gulp of wine, I left him in no doubt about what he had agreed. 'Before we go, do you understand exactly what you're getting yourself involved in?'

'Yes, of course I do,' he replied. 'Frankly, I'm grateful; I could do with the extra cash. Not bad for a day's work; I like it.'

Ben had to leave and I walked Risdon back to his nearby flat. He invited me in and introduced me to his girlfriend, Frances. She was holding a little girl who seemed about eighteen months old. After a coffee, Risdon walked me back to my car.

On the way he said, 'I'll leave her when I make some money. I'll find someone else.'

As soon as I got into my car I felt uneasy. I had real misgivings. I knew instinctively that if Risdon could even talk about betraying his girlfriend, then he could betray anyone.

Later that night I raised my fears with Ben, telling him of the conversation with Risdon.

'Don't worry,' Ben said. 'If he shops us then he'll be putting himself in the frame as well. So far, the jobs you've given him he's done well enough and at least we've known him almost a year now.'

'That's true,' I said, and added, 'just as importantly, he's shit-scared of McLaine. If he grassed anyone, Tom would kill him. And he knows it.'

With our robber in place, the time had now come to plan the entire operation. We determined to leave nothing to chance.

First, we increased our insurance cover at Lloyds from one to two million pounds. Our policy authorised us to travel with up to £500,000 worth of gems on our person at any one time. If, however, we wanted to transport gems to a greater value, then we had to give prior notification in writing to the three leading underwriters of the Jewellers Block Policy. In addition, we had to keep the gems in vaults overnight when we weren't actually carrying them to dealers' offices.

All trips abroad had to be handled by approved couriers and Inca used a London firm that specialised in transporting gemstones abroad and clearing them through Customs.

Throughout our plotting, we realised that after the robbery had occurred and the police and loss adjusters had been called in, we would have to prove that we had taken every appropriate precaution.

At that time Inca had approximately 50 per cent of its capital tied up in gems and 50 per cent in cash. In order to be able to claim the maximum amount against the insurance policy, the company had to spend all its cash balances on purchasing more gems.

If our plan succeeded, we could then put the two million or so pounds received under the Lloyds insurance policy on deposit which, in 1989, at interest rates of around 15 per cent, would earn Inca some £300,000 a year. This would be sufficient to pay the company's overheads and save it from ruin. As for the money that we would raise by selling the 'stolen' gems, this would represent Ben's and my personal gain. My half of it would not only pay back everything I had risked on the bullion-smuggling operation, but would also restore much of the money that my father had lost at the hands of Lloyds.

At that stage, Inca owned twenty beautiful stones, valued in total at about £750,000. Since we wanted to sting Lloyds for a total of almost two million pounds we decided to purchase another twenty gems, at least as far as the company's books were concerned. The reality, however, was that these purchases would be bogus and would be covered by using synthetic stones.

We decided to buy the twenty fakes, costing only £50 each, so that when the police or Lloyds began searching for forty stones we would already have thrown twenty away. It meant that Lloyds would be paying nearly £2,000,000 for gems worth little more than £750,000 and that investigators would be looking for at least twenty gems that had never even existed.

To confuse the investigative trail still further, we pretended to sell all our gems and purchase others of a different description, so that even as far as the twenty genuine stones were concerned, the authorities would be searching for gems of the wrong size, shape and weight.

To carry out these various transactions and convince the police and Lloyds of their authenticity, however, we needed to be able to prove that the gemstones as described in Inca's books were for real. This required the use of a dummy company. To this end, we approached Ishan Dutta and asked if he would consider becoming part of the plot. He was only too happy to help, one reason being that funds from the sting would be used to increase our gold-smuggling enterprise from which he was making a very good living.

He set up a dummy company called Rasiklal & Sons Limited and, in December 1989, opened an office using an accommodation address at Maker Chambers, Nariman Point, Bombay, posing as a Mr Mehta. He then had invoices printed in the name of Rasiklal & Sons and set up a bank account in Geneva in the same name.

In this way we reckoned that if there were any investigations, Ishan, as Mr Mehta, would be able to confirm that the gem transactions had indeed taken place.

From December 1989 to the end of January 1990 we purported to sell Inca's stock of twenty gems, and purchase forty others — twenty of which were the original stones that had belonged to Inca, though described differently, the other twenty of which were fake and almost worthless. In order to pay for these stones we used a mixture of banker's drafts, made payable to Rasiklal, and physical cash.

An investigation into the drafts from Inca's bank account to Rasiklal's Geneva account would show that money for the new gems had indeed been deposited with the company from which we purported to have bought them. The cash, perhaps two or three hundred thousand pounds at a time, would simply be withdrawn by us from our account in London. From there we would fly to Geneva, and deposit it, once again, into the Rasiklal account. Using large sums of cash in this way to carry out deals was in fact common practice among gem dealers. Quite often, stone merchants in London's Hatton Garden or New York or Amsterdam will walk along the street with perhaps one million pounds in a briefcase or the equivalent in gems in their pocket. It may seem strange to those unfamiliar with the trade, but this is how it works.

Having accumulated our forty stones, only half of which were genuine, we needed a trail of witnesses to corroborate the existence of these gems, which consisted of rubies, emeralds and sapphires. To even a half-trained eye, we realised that the twenty synthetic stones, bought in Hatton Garden, would immediately be recognised as fakes.

The trail we laid began at Heathrow. We made four separate trips to Geneva bringing back a few gems at a time, some genuine, some synthetic. HM Customs would inspect the stones, check them against the Rasiklal invoices, compute the VAT payable according to the invoice price and then impound the stones until the 15 per cent VAT had been paid, only to be reclaimed at a later date by Inca.

Ever since the inception of the company when we had begun to import gem stones into the country, it had appeared obvious to us that the British Customs Officers had no idea about the value or authenticity of the gems they inspected. They would always take a cursory look at them, more interested in the accompanying paperwork than the actual stones themselves. It was for this reason that we believed we would encounter no problem in importing the fakes.

On the final trip from Geneva to London, which took place in January 1990, Ben and I brought back only synthetics with us. The three previous journeys had occurred without a hitch and so we walked confidently into the red channel and declared our seven fake stones.

At that same moment Ben and I looked at each other, distinctly alarmed. For standing at the counter was a man we both recognised, a gems expert we had met on a number of occasions. What we had never realised before was that this man was also a Customs Officer .

We knew there was no going back.

He hurried over to us smiling. 'Good morning, gentlemen. Don't we know each other?'

'Yes, of course we do. How are you?' said Ben, trying to keep his composure.

'Well,' our friend said, 'what do we have today? Something interesting, I hope?'

'As a matter of fact,' Ben replied, 'we do have a few stones that might interest you.'

He turned to me. 'Go on, Darry, show our friend the invoice.'

I produced the invoice and passed it to him.

'Oh, I say!' exclaimed the Customs Officer. 'This is interesting. A twenty-one-carat Kashmir sapphire and an eight-carat Burma ruby.'

'I had a feeling you'd be interested,' said Ben.

'I suppose you wouldn't mind me taking a look, would you? I don't think I've ever actually handled a Burma ruby of this weight.'

Ben looked at me. By this stage, I was desperately thinking of an excuse for the moment when the Customs Officer would look up and inform us that all our gems were fakes. 'Oh, my God! I knew we should never have trusted those Indians. They've ripped us off!' was the best I could come up with.

In a hesitant voice, Ben said, 'Yes, yes, of course,' took them out of his jacket pocket and handed them over.

The Customs Officer took the sapphire, a piece of blue glass worth £50 that we had priced on the invoice at £133,000, and held it to the light.

'You haven't by any chance got a loupe I could borrow?'

'Yes of course,' Ben replied, convinced our gem-dealing careers were about to end in spectacular style.

The Customs Officer held the piece of glass to the light, examining it for ten seconds or more as we stood by, just waiting for the horrible moment.

'Oooohhh,' he sighed. 'What a beautiful stone! This is fantastic! I've never seen anything like this in all my life. Do you mind, gentlemen, if I look at the others?'

'He's taking the mickey,' I thought to myself and looked at him incredulously. Ben handed over the other fakes and our friend took them out of their brifkas, one by one, examining them in the light with the loupe, enraptured by their exceptional beauty.

'You don't mind if I show my friends, do you?' he asked excitedly.

'No, no, not at all,' Ben said, 'please go ahead. OK, Darry?'

'By all means,' I replied. 'It's not every day that you get a chance like this, is it?'

He called over four other Customs Officers. 'I've got something to show you. These here are probably the two most precious stones you'll ever see in your lives. You know, after years of experience such as I have you can always tell the genuine article a mile away.'

At this I really did think he was taking the mickey but he went on for several minutes giving his colleagues a lesson in precious stones, describing their chemical compositions and using technical terms such as 'inclusions', 'gardens', 'patterns', 'windows', 'bands' of colour, and so on.

Trying not to give our thoughts away, Ben and I looked at each other in disbelief but said not a word.

He returned with a smile of satisfaction on his face. 'That was a privilege, thank you both very much.'

He picked up the invoice, stamped it, and handed it back to us. Then he took the synthetic gems, which would be placed in a bonded warehouse until the VAT on them had been paid.

Warmly, he shook us by the hand. 'Gentlemen, may I say that you have made my day.'

Later that week we would show all forty gems, both the fake and genuine ones, to Inca's board members, ensuring their witnessing of the stones' existence was carefully recorded in the company's board minutes.

We also had to show the stones to a gemmologist. We knew this would be a gamble, for he would instantly pick out any fakes, but if it worked it would establish an authentication of the existence of our stock that would be hard to dispute. Our only recourse would be to show him ten of our genuine stones on four separate occasions, mixing them up and giving them to him to inspect over a two-month period. We knew that over this length of time he would be called on to verify hundreds of other gems and we hoped that he would not recognise the stones that we had shown him several weeks before. It was always an anxious time whenever we gave him ten to examine, but he never twigged.

This procedure proved a valuable exercise. We would later gamble that having successfully used such a ruse on a gems expert we knew and respected, the chances were in our favour that other gemmologists would fall for the same trick.

By mid-February nearly everything was ready. Now all we were awaiting was for Risdon to tell us he had acquired a gun. In December 1989, he had flown to Philadelphia to meet a contact and buy one. We had specified that the firearm should not be too large, because when the bullet was discharged in the hotel we did not want it to go through a wall or the floor and perhaps hit someone! We suggested that a .22, a .32 or even a 9mm would be fine, but we did not want anything bigger.

Risdon flew back to London leaving his supplier to buy a gun that could not be traced back to him. He had said he would contact him in the near future and impressed on him the urgency of his task.

On 20 February, 1990, I received a phone call at my home. It was Risdon. 'We're on,' he said. 'My man in Phili's just called. He's got the goods we asked him to buy.'

'Well done, Peter,' I told him.

'That's all right,' he replied. 'Now you know you're dealing with a true professional.'

'Quite,' I said. 'I'll contact you in a couple of days with details of our itinerary.'

At breakfast the following morning, Ben and I were poring over a large map of Manhattan spread out on our breakfast table. We knew that the vaults we were to use were located on 115 East 57th Street, only ten minutes' walk from the gem district. We also knew that the vault company employed a logging system, whereby visitors requiring access to the safe deposit boxes, that were all below ground level, would be logged in and out on a time sheet. This was vital for providing proof of our visits to and from the vaults with various gem dealers.

We drew a circle around the immediate vicinity of the vaults and began searching for a suitable hotel, one that had safes in its rooms. We found an ideal one, the Halloran House Hotel, on Lexington Avenue, ten minutes' walk from the vaults.

Throughout the planning of the operation, we continued to make sure that the gems trail could be corroborated in any investigation, and that every decision we made was consistent with those of two honest gem dealers planning a long-term sales drive in the United States.

We used a freight-forwarding company that specialised in the shipment of gems and was, happily, one of Lloyds' approved couriers. We made sure that they were always present at the exportation and importation of the company's stones and that their representatives saw the gems at each stage, adding yet further proof of their existence.

The courier's counterpart in New York was put on stand-by to arrange the importation of the stones at J F K airport and the payment of the necessary duties. This, too, would provide additional evidence of the existence of the company's stock of gems.

The US courier company contacted a security firm and arranged for them to pick up the stones from JFK airport once they had cleared U S Customs and transport them directly to the vaults in central Manhattan in one of their armoured vehicles.

In telephone calls from London, Ben and I booked a series of appointments from 28 February to 6 March with a dozen or so major New York gem dealers. We anticipated the robbery taking place on Friday 2 March, but it was clearly important to schedule further meetings beyond that date to avoid any possible suspicion that we had known all along that the robbery would occur on the Friday. We marked each and every appointment in the Inca company diary.

We also made sure to book a provisional return flight to London for 7 March for the same reason.

I booked my flight to New York for 25 February in order to open the safe deposit facility and Ben booked his flight for two days later, when he would follow with the stock of forty gems.

We reckoned that when Ben arrived in New York, as had occurred in London, the untrained U S Customs Officers would simply stamp the importation forms without any fuss, thereby authenticating the arrival in America of forty valuable gems worth almost two million pounds.

We knew, however, that we would need still more evidence to corroborate the existence of the stones. This, we hoped, would be provided by the various gem dealers with whom we had booked appointments from London. The aim was to create a general impression of having had numerous valuable gemstones on us by showing the same twenty stones twice over to different experts within the same company, but at different times.

On the morning of 25 February, I packed my bags, put them in the boot of my Mercedes, and shook hands firmly with Ben.

'See you in New York the day after tomorrow,' he said.

'Feeling OK?' I asked.

'Yes, fine, but I can't believe we're going to do this. Are you sure about it?'

'If we keep our cool, this will go fine.'

'I know, I know,' he said and looked at me, but I saw a faint sign of doubt in his face. It worried me, but I determined to put it behind me. I was convinced that we had left nothing to chance. I could see no way the sting would go wrong.

Sitting beside me as I drove down the M4 to Heathrow was a 23-year-old woman, dressed smartly in a navy blue Moschino suit that contrasted with her shoulder-length, platinum-blonde hair. I was taking her to Heathrow to catch a flight to Newcastle, where she would spend the next few days with her mother in her home town of Sunderland.

As we sped along she asked me, as she had on numerous occasions over the previous few days, why I was going to New York.

'Listen, darling,' I said to her, 'I've told you already, I'm going on a sales trip. You know the golden rule. You can talk to me about anything except my business. You just have to trust me.' I leant over and kissed her. I had decided from the moment I met her that she was too precious to me and that I would never endanger her by involving her in my schemes.

The woman's name was Patricia Holder.

*   *   *

We had met four months earlier. I was having a drink with a friend at the Groucho club in Soho one night and had noticed a beautiful young woman sitting on one of the sofas with two friends. As the evening went on we would give each other furtive looks, sometimes catching each other's eye. My heart was beating fast and I longed to be able to talk to her.

She had shoulder-length, platinum-blonde hair, green eyes, bright-red lips and she was wearing a simple black, fitted dress. She seemed very feminine and gentle in her mannerisms and I had an overwhelming intuition that one day she would be very important to me, so much so that I sensed, even before we had spoken a word to each other, that I would probably end up asking her to marry me.

In fact, the first words we spoke to each other were to criticise a man sitting at the bar who was becoming more drunk and noisy by the minute.

'I wish that man would leave,' I said to no one in particular.

'So do I,' she said, speaking so quietly that I could hardly hear her voice.

Later, in the club's dining-room the eye contact continued but, sitting at separate tables, we never had a chance to speak to each other. When she got up to leave, our eyes met once more and I wondered whether we would ever meet again. Somehow, I was convinced we would.

Some weeks later, I saw one of the two women who had been sitting with her that evening once again in the Groucho club. She was alone. 'Where's your pretty friend this evening?' I enquired.

'I'm afraid she's not in London. She's visiting her mother in the North East,' she replied.

We chatted for some time and I established that her friend's name was Patricia. Before we said farewell, I persuaded her to give me Patricia's London number, telling her that I couldn't get her out of my mind. 'I'm going to get into trouble for this,' she said, 'but I'll tell her you were very persuasive.'

A few days later, I phoned Patricia. She didn't seem surprised by

Oxford's most famous dining society, The Bullingdon, 1986

Top: Ben and Darius aged 10 on Wimbledon Common.
Below: The Gridiron Club, Oxford, 1986.

Graduation day with HRH The Princess of Wales, Oxford, Autumn, 1986.

Charles and Victoria Spencer with baby daughter Kitty at Darius' wedding, Magdalen
College, Oxford, September 1991.

Top: Darius with Charles and Patricia (centre). Darius' parents are on the left and Patricia's mother is on the right.

Below: Sir Napier Broom, Governor of Trinidad, with Lady Broom and Alice Guppy, Darius' great-grandmother (foreground, left). Prince George (later King George V), seated at the right of the photograph, was on a visit to Trinidad on board a British warship.

Top: Sarah Guppy, the wife of Thomas Guppy, as painted by Isambard Kingdom Brunel.

Above : The 'Guppy' fish, originally named *Girardinus Guppyi,* discovered by Lechmere Guppy aged 23, at the end of the last century. From a painting by Plantagenet (Jim) Guppy.

my call and we arranged to meet in a week's time. Although I had booked a table for 8.30pm that night at one of my favourite local restaurants just off the King's Road, when she arrived at my Chelsea home we stayed chatting and drinking champagne until 10.30pm. The more we talked, the more I became convinced that she would be someone very special in my life.

She told me of her childhood, how she had been brought up in Sunderland, how her father had died on the operating table while undergoing emergency surgery for a kidney transplant when she was just twenty, how she missed him desperately and how the pain of his death had driven her to the South to make a new life for herself.

Having worked in a factory for a short time in the North East to make ends meet, she was now earning her living as a hotel receptionist.

At the end of the evening we knew we wanted to see more of each other, and soon became inseparable. We would go to restaurants, the opera and the theatre and at weekends I would take her flying: a day out on the Isle of Wight with a picnic on the beach; to Norfolk for a walk along the coast; to Wales for lunch in the Brecon Beacons. Above all, I wanted to take her away for a long weekend to my favourite city, Venice, which I have always believed to be the most romantic place in the world.

Venice in January, with its peace and solitude, its narrow, empty streets and canals, its colours blurring in the fog, seemed like a Turner watercolour. We took private motor launches everywhere, always asking the captain to chug slowly through the low cloud, enjoying the isolation as we glided across the Lagoon to the islands of Murano, Burano and Torcello. We stayed at the Gritti Palace, visiting intimate restaurants by day and going to La Fenice, Venice's famous opera house, by night. We said nothing about our future together but, to me, it seemed the perfect honeymoon.

Our last morning in Venice, I awoke to the sound of church bells, while soft sunlight streamed through the shutters and on to Patricia's beautiful face as she lay sleeping. I realised at that moment that, for me, she had become the most important person in the world and I knew I wanted to marry her.

IX

On Sunday, 25 February, 1990, I flew to New York on British Airways flight number 175. My first hour in the United States did not bode well. 'The people's favourite airline' had lost my luggage.

Having reported the loss of my suitcase, I took a Yellow cab to the Halloran House Hotel and booked into a double room — room number 1207.

As I waited at the reception desk, I scanned the lobby to see whether there were any security cameras. I saw none. On the way up to the twelfth floor I repeated this exercise in the lift and in the corridors as the bellboy walked me to my room. Again, there were none. It was clearly essential to avoid Risdon being caught on camera as he entered or left the hotel.

The room was perfect. It was not too near the lifts, where someone might notice Risdon either coming into our room or leaving it, and it had a safe that was situated in a cupboard directly opposite the door.

First, I telephoned Dutta in Bombay to check on our latest gold shipment that was due to clear Customs at any time.

Having informed me that all had gone well with the consignment, he asked, 'When are you planning to go ahead with your little venture?' knowing that Ben was due to join me in New York in a couple of days.

'If you carry this out,' he added, 'then I must admit, you've got some balls.'

The following day, I opened a safe at the vault company for twelve months in the name of Inca.

After this, a second, secret safe was needed in which to place the twenty real gems just prior to the robbery. The idea was to return to collect these stones at some stage after the sting had occurred, when we considered the coast to be clear. This time I booked the safe using my own name, in a bank a few blocks away from the vaults. I decided to opt for a bank as opposed to a specialist safe deposit facility because I surmised that, after the robbery had occurred, the New York cops would, as a matter of routine, investigate the possibility of an inside job and check the safe-deposit firms for any facility recently opened under Inca's, Ben's or my name to see if the stones had been hidden there. It seemed unlikely that they would push the investigation to the extent of contacting, in addition, every single bank in New York that provided safe-deposit facilities for their clients. It was a definite gamble though, for had that second safe been found with the missing stones in it, the game would have been up.

I opened an account with $100 cash and then requested the use of a safe for twelve months.

Later that day, after my lost baggage had been located at the airport and delivered to the hotel, I received the phone call I had been waiting for. Risdon, who had flown from London on Virgin Atlantic, called from Philadelphia where he had arranged to collect the gun.

'I've got what you ordered,' he said.

'Good,' I replied. 'As agreed, I'll see you for a drink in PJ Clarke's on Third Avenue at one-thirty on Thursday. OK?'

'Fine. I'll be coming by Amtrak, arriving at Grand Central station that morning. I'll see you at PJ Clarke's.'

In London, earlier that day, Ben had met the courier company's representative, as arranged, at Inca's safe-deposit facility in a bank in Hatton Garden. He had handed the entire stock of the company's gems — twenty genuine and twenty fakes — to the representative who signed for them, having checked the contents of the packages. The stones were then transported from Hatton Garden to Heathrow where, once the Customs formalities were completed the following day, they would be handed back to Ben for his flight to New York.

Twenty-four hours later, Ben arrived on schedule at JFK airport and was met by the representative of another courier firm who cleared the gems, valued on paper at some $3,000,000, through New York Customs. Ben was then invited to ride with armed guards in an armoured truck from Kennedy airport to the vaults in central Manhattan, where I was waiting for him.

I met him downstairs in the vaults. 'Good flight?'

'Yes, no problems at all. Everything went like clockwork.'

With the gems safely stored, Ben and I went for a Japanese meal before going back to our room and watching the late TV news. We wondered whether we would be appearing on the same news programme in a few days' time, or whether an armed robbery of three million dollars' (two million pounds') worth of gems would be of little consequence for the American networks.

For the next couple of days before the robbery, we visited the various gem dealers with whom we had booked appointments from London, and in our spare time went for walks, saw friends, enjoyed good meals and generally tried to relax as much as possible. For most of the time we were ice-cool but sometimes we would suffer real doubts about our plan, wondering whether we were being very foolish and, perhaps, underestimating the diligence of the New York cops.

Among the dozen or so New York gem dealers we visited to show our stock, the most important was Tiffany's. The store's chief gems buyer, Roy Albers, expressed great interest in a sapphire and a large emerald and asked to keep them in order to examine them later with colleagues and consider a purchase.

'I'm afraid that won't be possible,' I said, thinking fast. I certainly didn't want Tiffany's to be holding two of our best stones when the robbery took place. 'We have to show the stock to other dealers. Perhaps we could bring them back again at, say 2pm on Friday, 2 March?'

He agreed and the meeting was fixed.

It was of course precisely at that time, according to our plans, that we would be acting out the robbery. We had always worried that one of our biggest problems would be to convince the cops that it had been necessary to keep the stones in the safe in our room rather than take them back to the safety of the vaults. Unwittingly, Roy Albers had provided the cover story we needed. We would now be able to argue that, having shown our gemstones to a number of dealers on the morning of the robbery and because we were running a tight schedule, rather than depositing the jewels at the vaults and taking them out again after lunch in time for our 2pm appointment with Tiffany's, we had decided instead to have lunch in our hotel room, in which there was a safe in any case, before going straight on to our meeting with Mr Albers.

Another area of concern for us would be how to explain the fact that the robbers must have known that we were staying in Room 1207 at the Halloran House Hotel with three million dollars' worth of gems on our person at the time in question. Our solution was to act throughout all our meetings with the dealers in a deliberately naïve way, leaving our business cards wherever we went, having written our hotel address and room number on the back of them. We hoped that the New York police and the Lloyds' loss adjustors would speculate that such action would almost certainly have alerted the whole of the New York gems district, which was full of shady characters, of our whereabouts. It would only require, after all, some employee or someone visiting the offices where we had liberally sprinkled our cards to tip off some of his criminal friends or else make use of the information himself to stage an armed robbery.

On Thursday, 1 March, at the agreed time, I walked into PJ Clarke's and saw Risdon. He waved and we sat and ordered a meal.

'How did it go?' I asked him.

'I've got what you want; it's in the bag at my feet. There's only one problem, no silencer,' he said looking a little sheepish, as though he had failed in his mission.

It was annoying that Risdon, the man with such remarkable contacts, hadn't been able to come up with a silencer. It would mean having to carry out some experiments with the hand-gun he had bought, to see how loud the noise would be when firing it.

'Have you found a room?' I asked.

'Yes,' he replied, 'quite near where you're staying; the hotel's called The Iroquois.'

At that moment Ben walked in and joined us. I told him about the lack of a silencer and it was decided that we should hire a car, drive upstate and experiment with the gun.

We hired a small Japanese car and paid in cash. Our first stop was a local department store where we bought some pillows to use in our experiment for muffling the sound of the gun. After driving upstate for an hour and a half, we left the freeway and stopped by some foothills, leaving the car in a lay-by. We walked a few hundred yards to a copse.

There we put on gloves and, from a canvas bag, Risdon took out a .22 Smith & Wesson, which I noticed immediately had an extra long barrel. He also took out three cartridge boxes, each one containing about fifty rounds — small, medium and long-length bullets, all of which could fit into the revolver's chamber.

Risdon took some rounds, placed them in the revolver's chamber, and clicked the gun shut with a flick of his hand.

'Hand me a pillow, please,' he said to Ben.

He placed the pillow on the ground and pushed the muzzle of the revolver into it.

'Stand back,' he said, 'just to be on the safe side. Remember I have many years of weapons training and you can never be too careful.'

Ccrraack!

The noise was undoubtedly louder than we had imagined it would be from a .22 hand-gun and Risdon, the highly trained expert, looked up, astonished.

'I fear we may be heard from those houses,' he said, pointing to a row of six houses, which must have been nearly half a mile away.

'I don't think so,' I told him.

'Noise carries,' he said, licking his index finger and holding it in the air to see if the sound had been carried down wind. I looked at Ben and winked. 'Remember,' he went on, 'I should know. I'm the one with all the experience. I'm not at all happy that we should continue with this experiment. We're likely to attract unwanted attention.'

After a short while, Risdon agreed to continue but this time he wrapped the entire gun, and not just its muzzle, in the pillow in an effort to stifle any sound completely.

The noise was appreciably quieter, but not quiet enough for the nervous Risdon. 'Gentlemen! Gentlemen! Please!' he insisted. 'We shouldn't continue this experiment here. We should find somewhere deep in some woods, far from all civilisation.'

After a short chat, Ben and I decided to go along with Risdon's suggestion.

As we walked back to the car I whispered to Ben, 'This chap's like Norman Wisdom.'

'Don't you mean Norman Risdon?' he quipped back. From that moment our colleague had a new nickname, but he would never know.

After another hour's drive we found a track leading to a cemetery.

As dusk fell, we discovered an old wooden shed perhaps eight hundred yards off the track. There, having completely covered the gun with a pillow, we tested the three different sizes of bullet, finding out which one caused the least noise when fired. Ben went outside to listen and returned to say he could hear very little. The shortest round proved the quietest.

After dining out, Ben and I were back in our hotel before 11pm. Throughout the meal I had become increasingly worried about Risdon's participation in the robbery. His reaction to the noise of the gun going off in the middle of nowhere showed he was prone to panic and I wondered whether he would go to pieces when called upon to carry out his role in the hotel the following day.

I shared my concern with Ben and debated with him into the night whether we should involve Risdon or plan something totally different. We even considered reporting to the police that we had been robbed at gunpoint while walking through Central Park, thereby dispensing with Risdon's services.

'Listen,' Ben said. 'We've planned this whole thing in great detail and Risdon is now in it up to his neck. He might panic but we'll just have to hold his hand and carry him through. It won't be that difficult for him. All he has to do is tie us up and fire a single shot. Even he can do that. And I can't believe he'd grass on us because then he'd be dropping himself in it.'

Persuaded by this argument, we turned in for the night. I slept soundly.

Friday, 2 March, 1990, was a bright, cold day in New York City. After breakfast in the hotel restaurant, we walked in the sunshine to the vaults to collect the stock. Deliberately, we left £10,000 worth of jewels — in the form of a matching ruby and diamond set, consisting of a ring, necklace and earrings made by the famous French jeweller, Chaumet — at the vaults.

We anticipated that the police would want to inspect our safe at the vaults and when they did so, they would see that we had some stock left there. Of course, gems worth ten thousand pounds out of a total of almost two million pounds' worth would be insignificant, but we believed that the psychological impact of seeing real jewels in our safe would lend yet further credibility to our story that, prior to the robbery, we had had in our possession a collection of highly valuable stones.

From 9.30 to 11.30 that morning we visited three medium-sized gem-dealing companies in the area, taking coffee, leaving our business cards, chatting, joking and trying to appear as relaxed as possible.

After leaving our last appointment Ben and I walked briskly to the bank where I had opened an account and the second, secret safe-deposit box. I put our entire stock of genuine gems, minus the Chaumet set, into my deposit box and got rid of the twenty fake stones by slipping them down a drain on Lexington Avenue. We were back at our hotel by 12.20pm.

Risdon, meanwhile, had gone that morning to a hardware shop on West 44th Street and bought a roll of heavy, rough cord and a pair of scissors. He had returned to his hotel room at the Iroquois and cut the twine into metre-long lengths. Having put these twine lengths in his coat pocket, together with four of the smaller rounds, and his Smith & Wesson in the back of his trousers, he had begun to make his way on foot to the Halloran House.

Ben and I were sitting watching television in our room, waiting for Risdon to arrive. On the dot, at 12.45pm as arranged, Risdon knocked on the door.

'Hello Peter,' Ben said. 'Fancy seeing you here.'

'Don't fool around, Ben,' said Risdon nervously, 'this is serious business; it's not a time for jokes.'

Risdon was dressed in a light beige, three-quarter-length weatherproof coat with large pockets. He was also wearing dark trousers, trainers and black leather gloves.

Thinking constantly of forensic scientists, throughout that hour Risdon never took his gloves off, fearful that he might accidentally touch some object and leave a print. He didn't go to the lavatory; he didn't sit down; he even turned up the collar of his coat in order to trap any hairs that might fall from his head on to the floor.

We phoned for two sandwiches and in less than five minutes, there was a knock at the door. Desperate not to be seen in the room, Risdon dashed to the bathroom and hid. Surprised that the sandwiches should have taken so little time to arrive, I got up from the bed, where I was watching TV, to answer the door. It was a waiter with a bottle of complimentary champagne and a message of welcome from the hotel manager.

We cracked open the bottle, hoping this unexpected present would bring us luck.

'To success!' Ben said.

'To our future. May it be bright,' I replied.

Risdon chipped in, 'I'll have a drink, but I'm not taking my gloves off.'

After he had drunk his glass of champagne, we were careful to ensure that he washed and wiped his glass with great care, in case any forensic examination should reveal that there had been three men in the room instead of two.

At 1.30pm, another knock at the door heralded the arrival of our sandwiches. Again, Risdon refused to take his gloves off and had great difficulty consuming half a sandwich with the mayonnaise dribbling through the fingers of his gloves. Ben and I couldn't help laughing and the more relaxed we appeared, the more nervous Risdon would become.

After quickly finishing lunch, I went down to the hotel lobby and used a pay phone, calling the hotel operator and asking to be put through to room 1207. When Ben answered, I put on a thick Brooklyn accent and asked if I could speak to 'Mr Schlomo'. Ben replied that I must have been put through to the wrong room number and I put down the phone and went back upstairs. We hoped the police would ask the hotel operator whether we had received any outside calls. With any luck, the operator would be able to remember the mystery call to our room just minutes before the raid.

When I returned to the room, I said to Ben, 'Don't you think we're over-egging this whole thing, trying to second-guess how the police will think and act in every respect?'

'No, no, no,' Risdon interrupted. 'You can never take too much care over a crime of this magnitude. This is no petty stuff, you know, this is the real McCoy. I wouldn't have anything to do with it if I had thought you weren't real professionals, like me.'

We waited a little longer and at precisely 1.45pm I said, 'OK chaps, this is it. We've had enough messing around. Let's get on with it.'

I picked up the TV remote control and increased the volume in the hope that the sound of the bullet being fired would be muffled even more to any one who was passing our room. I opened the door, checked no one was in the corridor and then said, 'OK Peter, go for it. Go outside, knock and when we open the door, throw it open and burst in. Make it as realistic as possible but remember, try not to make too much noise.'

Ben lay on the bed nearer the door and I lay on the bed next to the bathroom, both of us watching TV.

There was a knock and Ben got up to open the door with the remains of his sandwich in his right hand.

'Who is it?' he asked casually.

'Room service,' came the reply in what was meant to sound like an American accent.

As Ben opened the door, Risdon flung it open further and rushed in, the gun in his hand. Ben's sandwich was sent flying.

After kicking the door shut with his foot, Risdon put the gun to Ben's forehead saying, 'We've come for the gems! This is a fucking robbery! Lie down!'

'Hold on,' Ben said, 'don't be too realistic, do remember that gun's loaded.'

Risdon, however, would not be put off. He had now entered into the spirit of the robbery with a vengeance.

'Shut up, you punk!' he yelled. 'Lie down on the bed, face down. Shut the fuck up!'

Ben and I lay face down on our beds. Throughout the ten-minute robbery, we imagined that there were two robbers in the room. Risdon took out our wallets, containing our credit cards, which we had deliberately put in our back pockets. Later, he would throw away the credit cards on the side-walk in the Lower East Side in the hope that some dubious character would pick them up and use them. A subsequent check by the police of our credit card transactions would then corroborate our story that our cards had been stolen during the robbery.

Risdon went over to the safe and then turned on Ben. 'Where's the safe key?' he asked, pressing the gun against his forehead.

'There's nothing in there,' Ben responded, nonchalantly.

'Listen, punk,' said Risdon in his assumed accent, 'don't think I'm fooling around!'

He walked round to my bed, picked up the pillow, wrapped it around the gun and fired a shot into the mattress within six inches of my head. The noise sounded more like a light thud than a bullet, but we were relieved that no one, even if they had been passing the door that very instant, could possibly have heard it.

'The next slug goes through your brains,' Risdon said, and I almost burst out laughing.

He turned to Ben again and said, 'This is your last chance, punk; hand over the key or you're history!'

Ben replied with a smile across his face, 'OK, you win. It's in my jacket pocket, the one hanging in the wardrobe above the safe.'

Risdon, the consummate professional, was clearly irritated at our inability to take the whole affair seriously.

He went over to the jacket, took the key from the pocket, opened the safe and mimed removing the imaginary jewels. He then took the lengths of cord out of his coat pocket. All this time, Ben and I were pretending in our minds that the 'second' robber was standing guard by the door.

Risdon came over to me while I was still lying face down on my bed, tied my hands behind my back and then frog-marched me into the bathroom. 'Lie down,' he ordered, and proceeded to tie my ankles together very tightly with the twine.

'Hold on a minute, Peter,' I said, 'not so bloody tight.'

'I've got to make it look real,' he whispered back.

Risdon then returned to Ben and tied him up in the same way, bringing him into the bathroom and making him lie down beside me.

'We'll be here for another fifteen minutes,' Risdon said, 'and if either of you punks moves, I'll blow his head clean off!'

As he left he roughed the room up a little, opening drawers, disturbing the bedding and throwing our clothes out of the wardrobe on to the floor. His last act before walking out was to turn up the television volume, as if to prevent anyone from hearing our cries for help.

As we waited, we tugged at the ropes that bound us so that friction marks would appear on our ankles and wrists. That done, we lay on the floor for ten minutes, giving Risdon time to disappear from the hotel. Suddenly, the fun and the euphoria of the whole affair disappeared and the gravity of the situation hit me. I began to think of Patricia, of all the emotional energy she had invested in me, how hurt she would be if it all went wrong and how sad I would be if I was caught and let her down. Until those moments, Ben and I had been in control. We could always have changed our minds, reversed things;

but now, lying on the cold tiled floor, bound hand and foot, and with the marks of the muzzle flash in the pillow and the bedding, everything had passed from our control. We were committed and there could be no going back.

We had gambled our entire destinies on this mad escapade; from here we had to keep our heads and pray that the precautions we had taken would be sufficient to fool the police and the loss adjustors into believing our story. If it worked, all would be fine; if it failed, we were finished. Everything now hinged on our acting ability.

Ben and I managed to bring our hands from behind our backs, and up, still tied together, in front of our bodies. Having levered ourselves using our elbows against the side of the bathtub, on to our knees, we were able to open the bathroom door and shuffle back into the bedroom and on to our beds. Ben rolled over to the telephone, lifted the receiver from the cradle with his mouth, and dialled '0' for the hotel operator.

'Operator, this is room 1207. Come quickly, there's been a robbery.'

A long minute later, there was a heavy knock at the door. 'Who's that?' we both cried out.

'Security!' came the reply.

'We're tied up! You're going to have to open the door yourself,' Ben said.

Two hotel security men opened the door with a master key. 'What's happened?' the one in charge asked.

'We've been robbed! Untie us, please,' I said, trying to sound as plaintive as possible.

They reached for the knife that had been brought with the sandwiches and was lying on one of the beds, and cut through the twine.

Once freed, Ben immediately went to the safe and exclaimed, 'Oh my God! They've got the jewels!'

'No, no they haven't!' I said, putting my head in my hands. 'Surely not!'

'How much are these gems worth, Sir?' the senior security man asked me.

I paused, as though not sure whether I should tell them. Looking him in the eye I said, 'About three million dollars.'

'Jesus!' came the reply.

At that, both men, who were rather paunchy and in their late fifties, reacted as if they had been shaken from their lethargy. This was no longer a small-time robbery.

One of them grabbed his walkie-talkie from his belt and shouted into the mouthpiece, 'This is security! There's been a major felony in room 1207! Three million dollars of gems have been stolen! Get the NYPD and make it fast!'

The other security officer had taken out his pad and pencil, and was writing notes as he walked round the room.

'Who else knew that you guys had these jewels with you?'

'Well, no one knew,' Ben answered.

'Well, someone must have known.'

'Come to think of it,' I chipped in, 'we're gem dealers from London and we've been here on a sales trip. Of course, we've been showing our stock to a number of New York dealers.' I paused. 'But, surely not. I mean, they were all so highly respectable.'

'Are you sure?' the security man asked.

'It just couldn't have been them,' I said. 'I mean, they were such nice guys.'

'How do you know? This is New York.'

'Come to think of it,' I went on, 'we did leave our business cards. And on some of them, we wrote the name of our hotel and our room number.'

The senior man looked at us, shaking his head and tut-tutting. 'That means the whole of New York knew where you guys were staying.'

I looked at him again. 'I suppose we have been a little naïve,' I said, innocently.

'Naïve? Naïve isn't the word! Tell me, do you fellas believe in the Easter bunny?'

The two officers looked at each other in disbelief.

Ben butted in, 'We must do everything to find those men! The bastards! They've taken everything, everything we had.'

At that point, two young uniformed women police officers from the NYPD arrived at the door, both chewing gum and looking tough.

'OK, you guys, what happened here? Take it from the top. Tell us exactly what happened.'

No doubt Ben and I put on a very convincing display of nervousness, as if we had been genuinely robbed at gunpoint, throughout the questioning. What the police officers did not realise, though, was just how easily it came to us. The prospect of ending up in one of the worst hell-holes on earth, Riker's Island jail in New York, would have made anyone look decidedly agitated. However, our interrogators mistook such anxiety as a symptom of the trauma we had suffered.

Ben got to his feet and took the officers through everything that had happened, emphasising now and again that there were two robbers involved, both of whom had been carrying guns. He described how one man had threatened us, tied us up, shot into the bed and taken the gems while the other had stood guard by the door throughout, with his hand in his jacket as if holding a revolver.

Thirty minutes later, two plain-clothes detectives arrived. The senior officer, Detective Raymond Berke, tall, blond, athletic and in his mid-thirties, apologised for what had happened and told us we would be required to accompany them to the 17th Precinct Station House.

Just as we left, the crime scene unit arrived and began to seal off and secure the room for a full forensic inspection. As we walked down the corridor to the lift, Ben muttered through his teeth, 'Darry, that's the worst piece of over-acting I've ever seen. You'll end up getting us life!'

I winked at him, realising, however, that the police hadn't even begun interrogating us yet. Originally, we had hoped that the whole matter would be dealt with in a couple of hours. Now it was becoming obvious that we would be lucky to be in bed before midnight. I reminded myself that I had to keep my wits about me for Detective Berke seemed nobody's fool.

We travelled together in the lift and walked across the hotel lobby with the reception staff looking on.

Detective Berke escorted us to the police car. 'After you, gentlemen,' he said as he opened one of the rear doors and then went round to the front passenger door. 'You guys have had a tough time,' he reassured us, 'but don't worry. We'll take statements from you so that we find out everything we can about these two "perps".'

'Perps' was Detective Berke's word for perpetrators and he would use the term throughout the time he spent with us.

'I guess that by now,' he said, thinking aloud, 'the gems are already out of New York City. They might end up in Europe, but I reckon it'll be Miami or L A. That's where most of this kinda stuff gets sold.'

The scene inside the 17th Precinct Station House reminded me of the endless American crime series that are screened on English television. It could have been the set of an episode of *Cagney and Lacey*, *Starsky and Hutch* or *Kojak*, with people shouting abuse, telephones ringing, suspects arriving in handcuffs and plain clothes officers rushing around with their holsters dangling from their shoulders. Everywhere the paint was peeling off the walls.

Ben and I were taken to separate rooms for interrogation. Detective Berke sat and gently fired questions at me while another detective wrote down my evidence. I ran through the series of events exactly as Ben had done a little earlier in our hotel room. My description of the principal robber was of a 'white male, 5ft 10ins to 6ft tall, clean-shaven with mousy blonde hair, weighing about 170lbs, and wearing a waist-length tan jacket'. The second robber, 'perp number two', I described as a 'white male, clean-shaven and wearing a long grey coat'.

Ben, of course, would give identical descriptions. To make the task easier for ourselves and to ensure that our evidence was consistent, we had decided to describe two friends from Oxford who we had chosen at random. Both had distinctive faces. The first was Radek Sikorski, my Polish friend whom I had sponsored for election to the Bullingdon, and the second was Mike Ivey, a friend of Ben's from St Peter's College. The police would concentrate their attention on the man we described as the main perpetrator.

After interviewing Ben, Detective Berke came back to my room with Ben following behind him. 'OK, guys,' he said, 'you've helped a lot. We're just going to the Manhattan Catch Unit, located in the 20th Precinct because we want to show you some mug shots of known perps.'

He smiled and slapped me on the back. 'After that, you can go get a burger.'

'Thank you, Ray,' Ben said, now on familiar terms with Detective Berke.

For the first time I began to relax.

Ben and I spent the next four hours looking through thousands of photographs of known armed robbers, murderers and other criminals and, not surprisingly, we drew a blank. Occasionally, Ben would ask me, 'What about him?' and, invariably, I would look more closely and comment, 'No, I don't think so.'

From the way we were being treated, we had the feeling our performance was convincing.

At around 9pm, Ray Berke suggested that we had had enough and told us to go to Kennedy's, a burger bar near the Station House, to get something to eat. He told us to return later when he would take us to the Artists' Unit at police headquarters in Manhattan Plaza.

We said not a word until we were safely in Kennedy's enjoying a meal, at which point Ben asked quietly, 'How do you think it's going?'

'I think he believes us,' I replied. 'Why, what do you think?'

'He's a nice bloke, isn't he?'

'Funny you should say that, Ben, I was thinking the same. I feel very guilty about having to lie to him. He's such a straight and decent man. Still, we've got no choice. What's done is done.'

'Exactly!' Ben said. 'I don't feel like spending the next few years in some American slammer, I can tell you.'

During the meal we decided that Ben should be the one to do most of the talking during our session with the police artist because he knew Radek Sikorski far less well than I did and, consequently, his description of the robber would be vaguer than mine.

Inadvertently, while Ben and I had been scouring through the mug shots, Detective Berke had given us a clue as to how we should behave. He had turned round in his swivel chair, so that his back was facing me.

'Darius,' he asked, 'what colour tie am I wearing?'

'I don't know,' I told him, 'I have no idea.' I wasn't lying. In fact, it was bright red.

'You see,' Berke said, turning to face me. 'You see how little a witness actually remembers. Now let me tell you guys something. If you had remembered every tiny detail about these perps I would have been suspicious because, usually, victims can't remember every single fact about the person who has robbed them. If they can remember, I know something's wrong.'

For more than ninety minutes, Ben and I sat with the artist, a slim man in his fifties, while he sketched away, constantly asking for our comments. In the end, we murmured our approval, making sure not to be too convinced of a photographic likeness. Detective Berke didn't even bother with an artist's impression of the second 'perp' because he believed our recollection of him would be too inaccurate.

Driving us back to the Halloran House Hotel, Ray Berke gave little hope that the armed robbers would ever be caught. 'I have to be honest with you guys,' he said. 'I don't reckon you'll ever see those gems again. Sure, we'll put out a description to all the top gem dealers throughout the States and maybe we'll strike lucky, but don't count on anything.'

He paused, then went on, 'Coming over from London, this kind of thing must be quite a shock to you but, believe me, here it happens every day. In fact, you're lucky they didn't just kill you.'

He continued, 'They told you not to look at them. But they weren't wearing masks. So they can't have been that worried about being recognised. That tells me most likely they come from out of New York State. My guess is that they were brought in specifically for this job. Next time, bring some bodyguards!'

Back at the Halloran House, we were put in Room 1208, directly opposite our former room, which had been sealed off for further forensic tests. At police headquarters they had taken our finger prints so that they could eliminate them from others found at the scene.

After we had been shown into the room, Ben tugged my sleeve, put a finger to his mouth for me to keep quiet and led me out into the corridor. Speaking in a whisper he said, 'I know this may sound paranoid but we should act as if the cops have put a bug in the room, just in case. Let's just keep the act going, even in our sleep. OK?'

'Agreed,' I replied, and we returned to our room.

After a few minutes I said, 'Can you believe what's happened to us? They'll never believe this back home, robbed at gunpoint in our hotel room in the middle of New York.'

'Just our bloody luck,' Ben said. 'Mind you I guess Ray's right, we're lucky to be alive. I don't think we'll ever see those stones again. Those bastards; there were some real beauties in that collection.'

'This will ruin us, Ben. It could spell the end of Inca, you know that,' I said, 'unless we're covered by the insurance, I suppose.'

'I wouldn't count on it,' Ben mused, 'especially when you realise how tight insurance companies can be. They'll find something in the small print, more than likely.'

'We'll just have to see,' I said.

We had noticed two TV crews outside the hotel, so I flicked on the television, hoping to catch the local news. At that moment, the announcer said, 'Today, at Lexington Avenue's Halloran House Hotel, two young British gem dealers were forced at gunpoint to give a very large tip when room service called.'

As footage of the hotel came on the screen, the announcer went on, 'At two in the afternoon, British gem dealers Darius Guppy and Benedict Marsh were having lunch in room 1207 when they were robbed of three million dollars of gems by two Caucasian males posing as room service.'

Ben and I looked at each other. In a serious voice, Ben complained, 'Ha, ha. Very funny. I don't think they should be making a joke of it. We could have been shot.'

'Those bastards!' I added loudly for the benefit of any hidden bug.

We had been asleep for less than an hour when we were woken by a loud knocking at the door.

'It's Ray Berke. Wake up, guys.'

I opened the door, wondering what he could possibly want from us at this hour of the night.

With his first words I was reassured. 'I'm sure sorry about this, guys,' he said, 'but we've gotta go to Brooklyn homicide. The two perps you described match exactly the description of two suspects wanted for shooting a Jewish gem dealer in a robbery a week ago in Brooklyn.'

'He's winding us up,' I thought to myself.

As we were taken by police car to Brooklyn, however, my head cleared and I realised just what a stroke of luck this had been. The coincidence was incredible, but it would obviously help enormously in convincing everyone of the truth of our story.

In the Brooklyn Station House, once again Ben and I were separated and, in turn, given a far tougher grilling than we had experienced with Ray Berke. Both of us were questioned for about an hour and I was beginning to wonder whether they suspected us.

But, as before, I would relax because when they had finished they brought us together and gave us a cup of coffee. The Lieutenant in charge, who had interrogated us, looked tough and acted tough and I knew he would be ruthless if called upon.

'Listen,' he said, 'we're not sure but the guys we think are responsible for robbing you may also be responsible for the murder of a Jewish gem dealer in Brooklyn a few days back. That's why, gentlemen, you're being interviewed by homicide and not the robbery squad.'

'How many homicides do you have to investigate?' I asked naïvely.

The question was greeted with laughter and cynical looks all round. 'Shit!' said the Lieutenant with obvious feeling. 'The few blocks around this station house have one of the highest homicide rates in the whole of the United States, in fact, probably the whole world.'

Leaning forward for emphasis, he went on, 'I guarantee you that if we let a couple of smartly dressed Englishmen like you out of this station, within two blocks you'd be robbed, probably stabbed, and maybe even killed.'

I felt that I should appear distinctly awkward at that statement but Ben chipped in, 'In that case, Lieutenant, may I ask whether you will kindly drive us back to our hotel. We wouldn't want to be a further nuisance to you.'

The six cops in the room liked that and smiled. The Lieutenant said, 'I think we can find you a car.'

Walking along the corridor to our room at the Halloran House sometime after 4am, Ben whispered, 'I've got some good news, Darry. Just after my interview finished I overheard one of them say, "Could it be an insurance job?" And another officer said, "No way, these guys are too nice." They believe us, Darry.'

Within a matter of hours, however, we were both to feel that Ben may have spoken too soon. Before going to bed, Ben decided to phone his father to tell him the news. He was understandably reluctant.

'You've got to phone him, Ben,' I said. 'You've got to bite the bullet.'

'It makes me feel really bad phoning my father and telling him a pack of lies.'

'You've got no option.'

Ten minutes later, Ben told his father the bare details of all that had happened. Peter Marsh immediately took control of the situation. 'Listen, take the next flight home with Darius as soon as the police have finished with you. I'll arrange a board meeting, inform the insurance company and see where we can go from there. The first priority is to return to London.'

'Do you think I should phone Patricia now?' I asked Ben. 'I don't want to worry her.'

'It's up to you,' he replied, 'but she's bound to read about it in the papers or see it on TV.'

'You're right,' I said. 'I'll phone her.'

I dialled Patricia's number and waited to hear her voice. 'Darling, how are you?' I asked.

'Listen, what's happened?' she asked. 'I've been worried sick. Some reporters have been on the phone to me; they told me you were nearly shot. Are you OK?'

'Yes, I'm fine, Darling. Don't worry. A shot was fired, but it hit no one. Ben's fine, too. He's just spoken to his father.'

'When are you coming home?'

'Soon,' I replied. 'It might be a day or two, as soon as the police have finished with us.'

'But what happened?' she continued. 'Tell me, what really happened?'

'I'll tell you everything when we get home. For now just trust me. Remember our agreement; we never talk business. OK, Darling?'

'Yes, but ...' she began.

'No buts, sweetheart, I'll see you in a few days. Take care.'

It had been a difficult conversation and I was glad when I put the phone down. I didn't want to conceal anything from Patricia but I knew I could never tell her either. I just hoped that she trusted me sufficiently to know that anything I did would be for our benefit.

At 10.30 next morning we were packed and ready to leave for JFK when there was a knock at the door. It was Ray Berke again. Another officer was with him.

'Guys, just for my colleague here, I want you to take us through the whole damn robbery one last time. I'm sorry about this, but we have to make sure we've got everything straight. When you're back in London, it won't be so easy to reach you.'

They asked us to mime exactly what had happened during the robbery, from the moment the raiders burst into the room, until the time they left.

Throughout this interview, Ray Berke and his colleague made Ben and me feel distinctly uneasy. It was the way they looked at us this time, so very differently from the previous day, fixing us with their eyes, giving nothing away, as though doubting everything we had said to them in earlier interviews. I sensed that they were deliberately putting us under pressure because they suspected that we may have been lying and I could tell that Ben felt this, too. For an hour we were grilled intensely, the cops seeming sceptical about every answer we gave.

A terrible thought came to my mind. What if they had discovered the other safe-deposit box? Perhaps they now had the gems in their possession and simply wanted to break us, to make us confess under the pressure of re-enacting what they now knew to have been nothing but a charade.

When the re-run of our account had been completed, I decided to confront Berke.

'We've been in touch with the chairman of the company,' I said, 'and he has asked us to return to London on the next available flight.'

Without waiting for any reaction I continued, 'We will of course return to New York at a later date if we can be of any further help in your investigation but, if it's all right with you, we'd like to get back to England to sort things out. There's a lot of work to do there.'

'No problem,' Berke replied. 'We have your telephone numbers and your addresses. If necessary, we might be liaising with Scotland Yard.'

However, before we were allowed to go Ray Berke had two further requests. He wanted two authorities from us, one to allow him to talk freely to American Express and Visa so that he could check on all the transactions that might have been made on the cards that we had claimed were stolen in the robbery; and the second authority to allow him to inspect our safe at the vault company in order to check the Chaumet set that we had left behind. We were happy to oblige.

A few hours later, still wondering whether we were going to be arrested just as we were about to leave the country, we boarded the return flight home.

We slept for the entire seven-hour journey.

X

Twenty-four hours after we arrived at Heathrow, on Monday, 5 March, 1990, the telephone rang at Inca's offices in Jermyn Street. 'There's a call for you,' our telephonist announced.

'Who is it?' I asked.

'Personal,' she replied. 'He wouldn't give his name.'

I took the call.

'It's me, Peter.'

'Hi, how are you?'

'Very well,' he replied. 'Everything went very smoothly.'

'Good. I'm pleased to hear it. OK Peter,' I went on, 'when do you want to meet?'

'I'm not sure, I think we should wait a while. I read that piece in the *News of the World*. We should leave it for a bit, for security reasons, you understand.'

'Quite, why don't we meet in a week's time?' I suggested.

'Yes, fine. Where?'

'How about Aspinalls?' I replied.

'Where?' he asked. 'Never heard of it.'

'It's a famous club in Mayfair, about three quarters of the way up Curzon Street on your left as you walk towards Park Lane. Ask anyone in the area; they'll point it out to you. It's got a casino downstairs and some private rooms upstairs where we can talk. I'll meet you at about six o'clock next Monday evening. When you get there, ask the porter for me and he'll direct you to where I am. OK?'

'Yes, I understand,' Risdon said. 'Don't worry, I'll be there. If anything happens in the meantime you know where to contact me, right?'

143

'Yes,' I replied. 'Take care.'

A week later, Risdon walked into one of the upstairs rooms at Aspinalls where I was having a glass of Perrier water with Ben. He was wearing dark glasses.

'Nice to see you, Peter,' I greeted him, shaking him by the hand.

'Keep your voice down,' he said, 'you don't know who might be listening.'

'Don't worry!' I reassured him. 'What would you like to drink?'

'I'll have a pint of lager. Thanks.'

We sat in a quiet corner and Ben asked Risdon to tell us what had happened since we had last seen him in New York. I took out a white envelope from my inside jacket pocket and laid it on the table in front of him. Risdon knew that it contained the balance due for completing the job: £10,000. As we talked, he kept looking at it nervously.

'When I left your room,' he began, 'I went straight to the lift, but for some reason it took a very long time to arrive. I have to confess I was extremely nervous at that time, which I must say is most unusual for me since, as you both know, I'm usually highly professional.'

'As I waited by the lift,' he continued, 'I saw a maid half way down the corridor pushing a trolley. She looked at me ...'

'She saw you?' Ben and I asked in unison.

'Yes,' he replied, 'but she was some distance away and I don't think she really took any notice of me.'

He went on, 'There were three workmen in the lift. As we went down to the lobby one of them made a remark, but I just smiled. I didn't want them to know I was an Englishman. When we arrived at the ground floor, I walked straight across the lobby and out into the street. I don't think anyone took any notice of me. It took me about fifteen minutes to walk back to my hotel. As soon as I got to my room, I took the gun out of the back of my trousers and I put everything together; the gun, the empty ammunition case, the unused rounds, the spare bits of twine and I even took my shirt off. Anyway, I put everything into a carrier bag. I put that carrier bag into another bag and went to my rental car in the car park opposite the hotel.'

After taking several gulps of lager, Risdon continued, 'I drove north for about two hours as we'd done the day before and eventually saw a sign pointing to a national park where there were lakes. I drove on and stopped by the side of a lake. It was very remote and most of the lake was covered with ice. There was one part that was ice-free and I threw the carrier bag as far as I could. It must have gone twenty or thirty yards, I should guess.'

He went on, 'As I drove back to New York, I heard the radio reports of the robbery. I decided to drive past your hotel and I saw masses of police cars and TV trucks with reporters and camera crews outside. That made me nervous, because I didn't know whether you two would be capable of withstanding the pressure. I knew that if I'd been there with you, everything would have been OK because I could have fielded all the police questions.'

Ben and I looked at each other and knew instinctively that if Risdon had been with us at that time, the whole venture would have ended in disaster, there and then.

Risdon didn't notice the look. Instead he went on, 'I think you two did very well by the way. I should like to congratulate you, both of you.' He continued, 'After cruising slowly past your hotel I dropped your credit cards in the street, somewhere on the Lower East Side as agreed.'

Ben asked, 'Do you think anyone saw you?'

Risdon rolled his eyes towards the ceiling at the sheer impertinence of the suggestion. 'Please Ben!' he sighed. 'What do you take me for?' He went on to tell us that the following day he had booked out of his New York hotel and taken an evening flight back to London.

'That's great, Peter,' I said. 'It seems everything went like clockwork. Well done.'

'Thanks. I knew it would. Never doubted it for a second.'

'Shall we leave?' I asked.

'Yes, that's fine,' he replied. Picking up the envelope, Risdon laughed. 'Better not forget this. Not bad for a day's work, eh? A nice little earner.'

'By the way,' he continued, 'before we go can you tell me where the stones are now?'

'That's none of your business, Peter,' Ben replied, 'but you've no need to worry; they're safe and sound.'

Before saying goodbye outside Aspinalls, Risdon told us that he was very worried about the amount of Press comment concerning the armed robbery, in particular the suggestion in certain articles that perhaps the robbery had not been all it appeared.

'Don't worry,' I told him. 'Let the press speculate all they want. They can only rattle you if you allow them to. Only one thing can drop us in it. This,' I went on, pointing to my mouth, 'or, more likely, that,' I added, pointing to his lips.

'Darius,' he said, 'it's not in my interest to talk about this to anyone, not even Frances, my common-law wife. Don't forget that I'm in this as much as you are. All right?'

'Good, well then we can all sleep easy,' I replied.

As we drove away from Aspinalls, Ben remarked, 'Darius, that man worries me.'

'I know what you mean,' I said, 'but I think we should be OK. Remember, he's in this up to his neck.'

Risdon would probably have been very surprised had he known that the gems were already back in London.

Before our meeting with him, Ben and I had flown by Concorde to New York, taken a Yellow cab to the bank, collected the gems from our secret safe-deposit box and returned to JFK just in time to catch the Concorde flight back to London the same day. It had been a close call, because snow had been falling heavily in New York, causing huge traffic jams between the airport and central Manhatten.

We had flown to New York on the Tuesday after our return in order to retrieve the stones and had gone by Concorde so as to be able to make it back in time for our meeting with the Loss Adjusters, which had already been appointed by Lloyds. This meeting had been scheduled for the following day and it was clearly essential for us not to be missed as it would have seemed very odd indeed if, instead of being there, we were back in New York for no apparent reason so soon after the robbery.

'Good luck!' I said to Ben as we got off Concorde, having landed back at Heathrow, because he was carrying the gems concealed in his Y-fronts. 'Let's hope one or two of them don't fall out in front of Customs.'

As we drove to London along the M4 half an hour later, the feeling of relief subsided.

'Ben,' I said, 'that was a crazy risk we just took. Imagine if we'd been stopped by Customs and they'd found the stolen jewels wrapped around your gonads. It would all have been over. Or just suppose Ray Berke had discovered we were in New York for a few hours.'

'Or the bloody Loss Adjusters for that matter,' Ben added. 'Shit, we must have been mad!'

'Perhaps, but it's easy to be wise after the event,' I remarked. 'Let's not forget why we went back in the first place. Returning to the scene of the crime must be the oldest mistake in the book, but we just had to get those stones back and quickly, if only for our peace of mind. Every day that went by was a day more for Ray Berke to find that safe.'

'Exactly,' said Ben. 'That final interview with Berke the morning we left, it really unsettled me. I genuinely think he knew we'd pulled a fast one. It was just that look in his eyes. Anyway, we've got the stones now and that's all that matters. It's one worry out of the way. Let's just make sure we put on a good act for the Loss Adjusters tomorrow.'

We had then driven to Ben's flat in St George's Drive, Pimlico, and looked around for somewhere to hide the twenty stones. Everytime we thought of a hiding place, though, it seemed too obvious. It was late and we were both tired.

'I know,' said Ben, 'let's put them in this biscuit tin.'

'What's in it?' I asked.

'Some old biscuits, I think,' he replied, rattling the tin.

He opened the tin. 'It's full of Jaffa cakes.'

'Wait a minute,' I suggested. 'Why don't we conceal the stones in the Jaffa cakes themselves? Let's just put one gem in the bottom of each cake. At least it'll do in the short term. We can always think again in a couple of days.'

'Why not?' said Ben.

We spent the next fifteen minutes gently positioning a gem in each cake and placing the cakes back in the tin. It was our intention to leave the stones in Ben's flat for, at most, a few days until we found somewhere better. We realised that if the police suspected that the robbery was a hoax and that we still had the jewels, the first places they would search would be our homes and Inca's offices.

The following morning Ben and I prepared ourselves for yet another grilling, this time at the hands of the Lloyds' Loss Adjusters appointed to investigate our claim for almost two million pounds.

By sheer coincidence, the man who would conduct the investigation had previously been involved in trying to settle a claim by Ben's father, Peter Marsh, whose furniture had been damaged while being transported from London to his house in Nice. On that occasion, Peter had lost his temper with this man because he believed that he was being asked to accept a lower payment than he was entitled to receive.

'Gentlemen, nice to meet you,' the investigator said, introducing himself as we walked into the meeting that was being held in Inca's offices. 'You must both have had a terrifying experience, especially you Darius, considering the bullet missed your head by only a few inches.'

'It's been a shattering ordeal,' I replied.

We shook hands and sat down. During the entire meeting the investigator showed nothing but concern for Ben and me. At the end of it, we handed over all our documentation, including the Rasiklal invoices for the stolen stones, the company diary, minutes of board meetings and Customs Import and Export forms for the stolen gems, duly stamped.

Everything now hinged on these papers. Leaving aside the question of the robbery having been staged, we knew that Lloyds would find any excuse, no matter how trivial, to avoid payment and that the success of our claim depended almost entirely on the attention we had paid to detail.

Five days later, we received a copy of the report that the Loss Adjuster had sent to Lloyds for consideration. Ben and I flicked through the short, three thousand-word document.

The report indicated very strongly that there was every likelihood we would receive the £1.8 million claimed. The investigator had believed every detail of the story of the alleged robbery, just as the New York cops had done. The words that gave us hope in particular, read, 'As Underwriters will be aware, New York is a violent city and jewellers are not infrequently the victims of violent attacks. Indeed, police investigators have indicated that the two men were lucky not to have suffered serious injury, particularly when they declined to hand over the key to the room safe.'

It came as no surprise to us that Lloyds would try to pressurise the Halloran House Hotel into paying the £1.8 million compensation. The report read, 'Although it seems unlikely that any claim against the hotel would meet with success, we are writing to them on Lloyds' behalf, holding them responsible and will advise of their response.'

'They're worse than us!' Ben said, for we, too, had decided to make a claim against the Halloran House Hotel, though for a much smaller amount, asking that they reimburse us for at least the cost of our stay.

This seemed consistent with the behaviour of two outraged customers who had not expected their stay in a top New York hotel to include being robbed, tied up and shot at.

Ben had phoned them from London and, having introduced himself to the manager, said in rather a stern voice, 'We stayed in your hotel because it had been recommended to us. We do everything the hotel suggests, including putting our valuables in the room safe, and then you allow two armed hoodlums to casually walk into the hotel, into the elevator and up to the twelfth floor where they tie us up, rob us, shoot at us and threaten to kill us. I mean, does this sort of thing go on in your hotel all the time?'

A most contrite manager had offered his apologies and said that he would discuss the matter with the Hotel directors and would let us know their decision about reimbursing us for our bill as soon as possible.

That was the last we had expected to hear from them but, to our surprise, some days later a grovelling letter of apology arrived at Inca's office in London, together with a cheque for some $3,000, the full amount of our hotel bill.

On 30 March, we received the final report from the Loss Adjusters. Attached to it was an Acceptance Form offering Inca a little over £1.8 million as full and final settlement of its insurance claim.

'Don't let's celebrate yet,' I said to Ben, suppressing feelings of great excitement.

'I agree,' he said. 'Let's wait until we actually get the cheque. Just in case. But it's looking good. The Loss Adjuster phoned a few minutes ago while you were out and said we could expect a cheque for the full amount in about two weeks.'

I decided to try to forget for the next fortnight that we were within inches of success.

Patricia knew none of what was going on. She had been wonderful since my return from New York, understanding, kind and patient, and sticking to our agreement not to pry into my business, and yet I sensed she had a suspicion, an inkling that the New York robbery wasn't as straightforward as we claimed. Part of me yearned to tell her the truth about everything that had happened in that hotel room, but I knew that I could tell her nothing, for I did not want to compromise her in any way.

Later that day, as she and I walked along the Embankment I told her that the next couple of weeks would be critical for Ben and me and the company, and I explained that we were waiting for Lloyds to pay us out nearly two million pounds.

'Don't worry,' she said, 'they'll pay out. Believe me, I bet you they'll pay up. I've just got a feeling about it.'

On 12 April Inca received the cheque from Lloyds — for £1,825,419, the full amount of the claim.

Ben opened the envelope, took out the cheque and handed it to me. I looked at the figure, read the amount and turned and hugged him.

'We did it!' Ben exclaimed.

Still, we were taking no chances. We ran out of the office, jumped into a cab and went round to our bank, asking them to express clear the cheque.

That night, I took Patricia to the Connaught for a romantic candle-lit dinner. We never even mentioned the cheque, or Lloyds, or New York. We just talked of our future together.

The following morning Ben and I asked Peter Marsh, as Chairman of the company, to write a letter to the New York Commissioner of Police praising Detective Berke for his sterling work and, in particular, for his understanding of the trauma that Ben and I had experienced. A few weeks later, he received a reply thanking him for his kind remarks about one of his officers.

Ben and I were becoming more confident by the day that our venture had been a total success. The authorities left us alone; no one wanted any further details from us and we heard not a word from the New York Police.

One day, as we discussed the gems, Ben began to laugh.

'What are you laughing about?' I asked.

'The Jaffa cakes,' he said. 'At this rate, the cakes will soon be even harder than the gems.'

We decided to leave the stones where we had hidden them and, when the time seemed appropriate, to liquidate them by taking them to Geneva or Bombay and selling them on the market, perhaps having had a number of them re-cut beforehand.

With my new-found wealth I decided to put all my resources and energy into smuggling far greater quantities of gold than I had done to date, eager to maximise profits before the rumoured relaxation in the importation regulations regarding bullion occurred.

Besides my own money, Inca also invested in the gold-smuggling project, as did Ishan Dutta. Ben invested only £100,000. We agreed to divide the profits generated pro-rata according to each stake.

In order to check out the Bombay market once again, I flew to India soon after Inca received the cheque from Lloyds but took Patricia with me this time so that she could enjoy a ten day holiday.

Our time together in India was magical: riding horses along moonlit beaches at midnight, eating out under the stars, and walking and chatting for hours through the back streets of Bombay in the cool of the evening.

And, during the days, I would meet with Ishan and Goutti, fine-tuning the details of our enterprise.

On returning from India, I drove down to Althorp with Patricia so that Charlie and Victoria could meet her. We would go for long walks together in the Park and on Charles' birthday, his father, Lord Spencer, dropped into the Falconry with a cake. At the end of the weekend Charlie shook me by the hand and said, 'She's lovely, Darry, you're a lucky man. Victoria and I both think she's the one for you.'

A few weeks later, Patricia and I were walking through the churchyard of Christ Church, in Hampstead village, on a summer's evening when I stopped her, took her in my arms and said, 'Listen, my love, will you marry me?'

'Are you serious?' she asked.

'Entirely,' I replied. 'What do you say?'

'Of course I will.'

We fixed no date, but agreed that we would wed within the year.

In that time I wanted to make sure that I could become financially secure so that we could raise a family and have sufficient money for the children's education, as well as having enough for us to enjoy ourselves.

That meant there would be much hard work and risk-taking ahead. I was determined to hone the gold-smuggling operation to its optimum efficiency. Within a few months this had been achieved and the deliveries of the gold, the false-bottomed aluminium crates and the exhaust gas analysers were arriving at the premises I was then renting in Tabard Street, south-east London, two or three times a week. On occasions, I would spend the night carefully packing the gold bars and making sure they could not be detected, before driving to the airport at dawn to hand them over for air freighting to Bombay. Meanwhile, in India, the consignments were also dealt with in conveyor-belt style.

Such was the extent of the operation that by the end of June 1990, our shipments began to affect the entire Bombay gold market and Goutti would have problems disposing of the bullion quickly enough. The business sections of various Bombay newspapers commented regularly on the vast increase in the amount of gold circulating in the market. Some weeks we would export hundreds of kilos of gold in this manner but, despite the efforts of the Indian authorities to trace the source of this dramatic upsurge in the black market bullion trade, not a single gold bar was ever discovered.

Two days before flying out to Jordan for a scuba-diving holiday with Ben at the end of June 1990, I received a phone call from the Commissionaire who controlled the lobby of Inca's new offices in New Bond Street.

'Darius,' he said, 'you'd better come down. There's been some suspicious bloke poking around down here, asking after Inca. Come and see what the geezer wants.'

I ran downstairs assuming it was some journalist looking for gossip about Charlie or his sister, Princess Diana. Some weeks before, I had been told by the Commissionaire that journalists had been snooping around wanting to talk to me about the Spencer family.

'He left ten seconds ago,' said the Commissionaire. 'If you're quick, you'll catch him. He's a young bloke, about your build, mousy hair.'

I ran out on to the street, determined to catch whoever it was and warn him to stop snooping around my office. If it was a reporter, and he was looking for gossip about my friends, he would be left in no doubt that it would be a bad idea to trouble me again. But the man had disappeared. I could see no one that fitted the description. I returned, frustrated.

In Aqaba, a few days later, I would come within an ace of drowning. Shortly after arriving in Jordan, I went scuba-diving with a couple of friends to search a wreck site a few hundred yards from the shore of the Red Sea.

As I began to swim up from the wreck I felt a tug on my shoulder at a depth of about 120 feet. I looked around, but could see nothing. Then

I saw through the clear, crystal blue waters a small boat above me with fishermen leaning over the side and tugging at a line.

I realised that my aqua-lung had become entangled in one of their fishing lines and that I could not free myself. The more I struggled to fight free the more taut the line became, while the fishermen above were convinced they had caught a large fish. A large proportion of diving accidents are caused by divers becoming entwined in fishing lines or nets and I knew that if I could not free myself, I would be in considerable danger.

I signalled to the diver nearest me, waving my hand in the standard distress signal. He swam over and I pointed to my shoulder and then up, indicating the fishing boat above me. He came behind me and tugged at the line in an effort to release the hook that had caught my air-tank and become embedded in my wet suit. That didn't work, so he used his knife to cut out the hook.

In that instant, the hook flashed inches from our faces as the fishermen tugged hard on the line. I signalled my thanks to the diver and swam slowly back to the surface. But my mind wasn't fully on the near-miss. I felt for some reason that what I had just experienced had been an omen about my own life and that, in some way, I was now in danger.

I had just taken off my air-tank, and was standing on the hot sand in my wet suit looking across the gulf of Aqaba at the hazy Egyptian shoreline in the distance, when a young Arab boy came running up to me.

'Mr Guppy, Sir, there's a phone call for you, come quickly.'

I looked at Ben, who had come over as I walked up the beach.

'Who on earth can that be?' I said.

'God only knows,' Ben replied, 'but we'll soon find out.'

I walked to the beach hut where a phone extension had been fitted.

'Yes,' I said.

The line was faint, but clear enough for me to recognise the voice of Inca's telephonist.

'Darius,' she said, pausing.

'Yes,' I replied. 'I can hear you. What's up?'

'You know that man who was seen snooping around the office the other day?'

'Yes,' I said, 'the one I couldn't find.'

'Well,' she replied, 'it wasn't a journalist at all, it was a man from Customs and Excise.'

'Go on.'

'There are eight Customs and Excise officers here in the office. They seem to think you're still in the country. They tell me they have a warrant to search these offices and your homes. They also have a warrant for Ben's and your arrest.'

'Sharon,' I said, 'I hear everything you're saying. I'll phone you back shortly.'

I walked out of the hut into the heat, swearing under my breath.

'Ben,' I said, looking glum. 'I've got some bad news.'

'What's that?'

'Customs have arrived at Inca. They want to search our homes and the offices. Worse still, they've got warrants for our arrest.'

'Typical,' said Ben, 'they could at least have let us enjoy our holiday first.'

XI

As we drove by jeep to our hotel along the beach, I remembered that the last shipment of gold I had smuggled to India was at that moment awaiting unpacking in our Bombay warehouse.

I told Ben about the consignment, a large one. There were forty-four kilos of bullion, worth £500,000 at Indian prices, which I realised we had to get rid of before there was any possibility of the Indian authorities raiding the warehouse.

As soon as we reached our room, I went to the phone and dialled Ishan Dutta at his home in Bombay. 'Ishan,' I said, speaking quickly, 'I'm bloody glad you're at home. There's been a little local difficulty and we have to act fast.'

'What do you mean, difficulty?' he asked.

'Our offices in London have been raided by Customs and Excise,' I said, 'and I'm worried they may inform the Indian authorities about our activities at any time.'

'Relax,' said Ishan, not seeming to comprehend the gravity of what was happening, 'I have everything under control at this end. I can assure you there's nothing to worry about. The authorities here have no idea what's been going on.'

Speaking quietly but firmly, I reasoned with Ishan that the British Customs would be bound to discover that Inca, a firm supposedly dealing in gems, had been sending many shipments of gas analysers to Bombay. The records of Inca's phone calls would confirm that we were heavily involved in India and would also lead to his phone number.

Again, Ishan insisted that there was no cause for concern; that he was using a false name — Aklak Addewala, as well as a number of other aliases — and that, even if the British Customs were able to deduce that the gas analysers business had been a front for smuggling gold to Bombay, the Indian authorities would never make the connection between Ishan Dutta and Aklak Addewala and would, therefore, never be able to trace the bullion to the warehouse.

For more than an hour, I argued with Ishan telling him that it was better to play it safe and that the British Customs were bound to have had sufficiently compelling evidence against us to have warranted sending round eight men to search our offices. For all we knew, they may even have been tapping our telephones for weeks. It was a mixture of laziness and sheer stubbornness on his part that was holding him back from driving to the warehouse compound and, if necessary, working through the night to remove the gold from the crates.

'Ishan, it only takes a single phone call from the British Customs to their counterparts in Bombay and the whole operation will be blown wide apart. If the Indian authorities find that gold in that warehouse,' I warned him, 'then we're all finished and we all lose a lot of money.'

Still Dutta prevaricated.

I looked at Ben, who came over and grabbed the phone from me. 'Listen, Dutta, you bloody little punkawallah!' Ben shouted. 'I've got some of my money wrapped up in that shipment. Don't be so fucking arrogant to assume you'll never get caught. Just get that gold out of the warehouse now, immediately.'

He handed the phone back to me.

'There's no need for Ben to talk to me in that way,' said Ishan, a little hurt. 'We're all in this together.'

'That's right,' I remarked. 'We're all in this together, so pull your bloody finger out. You try your best to cover any tracks your end and we'll do the same our end. Now, please, Ishan get that gold out of that warehouse and liquidate it, tonight. If it's all just a false alarm, then you've lost nothing except perhaps a few hours' sleep.'

With a sigh, Ishan finally relented. 'If you feel that concerned I'll do it, but I really do think you're both over-reacting to the situation. You'll see.'

When I put the telephone down, I was still not fully convinced that

Ishan would act with the necessary speed.

In the previous twelve months we had assembled a complete smuggling network to ensure the smooth running of the operation. Our venture could never have functioned properly without a committed band of a score or more local heavies. To a certain extent, our bullion-smuggling enterprise worked on the model of the American boot-legging syndicates of the 1930s with a hierarchy of heavies, some with prison records, others on the run, each playing his part. And their roles would become increasingly necessary as our shipments escalated.

When runners went out to sell our gold on the black market, they would need protection and one or two local minders would be assigned to look after them. Just as importantly, those handling suitcases full of money, often with as much in them as £250,000 a time, would need four strong men to escort them around the city. In the Bombay gold market, the sight of an Indian carrying a large and heavy suitcase could mean only one thing and he could, therefore, be a potential target for local gangsters. The heavies were also needed to guard premises where the cash was kept. Most of these activities were co-ordinated and organised by Bancil, Goutti's illiterate deputy who had an intimate knowledge of Bombay's black market.

I phoned Dutta again.

'Ishan, listen. This is the way it has to be done. Instead of liquidating the bullion as we usually do, little by little, waiting for the right bid,' I told him, 'we must get rid of everything immediately, even if that means taking a 5 or 10 per cent hit on the price.'

'I hear what you say,' Dutta said. 'But ...'

'No buts, Ishan,' I insisted. 'We must go for it. Get rid of the stuff instantly. For that you'll need even more help than usual. We must bring in Bancil and his men to give you a hand.'

'OK Darry, you've convinced me. I'm going to the warehouse first thing in the morning. I can't go now because it'll be shut for the night. I'll be there at first light with Bancil and his boys.'

Later, Ishan would tell us what occurred.

Shortly after dawn the following morning, Ishan arrived at the warehouse compound with six heavies and together they smashed open the eleven crates where the gold had been hidden. They put all of it into two jeeps, hiding it under blankets. Ishan kept back one bar, worth about £12,000, and concealed it in the glove compartment. He reckoned that if stopped by a policeman or army officer he would resort to the time-honoured custom of a bribe.

As they drove into Bombay, Ishan was surprised to find the roads jammed almost solid. Wondering what had happened, he turned on his radio. It was then he heard that the Indian Army had been called out to patrol all the major roads into and out of the city because the 'DRI' (Directorate of Revenue Intelligence) had been informed that a large shipment of contraband gold was being smuggled into Bombay. The report went on to state that the DRI believed this particular consignment to be part of a much larger operation that had been smuggling vast quantities of bullion into the country for several months.

As they approached a road block, stopping and searching every third vehicle or so, Ishan was convinced he would have to make use of the single gold bar that he had hidden in the glove compartment. Just as a soldier put his head through the driver's window to make a cursory inspection, the bar dropped through a hole in the bottom of the compartment and fell on to the floor. The man sitting next to Ishan quickly concealed it with his foot and the soldier never noticed. He waved them through.

Within two hours of Ishan taking all the gold out of the warehouse, the Indian authorities, together with armed police, had arrived there.

That night Ishan liquidated the bullion in one deal and deposited two suitcases, stuffed with rupees, one with Goutti and the other with a black market currency dealer. He anticipated that the money would be deposited in our Geneva accounts within the next week.

The following night Ishan phoned us in our Aqaba hotel to tell us what had happened. He sounded pleased with himself.

'Everything went perfectly,' he said. 'We got the stuff just before the DRI raided the warehouse and I managed to liquidate everything in one hit. The money is fine. Goutti has half of it and my other friend has the rest. You can sleep peacefully now. We're in the clear.'

I wasn't so sure. 'It's obvious the British Customs have put two and two together,' I told Ishan. 'It's also obvious the DRI know where the gold was going to and now must also know that the warehouse was rented to a Mr Aklak Addewala. Is there any evidence you can think of that could link Aklak Addewala to Ishan Dutta?'

'None,' he replied.

Twenty-four hours later, however, Ishan was back on the phone, in a near panic.

'Darry,' he said, 'something terrible has happened.'

'What?' I asked.

'This morning I decided to empty the bank account that was in the name of Aklak Addewala. There must have been about £100,000 in there that I kept as a reserve. I went to the manager and took everything out in cash, putting the money into a suitcase.'

'So what?'

'An hour later, I phoned the bank manager just to see if there'd been any enquiries from the DRI and he told me that the DRI had visited him twenty minutes after I'd left with the cash and had demanded to see my bank account details. But instead of asking for Aklak Addewala, they had asked for Ishan Dutta. They now know exactly who is master-minding this whole operation. If they catch me they'll torture me, do you realise that?'

His old arrogance and swagger had abandoned him. He was close to tears.

I urged him to calm down while I took in what he had said.

'Where are you phoning from?' I asked.

'My house, of course,' he replied.

'How can you be so bloody stupid?' I said. 'If they know your real name, they'll be round there in minutes. You must get out now.'

'You're right. I'll take the first available plane. I don't know where to. I'll phone you when I've reached safety.'

Two days later, I received a call in Aqaba from Ishan. He had arrived safely in Geneva and he sounded elated.

'Darius, I made it, and just in time as well because I rang my family in Bombay and the DRI have raided my residence. They've even impounded my jeep.' He continued, 'I've checked the banks over here. One lot of money has arrived but we're still waiting for Goutti's. I spoke to him just before I left Bombay. He assured me that we'd receive the money within a week.'

'Ishan,' I said, 'well done. It's good to know you're safe. What are your immediate plans? Are you flying on to London?'

'No, I don't think so,' he replied. 'I think it would be more sensible for me to lie low for a while, you understand, until the dust has settled. I've already spoken to my father in Calcutta and he'll try to sort everything out. He's got good high-level contacts and is sure that, eventually, everything will be cleared up and I'll be able to return to India. It might involve paying out some money, but in India all things are possible.'

'Yes,' I said, 'I understand what you're saying. Ben and I intend to return to London in a day or two. When you're settled give me a call, or write, so that we can know where to contact you. OK?'

'Yes, I'll do that. See you soon.'

After the first phone call in the beach hut in Aqaba telling us of the Customs and Excise raid, Ben and I had decided to return immediately to face the music. However, our lawyers in London had advised us to wait in Jordan for a few more days so that they could ascertain our legal position and arrange for bail if we were to be arrested upon our arrival in England.

However, shortly after I had taken the fateful call from London, we had decided to telephone our offices and speak to the Customs Officer in charge of the investigation.

Ben made the call.

'Could I ask your name?' he asked.

'Yes,' the officer replied. 'Where are you Mr Marsh? Are you in England?'

'No. Mr Guppy and I are in Jordan, actually.'

'What are you doing there?' he asked.

'We're on holiday, scuba-diving.'

'Scuba-diving?' he queried. 'Isn't that a little flash, Mr Marsh?'

Ben chuckled and said, 'Not really. It's a package holiday and it only cost £300.'

'Oh,' he replied, somewhat taken aback.

'If you'd care to come here to interview us,' Ben said, 'feel free. I'm sure the trip would cost HM Customs a lot less than having eight officers hanging around our offices doing nothing.'

'Very droll, Mr Marsh. But I don't think we'll be taking up your invitation.'

Ben went on to ask the officer, 'What's this all about?'

'It concerns some gold purchases involving you and Mr Guppy. We have warrants to search your offices.'

Ben arranged for the Customs Officers to be let in to search the premises, but only if one of our accountants was present at all times.

The day after the team of Customs Officers had searched Inca's offices, I had spoken to our accountant, who told me what had happened during their inspection.

'They were very thorough,' he explained. 'But what struck me as quite remarkable was their reaction to finding papers relating to the New York gems robbery. They became like excited schoolboys. It was all that seemed to interest them and from that point, they seemed to take far less interest in the bullion transactions.'

When I had finished speaking to the accountant, I turned to Ben. 'Customs and Excise suspect New York.'

'What do you mean?' he asked.

I related what the accountant had told me.

'Shit! What happens if they find the gems hidden in my flat?'

'If they find those stones,' I said, 'it's curtains. I wonder if we can prevent them searching our homes.'

'Could we get the lawyers to challenge the Customs' right to do so?' Ben suggested.

'No,' I replied. 'I think that would be a mistake. They would immediately suspect we had something to hide. We have to stay cool as though we're totally innocent of any wrong doing. Let's just pray they don't find them.'

'But what about the gold transactions?' Ben said.

'Your involvement in that has been virtually nil. And my involvement has been mainly outside Inca. The worst case scenario is that I've committed some technical offences. In fact, all I've really done is to mislead Customs into thinking that the gold went to Switzerland when in fact it went to India. It's not as if Customs have been cheated out of a single penny. I don't give a damn about the gold, it's New York that could finish us.'

Two matters in particular were of real concern. The first was the possibility of Customs Officers finding the gems hidden in the Jaffa cakes in Ben's kitchen; and the other was the integrity of our accomplice, Peter Risdon.

I called Risdon at his offices in Tabard Street, where I rented the basement to pack the gold into the false-bottomed crates. He informed me that HM Customs had visited his offices and taken an innocuous statement from him about my use of the basement.

'What about the other matter?' I asked.

'Nothing,' he replied, 'it was never mentioned.'

'And I trust that if they ever did mention it at sometime in the future, you would divulge nothing.'

'Please, Darius,' he replied, 'don't insult my professionalism. You have my word. I have a reputation, you know. Also, remember, I have as much to lose as you as far as that particular incident is concerned.'

We arrived back at Heathrow on 8 July and were not arrested because our lawyers had arranged with Customs that we would surrender ourselves to them for interview a few days later. Before going to our lawyers' offices in Covent Garden, we called at Ben's flat in Pimlico.

'What the hell's happened here?' said Ben. 'Have we been burgled or something? Look at the place.'

Indeed, it seemed the investigating officers had been extremely thorough in their search. I wondered what mess they had left my own house in.

We went straight to the kitchen. Ben looked at me, shaking his head, as he noted that the coffee tin, which was on the shelf next to the biscuit tin, had been opened. We feared the worst.

Ben took down the biscuit tin and gently opened the lid. He removed one of the Jaffa cakes and turned it upside down. He gently prised open the small hole that we had made in the cake and there, inside it, was one of our gems.

'Thank God!' I whispered, my heart pounding.

Quickly we examined a few of the other cakes and it became clear that the Customs had missed them all.

'My God, we're lucky,' said Ben. 'What are we going to do with them now?'

'Funnily enough,' I replied, 'I think we should leave them here. They've searched the place. They're unlikely to come back. For the time being, it's probably the safest place in the world to hide them.'

'I agree,' Ben said, the worried frown that had been on his face ever since we had landed at Heathrow yielding to a broad grin.

Four days later Ben and I, accompanied by our lawyers, surrendered ourselves for interview at the Customs' headquarters on the Embankment.

At first, the questions concentrated on the gold transactions. As had already become obvious, they had soon been able to work out what we had been doing during the past few months, smuggling the gold into India rather than exporting it to Switzerland as we had claimed on all the paperwork. Ben and I were held in different rooms and investigating officers would regularly leave to cross-check our respective answers.

During the afternoon, however, another officer began asking questions relating to the New York robbery. Within minutes, it became apparent that the Customs' real interest lay not in the bullion operation but in the £1,800,000 insurance claim.

I kept comforting myself that the Customs Officers could have had no concrete evidence to prove that the robbery in New York hadn't been totally genuine, but their questions were always pointed and direct, and their technique of trying to make us feel that they knew more than they actually did was very effective.

After our interviews, we were both escorted to Snow Hill police station and charged with what were described as 'holding charges', essentially that Ben and I 'must have acted in a way that would have involved the commission of one or more VAT offences'.

'What the hell's that supposed to mean?' Ben queried, with his usual directness.

Our lawyers explained that this was standard practice when the Customs had not yet worked out the precise charges on which to indict a suspect. A more particularised indictment would follow in due course.

We were then given police bail to appear at Guildhall Magistrates' Court in early August 1990 and released. At that Magistrates' hearing we were bailed to re-appear in November while the Customs continued with their investigations. I was beginning to understand just how slowly the wheels of Justice grind. The prosecution asked the Magistrates to increase our bail from nothing to £30,000 each. Not surprisingly, the bench wished to know why such a request should be made, given that we had voluntarily returned to Britain from Jordan and had surrendered to the Court that day without any bail being involved. No doubt, we could have argued the point and would probably have won but we decided not to. Since Ben and I had no intention of absconding, the whole question seemed purely academic and not worth debating.

During the ensuing months, I would form a good working relationship with one of the senior Customs Officers assigned to our case.

Once, when I had gone round to the Customs' London Headquarters to collect some documents that had been confiscated during the search of Inca's offices, I asked the officer about the possibility of Ben and I settling out of court for a financial consideration or 'compounding', a power that is available to HM Customs & Excise.

'If we're strictly honest here, these allegations relate to technical offences that have cost Customs not one penny.'

'I agree,' he said, 'the allegations are technical.'

'Why can't we just cut a deal and stop wasting everyone's time then?' I asked.

The officer replied, 'You must get your lawyer to make a formal approach in writing. It will then be up to the Commissioners to decide what action to take.'

He went on, 'But, while these offences may well be purely technical, it's no small matter. The law is there to be obeyed.'

Shaking my head, I said, 'OK, I accept that what we did was wrong, but it was clearly not done to rip off the Customs since they haven't lost one penny.'

'Perhaps,' he replied. 'But you must realise, Darius, that there is a very thin blue line that has to be drawn between law and order on the one hand and anarchy on the other.'

'I know what you're saying, but the problem with that argument is that it's being used all over the world to justify increasing the State's power over the individual. "There are criminals everywhere," we keep on being told. "Give us more power and we'll protect you from them." You mark my words, the day will soon come when that thin blue line that you talk about will be used not to separate order from anarchy, but to justify absolute control on the part of the State over the individual.'

'Well, I've got a job to do, Darius,' he said, 'and if we can return to your own particular case, we both know that what we've been investigating is only the tip of the iceberg.'

Looking me straight in the eye, he continued, 'For example, while we have evidence against you in respect of in excess of one million pounds worth of bullion, we suspect there's significantly more.'

I remained calm, replying, 'Even if that were the case, the whole matter is entirely academic because Customs haven't lost any money.'

Speaking more slowly, he added, 'Please don't forget that your forging of a Customs stamp on an official form to show that your gold went to Switzerland rather than India means that, technically, we could charge you with impersonating a Customs Officer.'

'Come off it,' I replied, 'that really is stretching things too far.'

He smiled. 'Maybe, but the law's the law.'

I began to feel a little easier, but he was not yet finished.

'Darius, permit me to bring up the little matter of New York.'

'What do you mean?' I replied.

'I think you know exactly what I mean.'

'I'm sorry,' I said, 'but that incident has been investigated by the New York police and Lloyds and the matter is closed. I think we both know that Customs are just fishing.'

Changing the subject, I asked, 'Is it in order, therefore, to ask my lawyers to write to you proposing a deal?'

'By all means,' he replied, 'but we can't guarantee anything.'

As a result of our interviews with Customs, it was obvious to Ben and me that we needed to liquidate our hoard of gems as speedily as possible.

We had been given permission by the Guildhall Magistrates to obtain our passports from Customs when we needed to travel overseas on business trips and in early August, Ben and I decided we would — using aliases — sell the gems through the auction houses in Switzerland, and by passing them to Bombay black market contacts who would meet us in Geneva to take delivery of the stones before smuggling them back into India.

One August morning, we awoke at 5am and drove to Elstree Airfield where I had arranged to take a small private plane, a

Grummam 'Tiger' AA5 owned by a friend, for a day's trip across the Channel. After climbing into the four-seater aircraft, Ben took the gems from his pocket and hid them in the First Aid box under the front passenger seat.

Having carried out all the pre-flight checks we took off from Elstree and landed not long afterwards at Southend. At that time, every aircraft leaving UK airspace had to depart from a Customs-designated airfield and we had decided to make our official departure point Southend airport. We were concerned, however, that if our passports were checked and cross-referenced against the computer, our flight would probably be stopped and our plane thoroughly searched. It was a gamble we were prepared to take.

Having landed at Southend, I parked the plane near the Immigration offices. We presented the standard paperwork and simply flashed our passports at the Immigration Officer as nonchalantly as possible.

'That's all right, chaps,' he said. 'Have a cup of coffee while I sort out these documents with Customs.'

Sitting at the window of the café that overlooked the runway, we waited and watched, checking to make sure that no one went near the plane while the Immigration and Customs officials looked through our paperwork. Although the procedures at such small airfields are fairly lax, there are occasions when Customs will swoop and conduct spot searches on light planes. But no one stopped us that morning.

Two hours later, we landed at Le Touquet in France. We breezed through passport control and, after a cup of coffee, took off again for Dieppe. For fun we would pass low over the beaches, sometimes hedge-hopping across the fields. It was a glorious, cloudless day and it felt good to be free, however temporarily, from our problems.

After landing at Dieppe airfield on the French coast, we took a taxi to the main railway station and put the gems in a left-luggage locker. Four hours later, we were back at Elstree.

The following morning, we took a scheduled flight to Paris, from Heathrow. From Paris we travelled by train to Dieppe and recovered the stones from the locker a few hours later. We took the next train back to Paris, from where we caught the night train to Geneva. At 10am the following morning, we opened an account and a safe-deposit box in a Swiss bank and placed the jewels there.

Over the next few months we would frequently visit Geneva for meetings with international gem dealers, as well as Indian contacts from the black market. Before the end of the year, we had liquidated almost our entire haul of stones.

As the months went by, we became increasingly concerned about how to hide the money we had accumulated from the Lloyds sting, the gold-smuggling and the sale of the gems. We were convinced that Customs would eventually trace our bank accounts in Geneva and would endeavour, through the courts, to freeze the money contained in them.

Ben and I, therefore, decided to confuse the trail of the money, making it more difficult for Customs or any other investigators to find out exactly what had happened to it. To this end, we arranged for all the funds to be transferred from our accounts in Geneva to an account in Vienna, Austria.

A week later, we flew to Austria and withdrew every penny in cash.

At that point, we were still not absolutely certain what to do with the cash so we decided to have a cup of coffee and try to reach a decision.

I trusted Ben implicitly and I believe that trust was mutual. We both accepted, however, that at some point in the future we might find ourselves at the hands of the police or Customs investigators and subject to pressure so unbearable that one of us might crack.

Ben's suggestion was simple: 'What you don't know won't hurt you and what I don't know won't hurt me. So let's divide the cash and go our separate ways.'

I agreed. 'While we're sitting here, it's easy to believe that we would always be strong enough never to reveal each other's secrets. I'm sure we would be strong, but the harsh reality is that we can't know for sure whether either of us would ever crack or spill the beans because we've simply never been put to that test. And I pray we never are.'

We decided to go our separate ways. We divided the cash and arranged to meet back in London a few days later.

Two and a half years later I would tell the police that, after Vienna, I had smuggled my share of the money back into England, believing that this would be the last place any police or Customs officer would expect me to keep the cash. I told them that I had kept the money in a metal trunk in a storage unit off London's Goldhawk Road and that I had lived off that cash, paying for my legal fees and other expenses until I was left with only £200,000. I explained that I gave this money to an unnamed Middle Eastern businessman, who I had met and befriended at the Regent's Park mosque where I used to pray. This man had told me that he would either buy Grade 'A' bearer bonds, which could be redeemed for cash at any time in the future, or else place the money for safe-keeping with black market currency dealers in the Middle East.

I suspect that never, for one moment, did the police accept this story.

I realised that my tale sounded improbable, too far-fetched. In essence, however, it was indeed the truth with just one or two slight differences.

The police, the authorities and the judge at my trial were all convinced that I had stashed away far more than I claimed. In fact, more than one person had agreed to manage the money on my behalf. Since emerging from prison in February 1996 I have never traced them, nor the money. It is my aim to travel to the Middle East one day to locate the missing funds. Who knows?

While we dispersed our ill-gotten gains there was other serious business to attend to — weeks had passed since Dutta had escaped from India and still we had not received a single penny of the £250,000 he had left with Goutti to transfer to us. Instead, repeated phone calls to Goutti's home and office had prompted protestations of goodwill and endless excuses for not having had the money deposited into our accounts in Geneva, as he had promised.

A typical excuse would involve Goutti informing us, very politely and very sincerely, that the Indian authorities were spending hours at his office every day, interviewing him and pressing him to give details of the gold deals he had been involved in.

'It will be there soon,' he would assure me, 'but I have not had the time to transfer the money, you understand, Mr Guppy.'

I understood only too well. I regularly telephoned Ishan, who was then living in Paris, and told him of my doubts about Goutti.

'Have faith,' he would respond. 'I've also spoken to him a number of times and I know he's having real problems with the authorities over there. I believe he's a man of honour. He's never tried to cheat us before and I don't think he will now.'

After a further week, it was Ishan's turn to call me. He sounded upset and on the verge of panic. 'Darius, listen. Goutti's in terrible trouble. His offices have been raided by the DRI. They've confiscated the £250,000 I left with him. He tells me he can't get the money back.'

'Ishan,' I interrupted bluntly, 'do you really believe that story? It's obvious what's happened. He's been fobbing us off for weeks. He's a snake, Ishan, and he's not going to get away with it. I have an idea. I'll phone you tomorrow.'

As soon as I put down the receiver I knew what I would do.

Early the following morning I phoned Peter Risdon and asked for the number of William Hall, a former member of the security forces who knew Tom McLaine and who, I understood, had a first-class reputation for extracting money from reluctant debtors.

That evening, with Ben, I met Hall in the lobby of the Churchill Hotel. A squat, tough-looking man in his mid-forties with a bushy moustache and short, dark, wavy hair, he certainly looked the part.

After explaining the problem, Hall said, already calling me by my nickname, 'Darry ... you don't mind if I call you that, do you?'

'No, not at all,' I replied.

'Yeah, I'll help you out. But my job would be a lot easier if you could arrange some local support, if you know what I mean.'

Pausing, he went on, 'I've travelled a lot, but I don't know Bombay at all. And this bloke might have some friends he could call on.'

'No problem,' I told him. 'I should be able to arrange for some locals to give you a hand. I also hope to arrange for a friend of mine, Ishan Dutta, to meet you in Bombay. He'll be the one to introduce you to them. Now, what sort of fee will you want?'

Hall replied, 'I want four K up front, plus a grand a week, plus all expenses. That all right?'

'That's fine,' I replied. 'When can you go?'

'Whenever.'

'Good, I'll contact you as soon as the arrangements have been made.'

Later that afternoon, I phoned Ishan and told him that I had hired an ex-Special Forces soldier to go to Bombay with instructions to collect the money from Goutti by whatever means necessary. I went on,

'And you, Ishan, will have to be his guide. Our passports have been impounded and Customs are crawling all over us so we can't go, otherwise we would. I know you've got a false passport, so I suggest you fly to Kathmandu, take a bus over the Nepalese border into India and then make your way down by train to Bombay.'

'That will take me at least three or four days,' he said.

'That's fine,' I told him. 'I'll arrange for our man, Bill Hall, to meet you in the Fariyas Hotel in Bombay at 6pm a week today. Is that OK?'

'Yes,' he said, 'I can do that. I'll be there.'

'All I need you to do is to show him Goutti's office; point out Goutti in person and introduce him to a few of our boys. Leave the rest to him and then get the hell out of the country. Just make damn sure you never use your real name for anything. Don't call any friends and don't go to any of your old haunts. Any time you're not working, just stay in your hotel room. Any questions?'

'Understood. I'll go straight to Nepal.'

A week later I received a call from Ishan in his room at the Fariyas Hotel in the Colaba district of Bombay. He told me that he had booked himself in under the name of Malhotra and that he had also booked his Nepalese servant, Huri, into the room next door under the name of Parbhoo. Moreover, he had met Hall who was occupying a room down the corridor.

The first seven days were taken up with surveillance. At least two or three times a day I would call Ishan or Hall, co-ordinating the operation from public phone boxes in London. I would ask them for progress reports, after which we would agree the plans for the following day.

Ishan arranged to introduce Hall to one of the heavies' leaders, a man who was on the run from the law and on the 'most-wanted' list of the Bombay police. They met in a bar in downtown Bombay. After explaining the operation, Ishan agreed terms with the man and said he would be in touch soon. Hall told him that they might need half a dozen men, at the most.

They took a 35mm camera, hired a taxi and a driver for the day and followed Goutti from his office to his car. Having identified his car, they left him until the following evening when he returned to it from work. From there they followed him to his home. For the next three days they watched his every move, noting his arrival and departure times from his home and his office until, having learnt his routine by heart, Hall was satisfied that he could predict his movements with confidence.

At first light one morning Hall met up with the heavies, as agreed, not far from Goutti's home. They were armed with machetes and guns. Hall, for reasons unknown to me, took his umbrella. Together they walked into his block of flats and up to his third-floor apartment. Hall knocked at the door, which was opened by a servant.

'Mr Goutti not at home,' the servant told him.

'Where is he then?' said Hall, thumping the servant hard in the abdomen with the handle of his umbrella.

Struggling for breath, the servant informed him that his master had gone out of town the previous night and would be back later.

'Well, give him this,' said Hall, thrusting a piece of paper into the man's hand. Written on the paper was the number of a bank account in Geneva, which Goutti would immediately have recognised, for it was the account we had used in the gold-smuggling operation.

Hall then phoned me asking for further instructions. I told him to sit tight until I got back to him. That evening, I phoned Goutti at his home.

'It's Mr Guppy here,' I said. 'I'd like to speak to Mr Goutti.'

'Mr Goutti not here,' came the reply. 'He's gone away. He has left the country for six months.'

I had, however, recognised the voice.

'Tell Mr Goutti to come to the phone now or I'll send some people round to make him talk to me.'

After a short pause, Goutti, assuming a slightly different accent, said, 'Mr Guppy, how lovely to speak to you again. I'm so sorry about my servant. A slight misunderstanding on his part. What can I do for you?'

'I'll get straight to the point, Goutti. That story you told Ishan Dutta about the authorities confiscating our money is a pack of lies. You will hand it over immediately.'

'Mr Guppy,' he said, 'you don't understand. Events here have been terrible and the DRI came into my office and simply confiscated the money that was in the suitcase.'

Before he could continue, I yelled down the phone, 'You're not dealing with Ishan now, you're dealing with me. Don't insult my intelligence! You're a fucking traitor! You've taken a diabolical liberty and I'll stop at nothing to rectify things. In all our dealings with you we've been entirely straight, never once breaking our word, but you chose your moment, when you knew that Ishan was at his weakest, and out of the country and on the run. That is not acceptable. Unless you get the money you owe into that account in Geneva as you promised, those boys will come round again and this time they'll gut you like a rabbit. Do you understand what I'm telling you?'

There was a pause.

'Mr Guppy,' he said, hit by a sudden recollection. 'You are absolutely right. I have made a terrible mistake. That suitcase with the money the DRI took away was not your suitcase but another man's. You need not worry. Your money is safe with a well-known broker and I will arrange for it to be transferred tomorrow. Please, please Mr Guppy, forgive my temporary lapse of memory. I must be getting old.'

'Well let us hope you stay young. I will trust you, Mr Goutti, for one week only. Do you hear me?'

'Yes, of course. But Mr Guppy, please listen. You must understand that I did have to use some of the money to bribe senior officers and very important people.'

'Will £30,000 be sufficient?' I asked.

'Yes,' he replied, 'that would be very kind of you, very understanding.'

'Then we have a deal, do we, Mr Goutti?'

'Yes, I will always honour a deal with a gentleman like you, Mr Guppy. And do remember whenever you wish to take a holiday in India, you must come as my guest. And if you wish, you could bring your beautiful lady. It would be very good to see you again.'

I contacted Hall and asked him to remain in Bombay for another week, just in case the promised funds did not arrive in Geneva. I then suggested to Ishan that he leave India and return to Paris as there was nothing more he could do. Five days later, the money arrived.

Later, I piloted a light plane to Paris to discuss the whole affair with Ishan. He told me that he would not be able to return to India, because he had learned from his lawyers that the Indian authorities had issued a *coffe posa* order against him — a Draconian device primarily used by the Government against suspected terrorists, but which could be extended to cover many other offences against the

State. Such an order, Ishan explained, would enable the authorities investigating him to detain him in prison without charge or trial for up to three years.

Ishan assured me, however, that with the appropriate financial incentives, the authorities would drop the matter in due course. It was just a question of waiting for the dust to settle.

As the late summer months meandered into autumn, Ben and I began to relax believing that, despite all their suspicions, the Customs and Excise could have no hard evidence to suggest that we had organised and staged the New York sting. If they did have such evidence, we reasoned, then presumably we would have known about it by then. We were, of course, still facing the Customs charges that were due to be heard in November but we knew that, for such offences, a fine would be the most likely outcome.

Some weeks later, Bill Hall invited me to Hereford for a day's shooting. He knew that I often attended a shooting-range and that I enjoyed the sport. We met up and he took me to a deserted former military shooting range. There, we shot with a number of semi-automatic hand-guns and revolvers, ranging from 9mm Brownings and Berettas to a Colt .45 and .38 Magnum.

As we walked back to the car, Hall said, 'Not a bad bit of shooting there, Darry. Would you like a keepsake of the day's shoot?'

'What do you mean?' I asked.

'Here you are,' he said when we got to his car. He opened the boot and handed me a Browning 9mm semi-automatic with a couple of empty magazines and a tray of a hundred rounds of ammunition.

'That's very kind of you,' I said. 'Are you sure?'

'Yes, 'course I am,' he replied, 'otherwise I wouldn't have given it to you, would I?'

He went on, 'Only one point, Darry. Make sure you get the thing registered and get it licensed. We don't want you getting nicked now, do we?'

As he drove me back to his house for tea, I stripped the gun to examine it more closely and noticed that it had no registration mark.

'There's no registration,' I said, curious that he should own a weapon with no number.

'Darry. You don't need to ask any questions. I can assure you it's never been fired before and that's the main thing. It's a brand new, unregistered gun.'

I had always been aware of Bill Hall's links with the Special Forces and I assumed that he had obtained the gun from army pals. I wondered how easy it would be to register it since it was unmarked but, because I had so many other more pressing matters to attend to, I didn't get round to making the appropriate enquiries. Instead, I hid it in my attic and didn't think about it again.

In November 1990, Risdon phoned out of the blue and invited Ben and me for a drink because he had a proposal he wanted us to consider. We met in the Rosendale Arms in Dulwich just after six one evening.

From the outset, Risdon spoke in whispers.

'Ever since we did that job together in New York,' he said, 'I've been thinking.'

'What do you mean?' Ben asked.

'I'm thinking of doing the same sting, but this time for about one-and-a-half million. And I thought that, as the last operation was so well done, I would invite you two in to share the spoils.'

Ben and I looked at each other but said nothing, as Risdon went on to explain that a massive uncut diamond, which had been stolen from De Beers in South Africa, would be smuggled into London in January 1991 by some of his criminal associates and that he wanted to set up an insurance fraud.

'Peter,' I said, 'what we did in New York was a one-off operation, done with a specific objective in mind, to get back money that Lloyds had ripped off from my family and to help out our company. We would never repeat it.'

Risdon changed tack. 'We haven't yet reached a decision about an insurance job. We might just sell the diamond. If we did that, could you two help?'

'That's a different matter,' I said. 'In those circumstances, I'm sure we could steer you in the right direction. Most of the diamonds that end up in Hatton Garden have been smuggled across borders at some stage and I'm confident that Sotheby's for one would handle the sale, especially if the diamond is as big as you say it is, but they'd also want to know the provenance of the stone.'

Risdon, however, seemed more keen on the idea of an insurance sting. 'I've assembled a team to carry out this operation,' he said. 'We're talking a major criminal network here, all ready to take their orders from me, involving South Africa, London, New York and Greece.'

'What the hell has Greece got to do with this?' I asked.

'Because that's where I'll hole-up after we complete the job. I've decided to leave my girlfriend and to go underground with some very heavy-duty contacts I have out there.'

Ben and I exchanged glances. 'Listen,' Ben said. 'We're under investigation at the moment and we couldn't consider for one minute becoming involved in any such thing. It would be madness. Why don't you leave us out and we'll wish you luck?'

Risdon took a drink and then added, 'Yes, maybe you're right. If we were to split the proceeds on this one, then you would still be well ahead of me, bearing in mind how much you made from the New York job.'

His words alarmed me. For they showed that he was not simply some Walter Mitty character, but also envious and that was dangerous. 'What the hell do you mean, Peter? This isn't some race. There's no competition between us, is there?'

'No, of course not,' he protested.

'Listen Peter. Let me make one point. These operations are very difficult to carry out successfully. We were very lucky with New York. It could so easily have gone wrong. You have to be very, very careful. My advice to you is don't try any insurance fraud, just sell it straight. We'll introduce you to some contacts and I'm sure you won't have any problems disposing of the diamond, because a great many of the big gems that come on to the market have dodgy backgrounds and all the major gem dealers know this perfectly well.'

Ben and I drove back to Chelsea convinced that Peter Risdon could be a serious danger for us. 'The one consolation is that he's planning to emigrate to Greece. The sooner he's out of the picture the happier I'll feel. He worries me,' I told Ben.

Throughout the first few months of 1991 we tried to continue our main business — gems dealing through Inca — but the fact that HM Customs appeared to be dragging their feet over our court case caused problems. We hoped they would agree to settle out of court. From time to time they would reassure us that the case would soon be resolved one way or the other, but then we would hear nothing. We were beginning to lose patience, but were still convinced that the matter would end at worst in our receiving a fine.

One morning in March 1991, I took a phone call.

'It's Frances,' said a woman's voice.

'Sorry,' I said. 'Frances who?'

'Peter's girlfriend. Don't you remember you came round to our house one day?'

'Yes,' I said, 'I'm sorry. Of course I remember.'

'Listen,' she said, 'Peter's been arrested.'

My heart sank, wondering what on earth Risdon had been up to.

'What's he done?' I asked.

'Well, I don't know the details but it's concerning a large diamond from South Africa.' She went on, 'He was arrested by the police trying to get it out from a bank a few days ago with a forged passport. He's been in Wormwood Scrubs ever since. He's been granted bail of £20,000 and he's trying to raise the money. He wants you and Ben to stand surety for the whole lot.'

'I see,' I said.

'There's something else,' she said. 'He told me that if you weren't willing to assist him, he might be forced to reconsider his position regarding New York, whatever that means.'

My first thought, in fact, was not of anger at Risdon's pathetic attempt to get money from us, but of pity for Frances. She obviously had no idea that Risdon was planning to desert her. And now he was using her to try to get out of jail. I felt sorry that she had become involved with such a shabby man.

'Listen Frances,' I said, 'calm down and think about what I'm going to say. Because Ben and I are facing charges and are on bail ourselves, no court would accept our surety.'

'I see,' she said.

'Not only that,' I went on, 'when anyone stands surety the police or the court have to accept the person offering to put up the bail. Since we're already on Customs bail, they'd be very interested indeed to know why we were offering to stand surety for Peter and would be bound to investigate the connection further. Tell him very clearly that, bearing in mind what happened in New York, it would be absolute madness to invite the attention of the police. It would be asking for trouble. Tell Peter that if he can find someone to front for us then we'll provide the money for that person to stand surety. It would probably take a week to organise, but we'd be happy to do so. Whatever happens, the bail should not be in our names.'

'I understand,' she said, 'and I'll tell him.'

'One final thing,' I told her. 'Peter must know what type of characters we are. And he must realise that such behaviour will never work.'

I heard nothing more from Frances and a week later, received a phone call from a chastened Risdon. 'Darius, first I must apologise profusely for what I gather Frances told you on the phone. I think she misunderstood the message I was trying to convey and I really hope that our working relationship will not be impaired by this most regrettable incident. You know me. I am a man of honour.'

'Anyway,' he went on, 'as you may have gathered, I am a free man again. My parents put up bail.'

'Good, Peter. Well let's forget about the misunderstanding,' I said. 'What exactly happened? Are you OK?'

'It's all about that diamond, the one I told you about. For some reason, when I went to retrieve the said item from the bank last week, using false documentation, the police were waiting for me.'

'What's the net result, Peter? How serious are the charges against you?'

'At the moment,' he replied, 'I'm very confident because the charges relate only to handling stolen property. But I'm concerned in case the police try to implicate me in a conspiracy to commit an insurance fraud. Fortunately in that respect I'm lucky, because all my accomplices are out of harm's way, so to speak,' he guffawed, 'in South Africa. Anyway, the situation is under control.'

Risdon requested a meeting but this worried me. Whether instinct took over, I am not sure, but at that moment I had a strong feeling that if we met Risdon he would tape our conversation.

'For the moment that's probably not a wise idea, just in case you're under surveillance. Just keep in touch and keep quiet at your end and we'll keep quiet at our end. Let all this blow over, then we can all get together.'

When I put the phone down I turned to Ben and said, 'What do you think? Is this guy going to grass us?'

Ben replied, 'The pressure is off him since he's now out on bail. If he'd grassed us up, there would have been a knock at the door by now. Our best protection is that Risdon's implicated in New York as much as we are. What could he gain from informing on us? He'd only be dropping himself in it and he's in enough trouble as it is.'

Three weeks later, lawyers acting for Lloyds walked into Inca's offices and served us with a writ to recover the £1,800,000 they had paid out. They had obtained a Mareva injunction, a court order freezing the company's assets and bank accounts.

As soon as the lawyers left the office, I motioned to Ben to keep quiet and we walked out of the office to a coffee shop around the corner.

Once in the street I said, 'Ben, I didn't want to talk in there. Now that things have gone this far it's perfectly possible the police, or whoever, could have bugged the offices. I didn't want to take any chances.'

'Sure, I agree,' he said. 'What do you think?'

We examined the papers served on us in an attempt to ascertain Lloyds' case. It became obvious that HM Customs had conveyed to Lloyds their strong suspicions about the robbery in New York having been a put-up job but that, since there was no real evidence to substantiate such a theory, Lloyds had had to rely on the argument that we may have over-claimed on the policy to the tune of about £10,000. As a consequence, Lloyds claimed we had to return the full £1,800,000 since the policy would be null and void in such circumstances. There was no mention of Risdon and no allegation of fraud.

It was now clear why Customs had been using delaying tactics over the previous nine months. In fact, they had taken comparatively little action over the gold-smuggling matters, but had been spending their time trying to convince Lloyds of London that the gems robbery had been staged and attempting to gather the evidence to demonstrate this.

It had been fortunate for Ben and me that we had decided, nearly a year earlier, to move most of Inca's assets overseas, including nearly all its money. This meant that the Mareva injunction had very little bite because, in effect, it could only freeze the company's UK bank accounts in which we had kept only sufficient funds to cover our overheads.

A few days later, we went to the High Court and won permission to enable Inca to continue trading as before on condition that the company's expenditure be monitored by Lloyds' lawyers.

Outside the courtroom that day, we met the solicitor who was dealing with Lloyds' action against Inca, David Reynolds of Messrs Clyde and Co., a slim man of average height with dark, thinning hair and aged about forty-five. He would play a major role in determining my attitude and behaviour towards Lloyds over the next few years and from the moment I met him I disliked him intensely.

A few days later, the London *Evening Standard* published an article outlining Lloyds' action against us. Hours later, I received a call from Peter Risdon, again reassuring us of his honesty and his discretion. 'Listen,' he said, 'I read that article but I want you to know that you've got nothing to worry about from me. I'm in enough shit as it is. It's not in my interest to create any more bother for myself. Also, please let us not forget that I am not only a professional but a man of honour. You can rest assured that I would never let you down. After all, I do have my reputation to consider.'

I was not convinced.

Realising that a search by the police of my house was a distinct possibility, I remembered the gun that Bill Hall had given me and was now in my attic. I had been meaning to enquire into how to have it registered, but hadn't yet got round to it. I knew that Patricia had a safe-deposit box in Knightsbridge and asked her to store the gun there. The ammunition tray, however, was too deep to fit so she decided to keep it in a safe at her workplace.

At 11am on 15 May I phoned Patricia at work, as I did every day at that time. The telephonist seemed nervous and told me, 'I'm afraid she's not here. She's gone out. I don't know when she'll be back.'

I said that I would call back later and went to visit the offices of HM Customs on the Embankment, to collect my passport for a business trip the next day. As I left the building I was approached by two smartly dressed men and realised instinctively that they were plain clothes police officers. I was convinced they were about to arrest me for the New York robbery.

'Are you Darius Guppy?' said one of them.

'Yes,' I replied.

'My name is Detective Sergeant Webb and I am arresting you on suspicion of possession of a hundred rounds of ammunition.'

I breathed a sigh of relief and almost smiled.

The two officers behaved like gentlemen. 'Is that your car, Sir?' they asked, pointing to my black Mercedes.

'Yes, why?' I asked.

'Well, we don't want you to get a parking ticket while we're detaining you for questioning so we'll write a note to the traffic warden.'

I was surprised and rather taken aback. 'That's very thoughtful,' I said. 'Thanks very much.'

I was taken to Holborn Police Station where I noticed Patricia's name, written in chalk, on a cell door and the words 'possession of ammunition' underneath it.

'Darling, are you all right?' I shouted, wanting to let her know that I was there with her and that she was not alone.

I looked through the slit in the cell door and saw her sitting down, eating an apple and doing *The Times* crossword. She seemed remarkably composed. As I was shown to my cell I felt guilty that Patricia, who was a completely innocent party in all this, should have been arrested and embarrassed in this way, for no good reason.

When questioned by detectives later that day I told them the facts — that I was a member of a shooting club, that I had been given the gun, that I intended to register it one day and that I had asked Patricia to conceal the gun in her safe-deposit box because I suspected my home might be searched. I told them that neither the gun nor the ammunition had anything whatsoever to do with Patricia and asked them to let her go free.

They accepted that I was no terrorist and that I had no intention of using the weapon other than in a gun club. They were, however, insistent that I tell them who had given it to me.

'You know this weapon is almost certainly an army gun and, more than likely, Special Forces. This seems the most likely explanation since it's not a question of it having had its serial number filed off; it never had a serial number in the first place. It looks like it's come straight off the production line. We have to know who provided you with this weapon.'

I replied, 'I promised the man who gave it to me, as a present, that I would never divulge his name, but I can assure you that it didn't come from a criminal source.'

For several hours they insisted that I tell them, but throughout, on this one point, I refused to co-operate. At midnight, they charged Patricia and me with possession of the gun and the ammunition. We were released on police bail. As we left the station one of the officers said to me, 'Off the record, Mr Guppy, we're just doing our job and I respect you for not informing on that man. If you'd told us who it was, we'd have let you off with a warning.'

As we drove back home I felt terrible about having dragged Patricia into this messy business and I said to her, 'I can't tell you how sorry I am. I broke our golden rule that I would never involve you in any of my affairs. I promise you I won't break it again.'

I also told Patricia, however, how proud I was about the way she had handled the entire matter, never telling the police a thing and keeping cool throughout.

I was angry with those senior police officers who had decided to charge Patricia as well as me for something that they must have known perfectly well did not really involve her. Surely, I argued, they could have released her with a caution.

Six weeks later in June 1991, Patricia and I pleaded guilty at Clerkenwell Magistrates Court to two charges of possessing ammunition and a firearm without a certificate. I was fined £100 on each count while Patricia was fined £50. The Magistrate accepted that Patricia and I had acted responsibly in keeping the ammunition apart from the weapon and also accepted that it had been an oversight on my behalf not to have had the gun registered.

Even though Ben and I had tried to deny the signs of the past few months — Risdon's arrest, Lloyds' action against Inca, my arrest over the gun and growing speculation in the newspapers about what had really happened in New York — all our instincts told us that the net was drawing closer. We could feel it in our bones.

After the Clerkenwell court hearing, Ben and I discussed our predicament and we resolved not to panic and to keep our nerve.

But the signs kept revealing themselves. A few days later, I received a call from Bill Hall inviting me to meet him at the London Hilton in Park Lane. Immediately I became suspicious, but I decided to go along.

Over tea, Hall told me that Risdon had contacted him and was trying to arrange a meeting with me. This seemed odd. There was no reason that I knew of why Risdon should not telephone me direct, rather than go through Hall.

'What does he want?' I asked. 'Do you know?'

'He says it's got something to do with New York.'

I feared the worst. Several times during the following few minutes, Hall would return to the question of New York and I wondered whether he was secretly taping our conversation. In due course, such suspicions would be confirmed.

Whenever he raised the matter, I would reply, 'That business was fully investigated by the New York police. What possible reason could Risdon have to talk to me about it? If he wants to chat to me about something, tell him to phone me.'

There were other signs.

Towards the end of June, Ben returned home one evening and noticed a young man, who was walking along the pavement, look up for a few seconds at his second-floor apartment. It may have meant nothing but Ben was instantly suspicious and told me about the incident. I was convinced that the man had been either a police or a Customs officer.

A few days later, I returned home and my cleaning lady told me that she had met a man on the street when leaving my house. He had asked her whether a Mr Guppy lived there and she had told him, in colourful language, to mind his own business.

At 6.50am on Monday, 1 July, 1991, I awoke in my home in Hampstead. I could hear the trees outside rustling in the wind and had a premonition that I would be arrested that morning. Minutes later, I heard a car drive up the cul-de-sac where we lived. As I listened to the sound of the car, I looked at Patricia sleeping peacefully beside me and kissed her on the forehead.

I heard the car come to a halt and the sound of four doors banging shut, in quick succession, whereupon I went to the window and saw four men walking towards the house, two with dishevelled long hair and earrings and all four dressed in jeans, T-shirts and trainers. They were chewing gum. I shook my head in disbelief and muttered to myself, 'What has the British bobby come to?' One looked up and noticed me.

I put on my dressing-gown and went downstairs. When I opened the door, one of them, a tall, solid-looking man said, 'Are you Darius Guppy?'

'Yes,' I replied. 'What can I do for you?'

'My name is Detective-Sergeant Redgrave of the South East Regional Crime Squad. I am arresting you for conspiracy to defraud Lloyds of London.'

Top: The Pond, Darius' father's home, 1980.

Below: Darius' father, Nicholas, after paying his debts to Lloyds at his tiny rented cottage in the centre of Cambridge, June 1996.

Top: A happy family reunited after Darius' release from prison, February 1996.
Below: Darius after his release at his Northamptonshire farm house on Earl Spencer's estate.

Top: Darius, a keen pilot, by a Seneca twin-engined aircraft.

Below left: Patricia with two-year-old daughter Isabella, 1995.

Below right: Darius with Weimeraner puppy Rufus, which he gave to Patricia for their first wedding anniversary.

Top: Patricia with Isabella on a day trip to the zoo shortly after Darius' release from prison, February 1996.

Below: Darius with Isabella on the same occasion.

Top: Darius and Patricia out for an evening in Patricia's home town of Sunderland shortly after Darius' arrest, August 1991.

Below: Photo of Patricia on holiday, which she sent to Darius in prison, Summer 1994.

Top left: Patricia, seven months pregnant, shortly after Darius' conviction, March 1993.
Top right: Patricia modelling Chanel for the *Daily Mail*, 1995.
Below: Patricia in her early twenties before meeting Darius.

Top: Patricia's mother, Maria.

Below: Patricia in her early twenties, before meeting Darius, on holiday in the Canary Islands with friends.

Charles Spencer and Victoria Lockwood – engagement photo, Summer 1989.

XII

For three hours the four officers systematically searched my modest two-bedroom, semi-detached cottage. Every cupboard and wardrobe was checked, every item of correspondence, invoice and credit-card bill read through. Even the invitations on my mantlepiece, it seemed, were worthy of inspection. Patricia made them tea and coffee as they worked their way through the house, room by room.

After an hour or so one of the officers came downstairs and said to Patricia and me, 'Well, is this it?'

'What do you mean?' I enquired.

'Is this it?' he repeated, emphasising the last word and looking around the room with disdain.

He seemed surprised at the spartan life we led. Where were the art treasures on the walls, the vintage wines, the gold Rolex watches, the hand-tailored Savile Row suits and shirts, the wads of crisp fifty pound notes? And where in the name of heaven were the yachting brochures?

'I'm afraid it is,' I replied dryly. 'I'm sorry to be such a disappointment.'

'I must confess I was expecting a bit more than this,' he said. 'I mean this is just plain ordinary; it's not like they made you out in the papers at all.'

'And to think you had to get up at the crack of dawn,' I remarked. 'Life really isn't fair.'

A few minutes later, however, the police perked up considerably.

Detective-Constable Michael Ellis, an officer who would play a vital

185

role throughout the investigation, had been sifting through a box of correspondence in one of the wardrobes when he looked up, as though he had found gold.

'Come here,' he said excitedly to one of the team. 'Look at this lot! What's this, then?' He handed me a sheaf of papers, which were minutes of meetings relating to the family trusts of Charles Spencer's grandfather.

Some years earlier, Charlie had asked me if I would become a trustee of his grandfather's estate. I explained all this to D/C Ellis and he nodded.

Then he took out a single piece of paper, a letter from Charlie. 'What's this, then?' he asked. 'Ah-ha, a letter from Lord Spencer. That's Princess Di's brother, I presume.' Excitedly, he beckoned to his colleagues.

Two other officers went over to look at the letter and it seemed to me that their lips moved, almost in unison, as they read the simple thirty-seven word note.

Addressed to me from The Falconry, it read: 'Dear Dino, If you're not inside, please come and shoot here on 15 December. Stay the weekend — Patricia's welcome — or else make a daytrip of it. I'll warn Ivor that you are returning. Love, C.'

I did not guess it at the time but this letter was one day to have a special significance.

'We'll have to take this away,' said D/C Ellis.

'What on earth for?' I protested. 'This is simply an invitation from a friend to go shooting. What possible connection could it have with your enquiries?'

'That is for us to discover,' he remarked, sounding rather superior.

Before the police took me out of the house, Patricia asked them, 'When's he coming home?'

'Don't worry, love,' one of the officers replied, 'he should be back tonight.'

I kissed her goodbye. 'Stay calm, darling, everything will be fine, you'll see.'

I sat between two officers in the back of the car, handcuffed to one of them, for the hour-long journey along the North Circular Road to Redbridge Magistrates' Court in Essex where I was put in the cells.

Throughout that journey I wondered how Ben would be coping with his own arrest, as there was little doubt that he would be undergoing an experience similar to mine. I was also asking myself what evidence the police could have against us, whether they had been tapping our phones or listening to conversations in our offices, debating in my mind whether we had made some cardinal error that we had overlooked and going so far as to imagine that the arrest had been nothing but a bluff to unnerve us, the police hoping that one of us might break and confess all.

Every time, however, my mind went back to Risdon, for I realised that he was the weak link. After the events in New York, we had not told a soul the truth of what had happened in that hotel room, so he was the only person other than ourselves to know for certain. I had no evidence that he had said anything to the police and for all I knew, he, too, could be under arrest, protesting his innocence.

Shortly after I arrived at the court house Ben arrived, accompanied by four more officers, dressed in the same style as those who had come to my house. He looked depressed and I told him that I had telephoned our lawyer, Harry Travers of Burton Copeland Solicitors.

I asked Ben, 'How did they treat you?'

'Fine,' he replied. 'They just seemed very disappointed by my less than lavish lifestyle.'

'They were exactly the same with me,' I said. 'It's amazing how so many people think in clichés. I suspect they actually believe what they read in the papers.'

While the officers went off to search Inca's offices in New Bond Street, I fell asleep in my cell. Shortly after 5pm that evening, I was taken from the cell for my first interview.

In the interview room were not only Harry Travers, our solicitor, and D/C Ellis but also, casually sitting back in a chair behind the desk, Detective Inspector Peter Avery, a tall, powerfully built man who was in charge of the investigation. He wore his thick brown hair collar length and appeared smartly dressed compared with the other officers, in a light sweater, dark trousers and brand-new Hush Puppies.

Twelve minutes later, he announced that the interview was at an end and switched off the tape recorder. I had told him that I was entirely innocent of the allegations regarding the robbery in New York and that I had nothing to add, despite his repeated attempts to engage me in a dialogue. He did not look a happy man.

That night Ben and I managed to exchange a few words as our cells were next to each other. We agreed that it seemed the police were trying to soften us up, keeping us in custody overnight, hoping we would confess all the following day. For most of the past sixteen months, while there had certainly been indications of the authorities' suspicions about the events in the Halloran House Hotel, there had been no hint that any firm evidence had been obtained to substantiate such theories. Now, all of a sudden, we had been arrested. The police had to have something more than they had let on so far and we feared that they were keeping their major surprise for the following day.

At 11am the following morning, I was taken to the same room for my second interview. For three minutes, Avery cross-examined me over a series of photographs taken inside room number 1207 of the Halloran House Hotel by the New York Police Crime Scene Unit. I had nothing to say. To all his questions I simply replied, 'I have nothing further to add.'

Then he paused.

'Do you know a man called Peter Risdon?'

My heart sank and an image of Patricia flashed across my mind. I hated myself for having hurt her.

'What a filthy grass Risdon is,' I thought to myself, for it was obvious he had betrayed us.

Despite the turmoil within me, however, I would not be side-tracked from the refrain with which I had answered every question: 'I have nothing further to add.'

Avery said, 'Mr Guppy, I can see that you are swallowing hard.'

Immediately I turned to my lawyer and for the benefit of the tape recording said: 'I'm turning to my lawyer, Mr Travers. Mr Travers, can you confirm whether I am showing any signs of nervousness?'

He replied, 'I can say that you don't look remotely nervous.'

Step by step, Avery took me through the New York robbery and towards the end of his statement said, 'This was a very, very complicated cleverly thought-out conspiracy. It was done in such a way that everybody would have been fooled. The part that you knew very well, you had to have the gun, you had to have the shooting to make it look good. You thought that travelling to New York would cause jurisdictional problems that we, as an investigating force, possibly wouldn't be able to cope with. But at the end of the day, you paid Risdon thousands of pounds. Peter Risdon has decided to tell the full and frank truth about being your accomplice.'

The next question worried me. 'Do you know a man called Dutta?'

I was concerned because Ishan had recently moved from Paris to London where he was working in an investment bank in the City and would doubtless have heard the reports that had begun circulating in the media that day about my arrest. I feared that Ishan might think I would crack under questioning and betray him.

To Avery, I gave my habitual reply: 'I have nothing further to add.'

At the end of this thirty-minute interview, Avery growled: 'We'll be opposing your application for bail.'

'Why?' I asked angrily.

'We have reason to believe that you would abscond.'

'Rubbish,' I said. 'We've had enough hints that the net was drawing in. Do you honestly think that if we'd wanted to skip during the last few months, we couldn't have done so? We've been on Customs bail for the last year and have been overseas on twenty separate occasions. There have never been any problems.'

Avery replied, 'Well, we have our own views about Customs. We want you in prison on remand and that's all there is to it.'

I looked him in the eyes, believing his tough stance to be a ploy to pressurise me into caving in. I realised that, while in prison on remand, any man would be far less able to organise his defence, would have limited access to telephones and his legal advisors and, more importantly, would be psychologically at an enormous disadvantage. I was beginning to understand how the system worked.

That evening, Patricia came to visit me at the police station. She was accompanied by Ben's girlfriend, Katrina Kelshaw, an attractive, vivacious girl with long brown pre-Raphaelite curly hair. Patricia was clearly very distressed.

'What's the matter, sweetheart?' I asked as soon as I saw her.

On the verge of tears, she told me that she had received a mysterious phone call at about 2am that morning. She went on, 'There was no one on the other end of the line but then I heard a record playing. It was that song 'Are you Lonesome Tonight?' I kept asking who was calling, but no one spoke. After a minute or so, I just put down the phone and I couldn't control myself. I cried and cried, wishing you were there. And I felt frightened, too, not knowing what kind of sick person would play that tune to me. It must have been someone who knew you weren't there.'

The call worried me. In my view it was unlikely to have been any journalist nor anyone who had read a newspaper, because the telephone call had been made before news of my arrest had been given to the media. Only our closest friends knew Patricia's number, which was ex-directory. Even they hadn't known of my arrest at that stage.

Such an act was cowardly and cruel and I could hardly believe that anyone would behave in so despicable a manner. To frighten a highly vulnerable young woman who was already distressed and worried about her fiancé was as low as anyone could sink.

Patricia tried to put a brave face on the incident. 'Forget all that,' she said. 'Look what I've brought for us.'

She opened up a plastic bag and took out a meal of French bread and cheese, grapes and a fresh fruit salad.

She could see that I was seething with anger at the phone call incident and I had great trouble trying to concentrate my mind and enjoy the meal. I didn't feel like eating a thing.

After a while, I summoned up the courage to tell her that the police were going to oppose bail, a matter that I had to reveal to her but which I was convinced would upset her even more than the sadistic telephone call she had received.

'Darling, they want to keep me in prison on remand.'

'No, no, no!' she cried, the tears flowing down her cheeks. 'What have you done? You could have fled a hundred times if you'd wanted to. They must know that!'

She went on, 'It's not as though you've killed someone or anything like that.'

I held her close and tried to explain away the police action. 'Listen, Patricia, don't worry. It's just a police tactic.'

'But what about our wedding?' she said.

'Don't worry. I'm certain everything will be all right. We have very good lawyers and I'm sure the magistrates will believe that we have no intention of running away.'

She looked up at me, wiped away the tears and said, 'If they don't give you bail, my love, I'll marry you in prison.'

Now that I knew the police would oppose bail and feared they might persuade the magistrates to keep us inside, I was worried for Ishan Dutta. I knew that news of our arrest would be in the papers within hours and I was also aware that Ishan had used a false EU passport whenever he visited Britain. Now the matter was far more serious because he had moved from Paris to take up a job in the City and he had told me that he had managed to obtain a National Insurance number and a P45, all on the basis of the false passport.

Avery had mentioned Ishan Dutta's name in my interview and I wanted Ishan to know that I had said nothing about him. I was also concerned that if ever the police paid him an official visit, he had to make sure they did not find his false passport. If they did, I knew that they could then put enormous pressure on him and, if they wished, have him instantly deported to India where he was in serious trouble.

Before she left that evening, Patricia said she would contact Ishan and give him my message. An hour later, my father came to see me. He appeared sad and downcast and somehow older than when I had seen him only a few weeks earlier.

'I'm very upset to see you like this,' he said. 'I hate the thought of you being locked up. I know the allegations that you're facing and I'm not going to pressurise you now. But, between you and me, the minute I heard that you'd been robbed in New York I knew it was all a load of baloney.'

'Of course it was a load of baloney,' I whispered.

'That's a matter for you,' he said, looking me straight in the eye, 'but it doesn't alter the fact that I don't like to see you in here, locked up like this.'

We would not discuss the matter again until after my release from custody, but he did try to comfort me that night and I respected the fact that he was too tactful and understanding to cross-question me or make moral judgements when I was under such pressure. When he left, I felt sad and guilty because I knew that I had let him down.

An hour after I had said farewell to my father, a duty police officer brought me a cup of tomato soup. While sitting on the wooden bench and reading the graffiti on the walls, I heard the clank of the key being put into the lock of my cell door. It cranked open and Detective Inspector Avery walked in. Spread over the stone floor of the cell were my legal papers.

'Right, Mr Guppy,' he said. 'You're going to be charged later tonight. This is your last opportunity to put the record straight. Have you got anything to say?'

'Sorry Mr Avery,' I replied. 'My position hasn't changed. My lawyers have advised me that I should say nothing and I'm sticking to that.'

Before midnight Ben and I were taken from our cells, charged with conspiracy to defraud Lloyds of London, photographed and fingerprinted. The officer who took the finger prints, a man I had never seen before, told me casually, 'You know you're going down for a long time, don't you.'

I replied, 'We'll have to see.'

Throughout that night the police kept on the stark fluorescent light that hung from the ceiling, despite my repeated requests that they should switch it off and permit me to sleep. Whenever I asked for the light to be turned off, the young duty officer would bark, 'No! It's staying on.'

Finally, at 4am they did switch off the light and I managed to sleep for three hours.

Throughout that night I kept thinking of Patricia and regretted that I hadn't fixed an earlier date for our wedding. I had hoped to resolve the Customs matter and then to marry Patricia without any charges hanging over me. Rather than delaying our marriage, I should have brought it forward. Now I had no idea when we would be married or when we would be able to resume our life together and I felt that all this uncertainty would put a huge burden on Patricia, one she did not deserve.

At 7am I was allowed to shave, shower and change into the suit Patricia had brought for me the night before. While waiting to be taken upstairs to the court, I heard a racket in the corridor as a fit, young black man was being bundled into the cell opposite mine by several officers .

'Oi! Get off me, you fuckin' slags!' he shouted.

Seconds after the officers had slammed shut his metal cell door, the man began to hammer on it, using his fists and feet. 'What a fuckin' liberty!' he shouted time and again as he continued to bang away. 'Let me out of 'ere, you slags!'

Eventually, after he had quietened down, I shouted across to him, 'What are you in here for?'

'They've got me up on some wankin' robbery charge,' he replied. 'They think I've been bang at it. P'raps I 'ave, p'raps I ain't, but this charge is a fuckin' stitch up.'

I asked him, 'Are you all right?'

'Sweet, man, sweet,' he replied, almost dismissively. He continued, 'What you in 'ere for?'

'Insurance fraud,' I replied, 'involving some gems.'

Seeming to ignore my response, he said, 'D'ya want some water, mate? 'Cos I do.' He looked at me again. ' 'Ere, wait a minute. Ain't you that geezer that's related to Royalty? I read 'bout you in the papers.'

'No, not quite,' I laughed, 'I think that's an exaggeration on the part of the tabloids.'

He then resumed banging on his door. ' 'Ere! 'ere!' he yelled. 'This is no way to treat Royalty! The man needs water, you fuckin' slags!'

After a few more minutes of shouting at the officers on duty, D/C Ellis walked into my cell. He was smartly dressed in a dark suit and tie for his appearance before the magistrates. He seemed nervous and forced a laugh. 'You won't get bail,' he said. 'We've got something up our sleeves.'

From outside the cell we heard my new-found friend yell, 'He's just trying to rattle ya, Guppy mate! Stay strong!'

Ellis turned and looked through the open door across the corridor. 'Listen Guppy!' my friend shouted. 'One of the fings you learn quick is to give these muppets nuffink. You ain't got nuffink on the geezer and you know it, you filf!' he yelled across at Ellis. 'I'm tellin' ya, Guppy mate, it's your first offence, you ain't killed nobody and you come from a lah-dee-dah family. Unless these muppets have nobbled the magistrate you'll get bail, I'm tellin' ya!'

As Ellis walked out of my cell and into Ben's, his tormentor yelled, 'They ain't got nuffink; that's why they keep comin' into your cell, to turn ya 'gainst Guppy. Don't fall for it, mate.'

He continued, 'Oi, get out his fuckin' cell, ya muppet! 'Ere, you're not supposed to do that without his brief being there. That's against the law, that is!'

Ten minutes later Ellis walked out of Ben's cell and pretended to lunge towards the black man as he passed his cell door.

'You want it, mate?' he shouted at Ellis. 'Unlock this door and we'll see how much of a man you are. I'll wipe that silly smile off your ugly mug.'

Some time later, as my friend was taken away by the jailers for his bail application before the magistrates, I wished him 'good luck'. He laughed. 'You seen the colour of my skin? Not a prayer, mate. By the way, my name's Fred.'

In court, Fred put on a remarkable act. Ben and I watched from outside, the next to appear in the dock.

He turned towards his relatives and friends sitting in the well of the court. Shaking his hands and gyrating his hips as if engaged in a limbo dance, he cried out: 'Yeeeeeeeeah!', rejoicing at their presence.

'Got the gear?' he called out. 'Bring any drugs? Wicked! Wicked! Bring 'em on the next visit! OK?'

The Chief Magistrate snapped furiously from the bench: 'Sit down! Sit down!' Fred looked over his shoulder towards the bench and waved his hand contemptuously. 'Yeah, yeah,' he said. 'All right, all right. Hang on a minute, keep ya hair on fa fuck's sake, will ya?'

It appeared that Fred's entire family, all smartly dressed, was present for the occasion — a proud mother and father, his brother and sister and his girlfriend with their baby boy on her lap.

Ben and I could hardly stop ourselves laughing out loud. 'You have to admire him,' I said to Ben.

'He's great,' answered Ben. 'I love him.'

Fred's family clapped, cheered and whistled and he turned to them, a huge smile across his face. But his application for bail was refused and he was remanded in custody for a further two weeks.

I looked at the Chief Magistrate as we walked into the dock and saw a man in his forties. He appeared reasonable and intelligent and I felt we had a chance of being granted bail.

However, David Markham, the young prosecuting solicitor assigned to our case by the Crown Prosecution Service, seemed determined that we should remain in custody. He began by complimenting the bench. Then he turned his attention to us.

'If I may be so bold, the prosecution vigorously opposes the granting of bail to these two young men on a number of grounds, your Worships.' He continued, 'If granted bail, these two men will abscond from the jurisdiction. The defence will doubtless argue that they have been abroad on several occasions while on Customs bail and have always returned, but the prosecution is convinced, may it please your Worships, that were bail to be given by your Worships then this court could not expect to see these two men again.' Mr Markham then told the court that my mother was Iranian. I was amazed that he should employ such a tactic. Apart from anything else, my mother had lived in Britain for the past thirty years.

Then he turned to what he described as his central argument, the possible intimidation of vital witnesses. He explained that Peter Risdon would be the prosecution's star witness. 'In this regard', he said, 'your Worships should be aware of a matter involving Mr Guppy and a 9mm Browning semi-automatic hand-gun.' Detailing my arrest for possession of the gun that Bill Hall had given me as a present, he went on to describe me to the court in terms that made Al Capone seem an utter sweetie. At that moment I realised that this was the trump card that D/C Ellis had claimed to have up his sleeve and that he thought would prevent us getting bail.

'Your Worships may consider that this gun may have been intended for use against Mr Risdon. And, indeed, it is the prosecution's contention that Mr Risdon is frightened for his very life. He has had to move to a secret address and is even now under twenty-four hour police protection.'

I whispered to Ben, 'Not only is the man a grass, he's a coward as well.'

In reference to Bill Hall's debt-collecting activities in India, Markham continued: 'Another witness for the Crown will state that he has collected a debt from a man in India. Guppy and Marsh have shown themselves able to resort to such means. The prosecution is very anxious about the influence that these two young men can exert.'

One by one our barrister, Martin Barklem, rebutted the prosecution's arguments, pointing out that we been abroad no less than twenty times while on Customs bail and had always returned. He drew attention to the facts that not only had there been much speculation in the press about the authenticity of the New York robbery and that Lloyds of London had even issued proceedings against our company, but that despite all this and having had ample opportunity to abscond, we had never done so. He added, 'Mr Guppy's wedding has been planned for this summer. Is it really likely that he would abscond in such circumstances?'

As for the firearms charges, he produced the conviction slip from Clerkenwell Magistrates' Court showing a mere £100 fine, which he suggested was hardly in keeping with the gangster image portrayed by the prosecution.

He continued, 'As for Mr Risdon being terrified of the defendants, according to the prosecution he was supposed to have been the tough guy hired by these two young men to commit the robbery.' He paused and added, 'Some tough guy!'

This last remark prompted a ripple of laughter in the court, including from the three magistrates.

When the magistrates returned from their deliberations we feared the worst, for the speech from the bench appeared to be leaning towards the prosecution's case. Finally, the Chief Magistrate ruled in our favour: 'Bail will be granted on condition that each of the defendants provide two sureties of £250,000.'

XIII

Two days later, I awoke with the early morning sun streaming through the window of my home in Hampstead. For the couple of days before my bail application, I had had considerable doubts about whether I would be released from custody. It felt exhilarating to be free again.

When bail was granted Ben had been able to leave the courtroom that morning because his parents, Peter and Nicki Marsh, had been available to stand surety immediately. Unfortunately for me, however, although my father had been happy to stand bail, my mother was abroad. As a result I had had to spend another twenty-four hours in custody, this time in Wormwood Scrubs, until I could raise the second £250,000 surety.

As I was driven away in the prison van to Wormwood Scrubs, sitting in one of the cramped cubicles that cons call 'sweat boxes', I had looked through the tiny tinted window and smiled, watching Ben drive away in his burgundy Porsche 928.

The following morning I had been met at the Prison gates by Patricia and my lawyers. Patricia told me, 'Charles put up the bail. He heard the news on the radio and immediately phoned your lawyers. Thank God for Charlie.'

As we were driven away in the taxi I had said to Patricia, 'All right, darling, the minute we get home I'm booking the civil ceremony at Chelsea Registry Office. We'll marry as soon as possible.'

She had thrown her arms round my neck and given me a long kiss.

Later I had told her, 'I'm very sorry I delayed so long. I wish we had married before all this trouble began. All I could think about when I was in those police cells was getting out so that we could be married.'

Although I had written some months before to Patricia's mother, Maria, asking for permission to marry her daughter and had obtained it, I thought it only fair in view of recent events to seek her renewed approval. I telephoned her and put the question to her again a few days after being released from custody. Maria's view was completely unchanged and she gave us her full support.

Fifteen days after my release from Wormwood Scrubs, on Friday, 19 July, 1991, I walked into Chelsea Registry Office with Charles, Victoria and a few other close friends and saw Patricia, looking beautiful, dressed in a white Donna Karan suit waiting in the ante-room. After the ceremony eight of us dined at San Lorenzo restaurant in Beauchamp Place.

Some time later, my mother would tell me, 'Patricia is just like me when I married your father. Although your father came from a good family, he was a not very wealthy writer at the time. The fact that Patricia wants to marry you in these circumstances shows that her motives are entirely genuine and I love her for that.'

During our honeymoon at the Lucknam Park, a country hotel outside Bath, Patricia and I determined that during the next few months before my trial we were going to enjoy life to the full and, indeed, the prospect of our being separated gave our lives during this period a very special intensity.

I said, 'Darling, I might be sent away for several years or I might, God willing, be let off scot-free. The police said at the bail hearing that the committal proceedings would start in four weeks, but they always say that. I bet you anything it'll take at least twelve months before we go to court. So whatever happens let's not lead our lives according to the timetable the prosecution are going to set. Let's just ignore them and live life to the full.'

For the next week we enjoyed fine weather and forgot all about my troubles. During the day we swam in the hotel's swimming-pool and explored the beautiful city of Bath as well as going for picnics in the Wiltshire countryside, and in the evenings we would talk over long candle-lit suppers, discussing the future and our love for each other.

I longed to travel abroad with Patricia and to see some of the beautiful parts of the world with her. However, because my bail conditions prevented me from going overseas, instead, over the following months, we spent many weekends exploring various parts of Britain, staying in remote hotels and friends' houses in Scotland, the Lake District, Devon, Dorset, the Yorkshire Moors and Norfolk. We also spent weekends with Charles and Victoria at Althorp and with Patricia's mother, Maria, in Sunderland.

In Sunderland, Patricia took me to the cemetery where her father was buried and we paid our respects. Her father, who had suffered from diabetes most of his life, died of a massive heart attack during a kidney transplant operation at the age of forty-four, when Patricia was twenty. Shortly after that, and with very little money, Patricia had come to London. The fact that she had had to cope with such adversity at a young age, I felt accounted for much of her strength.

Throughout the period before my trial, I was required to attend Redbridge Magistrates' Court every few weeks for further remand hearings. At these hearings the prosecution would inform the court how their investigation was progressing and how much longer they anticipated we would have to wait before bringing the case to trial.

The first of these hearings took place four weeks after our successful bail application. We met our barrister, who was dressed in a navy-blue pin-stripe suit with a colourful, silk handerchief that dangled rather fashionably from his handkerchief pocket. He seemed to exude the confidence of Drake playing bowls before his battle with the Armada.

Standing opposite us was a particularly robust-looking man, who was chewing gum slowly and very noisily. About forty-five years of age with shaggy, shoulder-length brown hair, he was over 6ft tall and had a prodigious beer belly. Dressed in an arresting, Hawaiian-style shirt that flopped out over his baggy jeans, he wore a large gold chain around his neck as well as a number of gold sovereign rings on his fingers. Speaking in a whisper I nodded towards the man and asked our barrister, 'Policeman or armed robber?'

Having looked the individual up and down, he replied in his typically urbane manner, 'I don't know. It's so difficult to tell these days.'

In court, the prosecution explained how a team of twenty police officers had been assigned to work full-time on 'what is a highly involved and complex matter'. In view of this, the prosecution argued, an adjournment of a further four weeks would be required.

I whispered to Ben, 'Four weeks! At this rate it'll take more like a year.'

During the following fifteen months before our trial, as the case was put off time and again, Ben and I formed a jokey relationship with some of the officers working on the investigation whom we would invariably bump into outside court at the various remand hearings. In particular, we noticed how some officers seemed to have permanent suntans and from our conversations with them, we learned that they had travelled to far-flung destinations such as Sri Lanka, India, Thailand and South America. In short, any exotic location that Ben or I had ever visited.

On another occasion we were chatting outside the court and a bronzed D/C Ellis came up to us. At the original bail hearing the prosecution had stated that Ben and I had purchased two pillows from Bloomingdales to use when test-firing the gun before the robbery. This small detail was, in fact, inaccurate because we had purchased the pillows in question from Macy's, a less well-known store.

Ellis took a pair of dark glasses from his top pocket and with a certain flourish put them on. 'Know where these shades come from, then?'

'No idea,' we chorused, wondering why he should ask such a question.

Looking over the rim of the glasses he replied, 'Would 'ja believe it, I bought 'em in Bloomingdales; you know, the one in New York where, if I am correct, you two both went shoppin' one day. Know what I mean?' And he guffawed.

I commented, 'It's very reassuring for us to know, Mick, that taxpayers' money is being spent so wisely.'

In late September 1991, only days before our wedding blessing was due to take place at Magdalen College, Oxford, I received a phone call from an old friend called David, who had contacts at Scotland Yard.

I had wanted to keep the investigating officers guessing. It seemed clear that the magistrates were losing patience with the prosecution, who had originally stated that the case would be ready for committal proceedings within four weeks of our arrest. I considered that with every blind alley the police pursued the more frustrated they would become and, in turn, the more impatient the magistrates would become as yet further extensions of time were requested.

I knew that the police could have no idea where the gems were hidden because we had smuggled them out of the country by private plane within weeks of being arrested by Customs & Excise over a year before. In fact by now, nearly every one of the gems had been sold. It seemed likely that one of the reasons the police investigation was taking so long was because they were convinced that the gems were still in the country and that, if they found them and could connect them to us, this would be the final proof of our guilt.

I had suggested to David some weeks before that it might be an idea to inform the police that the jewels were still in our possession and I had left the matter with him.

When David called that day he informed me that he expected the police to raid our offices the following morning at 11am as they had been erroneously tipped off that a fence would be at Inca's offices at that time to collect the missing gems.

The following morning Ben and I waited in the foyer of the Westbury Hotel, directly opposite Inca's offices. Bang on time we saw an unmarked police car drive up to the offices and four plain clothes officers jump out and run into the building. Five minutes later they emerged, visibly disappointed. They drove off and Ben and I walked back across the road.

Our secretaries told us that the four officers had just run in and barged into our office as if expecting us to be there.

'We told them that you hadn't been in the office all morning,' one of the secretaries informed us.

'Did they produce a warrant?' Ben asked.

'No. They didn't produce anything.'

'Good,' I said.

Ben and I knew that once we had been charged, the police were not entitled to barge into our offices without a warrant in this way or even to interview us again concerning our alleged offences unless our lawyers had been alerted and we had given our consent.

Immediately, we telephoned our lawyers to inform them what had happened. They, in turn, contacted the Crown Prosecution Service to complain, only to be informed that the CPS had no knowledge of what the police had been up to that morning. Our lawyers were therefore advised to seek clarification from D/I Avery.

They were then informed by the South East Regional Crime Squad that there had been no attempted 'raid' of Inca's offices as such, but that four officers had simply dropped in to 'verify some paperwork'.

Following this line of enquiry, our lawyers then telephoned the officer in charge of all the 'paperwork' on our case, a D/C Rowlands, who denied any knowledge of his colleagues' unexpected visit to Inca's offices.

When our lawyers subsequently informed D/I Avery that D/C Rowlands had had no knowledge of any visit to our offices, Avery stated that the four police officers had simply been in the area at the time and had wanted to make a routine enquiry.

Our lawyers made it clear to Avery that they considered such an explanation ludicrous and pointed out that, in any case, such practice was against the police code of conduct and was, therefore, outside the law.

After an exchange of correspondence, Avery wrote saying that he would conduct his enquiries in any way he felt fit. Our lawyers described his actions as 'reprehensible' and informed him that they would report the matter to a higher authority.

Although our tactics may have been a little devious, we felt totally vindicated because we had proved to our legal advisors and to ourselves, the extent of the measures to which the police would resort in order to convict us. To this day, I do not believe the police have ever realised that we were behind this little operation to expose their methods. It had been a small but important psychological victory, because we were aware that lawyers in this country are reluctant to attack police methods in general unless they have the strongest evidence to justify doing so.

*   *   *

On Sunday, 29 September, 1991, having gone through a civil ceremony with Patricia two months before at Chelsea Registry Office, our marriage was blessed in the beautiful chapel at Magdalen College,

Oxford, in the presence of our families and two hundred friends.

The service was conducted by Father Jeffrey John, the Magdalen chaplain who had been such a close friend during my years at Oxford. Father Jeffrey concluded the hour-long blessing with the words: 'I do wish you, Darius and Patricia, and all the rest of you who perhaps made these same promises many years ago, God's continued blessing for the very happiest of marriages.'

I was then invited to kiss the bride and Patricia and I embraced.

Father Jeffrey was in such good humour that he asked, 'If I may, I would also like to kiss the bride,' whereupon Patricia and he kissed Continental-style on both cheeks.

At that point, carried by the joy of the occasion, Father Jeffrey and I also warmly hugged each other.

Boris Johnson, now a journalist for the *Daily Telegraph*, who had been at Eton and Oxford with me, was a guest that day. When he later reported back to the Peterborough Column, the story that was printed claimed that, when asked to kiss my bride, I had in fact ignored her and kissed the priest full on the lips instead. This somewhat exaggerated version of events caused much amusement among our friends.

Patricia and I walked out of the chapel and into the sunshine to the accompaniment of Bach's *Toccata and Fugue in D Minor* on the organ. Outside, the bells were ringing and we were greeted by cheers and applause.

For the following half hour, everyone posed in the college's beautiful medieval cloisters for the traditional wedding photographs. Patricia was wearing a long, ivory-coloured dress that had an intricate pattern of beads, created for her by the designer Philippa Lepley. It was simple and elegant and she looked truly lovely in it. I was a very proud and happy man that day.

Unknown to any of the guests, however, Patricia was also wearing a magnificent emerald bracelet, part of the gems haul that Lloyds of London, the Regional Crime Squad and HM Customs & Excise had been searching for during the past eighteen months.

I had decided to take such a risk because I wanted very much for Patricia to wear something spectacular on our wedding day. When I had smuggled the gems out of the country in a light aircraft, with Ben's permission I had retained a set of matching emeralds purchased in India from the Maharajah of Jaipur's personal collection. Subsequently, I had asked a friend of mine in Hatton Garden to mount the gems into a bracelet, mixing the emeralds with diamond 'baguettes'.

In our hotel room on the morning of the blessing I had presented Patricia with the bracelet and, although I would have loved her to keep them, in order to prevent her being compromised I had told her a white lie, claiming that the gems were part of Iranian family heirlooms and that I would need to have them back after the blessing.

The reception took place at the Studley Priory, a lovely Elizabethan manor house outside Oxford. The atmosphere was just as I like it, completely relaxed. Champagne flowed throughout the afternoon and couples danced to the music of jazz bands and classical quartets. Only one incident marred the occasion.

Charles Spencer, my best man, spotted a guest whom neither of us recognised, moving from group to group and holding a mini-cassette recorder. It was obvious that he was taping private conversations and we guessed immediately that this gatecrasher was a journalist.

Charlie, not wishing to create a scene, went over to one of our guests, an intimidating Greek-Cypriot weighing twenty stone, and over 6ft tall, and asked him to deal discreetly with the man. My Greek friend approached the interloper, picked him up by the scruff of the neck and, with the man's feet off the ground, carried him out of the hotel. Leaving the reporter in no doubt about what would happen to him if he was caught snooping again, he threw him on to the driveway.

Charlie's speech about me caused much laughter. He began, 'I first met Darius fourteen years ago, an earnest figure of obvious intelligence and a great deal of energy but we were thrown together when we arrived at Magdalen, where we both read History.'

After recounting some of my more notorious activities at Oxford, such as my practising knife-throwing in my rooms, Charlie went on, 'I believe that exceptional people attract enemies as well as friends; that only the harmless are generally regarded as nice. Darius bears this out. The passionate and romantic nature which comes from his mother's side, blended with the adventurous, slightly eccentric style of his father, have resulted in a true original, and some people love that, and others feel threatened by it. Whatever, Darius has never been one to compromise. When I was leaving Oxford five years ago, I thought about what would happen to my friends. Some, I thought, would end up with good, solid jobs; some, I could see, had probably already peaked, and would have difficulty in the outside world; but Darius, he was easy. He would either be a millionaire by the age of thirty, or he would have visited Wormwood Scrubs. How typical that he's done both already.'

In my own speech I said, 'Because I believe that in a fair world people should be rewarded for the risks they take, I promise to ensure that Patricia's gamble in marrying me will have won for her a fine husband. I promise to be good to her, kind and loyal for the rest of my life because she has given me everything she has. I've had some pretty incredible adventures, particularly over the two years that I've known her and, where most women I have known would have run for cover, Patricia has always been there, brave and defiant.'

I had decided to whisk Patricia away on honeymoon by helicopter, one reason being to avoid the photographers and journalists who had not been permitted to attend the blessing ceremony at Magdalen or the reception and who I had felt sure would gather outside the Studley Priory. As we took off, I saw with what enthusiasm all our friends were waving at us from below and I was filled with optimism. We flew over the manor house and circled above the guests before heading North.

Days after we returned from honeymoon, my lawyers phoned with alarming news. Ishan Dutta had been arrested by the Regional Crime Squad and, worse still, he had been remanded in custody and had agreed to give evidence against us.

*   *   *

Prior to my arrest, in July 1991, Ishan had contacted me to say that he had returned to London looking for work in the City as he was short of money since all his assets had been frozen by the Indian authorities. He had also told me that he had used a false passport to gain entry into Britain.

This had caused me concern because I feared that if the police discovered him living in Britain with a false passport, they would use this fact to pressurise him into revealing all he knew about the New York robbery by threatening to deport him to India.

When Dutta had informed Ben and me that he had taken a job at an investment bank, we had naturally been very worried that he should have been so foolhardy. The police knew that he had worked previously in the City, and if they were searching for him, the City would be the first place they would check.

After being granted bail, I had warned him that the police had asked me during my interviews about his involvement in the gems robbery as well as the gold smuggling. I had told him, 'The police have been asking all sorts of questions about you so you must lie low. Another point; you should not keep your passport in your apartment because if they find it they'll know it's a fake and they'll have you over a barrel.'

I had continued, 'The police tried every trick in the book to coerce me into spilling the beans and naming all my accomplices, including you. I can assure you Ishan, that I told them nothing about you; not one word. I would expect you to do the same if ever the positions were reversed.'

He had replied, 'You have my word, Darius. I would have done exactly the same in your shoes, so don't worry. I would say nothing, even if they pulled my fingernails out.'

The following month, November 1991, Ben and I arranged to meet our lawyers in their offices in order to read the prosecution papers which had at last been served on them. One of the vital questions Ben and I wanted to know the answer to was why it was that Peter Risdon, our co-conspirator, had not been charged with any offence. We had wondered whether plea bargaining was permitted in British courts and our lawyers had replied, 'No, never. Well, not in theory.'

They had explained that in a case such as ours, where one of the conspirators turns 'Queen's Evidence' and becomes a witness for the prosecution, typically he would plead guilty to the same charges that his colleagues faced and would be rewarded with a reduced sentence in return for his co-operation.

The rationale for not allowing the accomplice who testifies against his co-conspirators to get off scot-free is that, if he is let off in such circumstances and his crimes are completely ignored, then not only would this offend against principles of natural justice, but it could also potentially lead to miscarriages of justice as he might be tempted to say absolutely anything against his co-conspirators simply to avoid being charged himself.

Risdon's various statements to the police, which were included in the prosecution papers, provided the answer to our questions. As Harry Travers, one of our lawyers explained, 'The line that the prosecution is adopting is what we will call the "innocent dupe theory", Risdon being the "innocent dupe".'

In one of his statements, Risdon claimed, 'Mr Guppy explained to me that he had administrative irregularities at Inca Gemstones, that resulted in him effectively having to justify the disappearance of a certain amount of stock. He explained it was a technical matter but very inconvenient to him, more an exercise in book-keeping that anything else. I had no reason to enquire what the irregularities were. Mr Guppy went on to explain that he and Mr Benedict Marsh had decided that the best place for this apparent disappearance would be New York. Mr Guppy asked if I would be prepared to help. He explained the problem had arisen because he had paid someone overseas in gemstones for services rendered and that part of the deal was that he didn't declare the payment for tax reasons. He, therefore, had to find another way of losing the gemstones. He told me the amount of money was £25,000.'

Risdon went on to outline the details of the robbery and how the police had taken him to New York, all expenses paid, in order for him to 'refresh his memory'. He had even subjected himself to hypnosis in order to help the police in their enquiries. Having read his statements, Ben and I did not know whether to explode in anger or simply to laugh.

I exclaimed to our lawyers, 'So we are going to pay this jerk £15,000, plus his expenses, plus our own expenses, all of which must have added up to more than £30,000. We're then going to allow ourselves to be tied up in a hotel room, shot at and risk jail, just for a £25,000 "book-keeping" exercise! The police cannot possibly believe such a cock-and-bull story.'

Having quietened me down, one of our lawyers said, 'Risdon has obviously told them that he won't testify if he's charged along with you two. It's simple; no testimony from Risdon, no conviction. So they've had to devise an excuse for not charging him. That's why they've come up with the idea of portraying him as the innocent dupe.'

There was another interesting matter that concerned Risdon. Included with the prosecution's evidence were the papers relating to Risdon's failed attempt to commit an insurance fraud, involving the large South African diamond, for which he had been arrested in March 1991.

These documents revealed that a South African named William Davis had attempted to defraud a well-known high-street bank by demanding the bank hand over a diamond, which he claimed he had put into their vault for safe-keeping. The bank had refused, telling him that he had never deposited such a diamond with them.

Later, Davis had teamed up with Peter Risdon who had persuaded him to copy some essential features of our New York sting. Together, Risdon and Davis had visited a number of London gem dealers and had shown them a fake South African rough diamond of 230 carats which they claimed to be worth £500,000, in order to authenticate its existence. They would later seek to insure and use it in their attempted fraud.

The plan involved Davis depositing the fake diamond at the Marble Arch branch of the same bank used in the earlier plan and having it included on the bank's insurance policy, valued at £500,000. Risdon would then collect the stone using a false passport in the name of William Davis. Some time later, the real William Davis would call to collect the diamond only to 'discover' that it had been handed over to the wrong person, enabling him to claim £500,000 on the bank's insurance policy, which he would then share with Risdon once he was paid.

In February 1991, Davis, a stocky, 5ft 9ins tall man with a dark complexion, had walked into the Marble Arch bank and deposited the replica diamond. As planned, on seeing certificates valuing the diamond at £500,000, which were in fact fake, the bank had agreed to insure it for that amount.

A few weeks later, Risdon had telephoned the bank, giving his name as William Davis, and had said that he would call in later that day to collect the diamond. Risdon, 6ft 5ins tall, gangly and blond, had arrived at the bank, shown his forged British Visitor's passport in the name of William Davis and, using a South African accent, had asked for the diamond.

Unknown to him, however, the bank had alerted the police and officers of the South East Regional Crime Squad, including D/C Ellis, were waiting for him as he had walked into the building. As soon as Risdon had asked at the cashiers to collect the diamond, he had been arrested and taken away for questioning.

As we read the papers, Ben muttered, 'Talk about Norman fucking Risdon. What a stupid, incompetent plan! Surely he could see that it would fail. To try the same trick on the same bank using the same name is beyond belief.'

The papers also included the transcripts of the interviews Risdon had given to the police after his arrest. He had betrayed every one of his accomplices in the failed diamond sting, providing names and addresses and any other evidence that he could. At that stage, however, he had said nothing about Ben and me or the events that had occurred in New York.

At the end of the interview, however, Risdon had laid the foundations of a plan to save his own skin, providing him with a way of escaping a prison sentence. He had told the interviewing officers, 'I'm trying to protect a couple of people for reasons that I don't propose to go into in a formal interview context.'

One of the officers had replied, 'Right, you say formal interview context. Obviously you're willing to speak in detail about something else later.'

I would have been fascinated to know what had happened during the informal interview that had obviously followed, because it was at that moment that our fate had been sealed.

Throughout our subsequent trial and after it, officers of the South East Regional Crime Squad would claim that Ben and I had been tracked down and brought to justice as a result of brilliant detective work. Instead, we felt it had been through our sheer misfortune, for they had stumbled on us only a year after we had been paid out by Lloyds and only as a consequence of the incompetence and subsequent betrayal of Peter Risdon.

Although Ben and I had always considered Risdon to be something of a Walter Mitty character, as indeed so many of those involved in the twilight world of 'security' tend to be, it was only after reading through all of his statements and the papers relating to his attempted fraud that we fully appreciated the extent of his fantasies. From a reading of the evidence, we learned that on one occasion he had even approached the Vietnamese Embassy in London with a plan to topple Pol Pot, the ruthless Cambodian dictator, by despatching a unit of ex-Special Forces soldiers to Cambodia where they would carry out the assassination. The Vietnamese Embassy had declined the proposal.

Annoyed at my own shortcomings, I commented, 'Why couldn't we have seen through him?'

Ben remarked, 'It's easy to be wise after the event but remember, Darry, that it worked for over a year. You can never insure against betrayal.'

Having devised an excuse for not charging Risdon, the next major problem was to explain why it had taken over a year for him to come forward about the events in New York. After all, he had claimed in his statement to the police that upon his return from New York he had been 'utterly shocked' to 'discover' from the newspapers the extent of the sting. If indeed, as he claimed, he, the innocent dupe, had been led to understand that the whole episode was nothing more than a 'book-keeping exercise', then why on earth had it taken him over twelve months to unburden his conscience to the police?

The answer was that he feared me.

His statement read, 'Mr Guppy told me that I could not report the matter as I was too involved in what happened. He threatened me, saying that in any court his legal people would be better than mine, because of his personal wealth and contacts. I have never been happy with the situation and have been keen to report the matter. I do feel intimidated by Mr Guppy's threats and I consider him to be a person to employ physical harm to those he sees as having crossed him.'

The statement continued, 'The events surrounding my arrest have given me the opportunity to meet police officers from Scotland Yard and, therefore, the chance to explain exactly what happened in New York.'

Ben cracked up laughing as soon as he read these words. 'The police can't possibly believe any of this crap!'

Three days after making his statement to the police, the Crown Prosecution Service had formally dropped all charges against Risdon relating to his attempted diamond fraud, despite his having been caught red-handed in a bank, with a false passport, trying to commit an insurance deception for £500,000.

'If you doubt that the police are aware of the sort of person Risdon is, read this,' the lawyer continued. He then handed us a transcript of an interview between D/I Avery and William Davis which had occurred when Avery had flown to Pietermaritzburg in South Africa. During the course of that interview, which had taken place on 10 September, 1991, in other words some four months after the charges relating to Risdon's attempted insurance fraud had been dropped against him, Avery had stated to Davis: 'You obtained or manufactured this replica rough diamond and brought that from South Africa to the UK. You subsequently deposited it at a bank and arranged insurance for the stone with the intention of defrauding the insurance company of the sum of half a million pounds. You produced in obtaining the insurance a false, fraudulent document. You then instructed your fellow conspirator in this matter, Peter Risdon, to retrieve the stone from the bank using a forged passport in your own identity. Your intention was to obtain the insurance money.'

After we had read the full transcript of the interview, Ben and I sat back in silence.

As we read on, Risdon's statements contained further pearls of nonsense that, had they come in less serious circumstances, could only have caused amusement.

'I met Guppy and Marsh one afternoon in the Rosendale Public House, Dulwich, in the autumn of 1990. They suggested repeating the events of New York. This time not with a view to the company gaining moneys from the insurance claim, but for them to get personal benefits. I was to get £500,000. I told them that they were silly and dismissed the matter out of hand. It was a most extraordinary suggestion.'

Risdon, however, had somehow failed to mention in his statement why it was that four months later he would be arrested by police officers attempting an insurance fraud for this very same sum.

'This is absolute rubbish!' I exclaimed.

'Listen,' said one of our lawyers. 'Risdon is a zero and the police know it. They can see from the way that he planned his fraud that he's no threat. On the other hand, they think that you two are far more dangerous. Also, there's glory for the police in convicting you two, especially with the so-called "Royal connection". Where is the glory in convicting a petty and incompetent crook like Risdon?'

There was, however, one distinct ray of hope as far as Risdon's statement against us was concerned — when the police had solicited his help in trying to find the hand-gun that he had thrown into the lake near Bear Mountain after the robbery, his attempts to pin-point the exact site had been to no avail. The detectives investigating our case had taken him to New York and a team of frogmen had even searched the lake that he had identified as the correct location. But they had found nothing.

Risdon, however, was not the only person we had employed who had been persuaded to give a statement to the police against us. Bill Hall, the former Special Forces operative we had sent to India to collect moneys owed by the bullion dealer, Goutti, and who had turned up at Goutti's house with half-a-dozen heavily-armed locals, explained in his statement, 'The day I visited Mr Goutti's house, I discovered he was out of the country. I had arrived at the house with a number of locals that Mr Dutta had employed to assist me in case of a language barrier with members of the house staff.'

Everyone in the room laughed at the same time.

I was surprised that Bill Hall had agreed to give evidence against us. It seemed out of character and I wondered what could have made him do it.

The prosecution papers also contained transcripts of interviews between Ishan Dutta and the police that had occurred after his arrest. It was obvious from reading them that he intended to give evidence against us.

Interestingly, however, Dutta's custody records showed that the police had been particularly keen to locate his false passport. The entry in the notes read, 'Nature of evidence sought: false passports and documentation re: trading in bogus companies', a reference to the dummy company, Rasiklal and Sons, Dutta had set up as a front for the purpose of our insurance claim. The records also revealed that, having conducted their search, they had indeed found Dutta's false passport and had confiscated it.

'Now it's obvious why he never made an application for bail,' our lawyer commented. 'They've got his false passport and they've made a deal with him. But, more importantly, they would simply deport him back to India where he would find himself in real trouble.'

By the time we had read and re-read all the evidence that had been collected and had discussed the matter with our lawyers, Ben and I both knew that we would only escape conviction with luck.

Determined not to be intimidated by the prospect of our impending trial, we continued to live each day, me with Patricia and Ben with his girlfriend Katrina, as if it were our last.

XIV

O ne of the most interesting events connected with our case took place on 13 March, 1992, when Ishan Dutta pleaded guilty to conspiracy to defraud Lloyds of London at Snaresbrook Crown Court before His Honour Judge Andrew Brooks.

Dutta's plea took just two hours from the moment he entered the courtroom.

Reading through the court transcripts shortly afterwards, Ben and I could hardly believe the extraordinary lengths to which the police, the prosecution and Dutta's lawyers had been prepared to go in securing, as they saw it, Dutta's future testimony against us and in setting the stage for our impending trial. But while we treated the whole episode with a certain 'gallows' humour, our lawyers were distinctly concerned that Judge Brooks appeared to accept what he was being told.

The deal struck between the police and Dutta had required the police to ensure that Dutta receive as lenient a treatment as possible from the Court, in return for his giving evidence against Ben and me a few months later.

To this end, Detective Constable Michael Ellis was called by the prosecution at the beginning of the hearing to give evidence on Dutta's behalf about his role in the New York sting. Ellis began by stating that before being remanded in custody in October 1991, Dutta had been earning £40,000 a year at an American investment bank.

Continuing, D/C Ellis said that I had exercised a considerable influence over both Dutta and indeed Peter Risdon due to my being 'a very strong personality'. It appeared, in short, that Risdon had not been the only innocent dupe in the whole affair.

He also told the judge that I associated with a number of 'ex-military men', a reference presumably to Bill Hall, as well as a number of 'major gangsters', a reference to no one we could think of.

'Who are these "major gangsters", Darry?' Ben asked ironically. 'They don't mean Peter Risdon, do they?'

D/C Ellis then went on to tell Judge Brooks that I was a man of sufficient wealth to put a contract on the life of anybody who I felt had crossed me. To illustrate his argument he referred to Bill Hall's trip to Bombay to recover the sum of £250,000 that Goutti had attempted to steal from us. In endeavouring to portray Ben and me in the worst possible light and Dutta in far more favourable terms, no mention was made of the fact that part of the money owed by Goutti was in fact Dutta's and that Dutta had been as responsible as me for co-ordinating the operation.

To hammer home the point, D/C Ellis went on to inform the court that I had been found in possession of a Browning 9mm semi-automatic hand-gun and some ammunition without a licence and had been charged and convicted. He added, somewhat sinisterly, that owing to my membership of a gun club, I had access to other guns.

In continuing his evidence to Judge Brooks, he stated that Dutta had expressed a genuine willingness to the police to give evidence against Ben and me at committal proceedings, which were due to occur in six weeks' time, despite having been severely assaulted in prison while waiting to plead guilty. He reported that only recently Dutta had been attacked by a fellow prisoner resulting in three of his teeth being 'smashed' and a fourth 'chipped'.

Asked whether there was any inference to be drawn from the injuries Dutta had received and his willingness to give evidence against Ben and me, D/C Ellis replied, 'Only in so much that it seems a coincidence that, having been in custody since October, my understanding is that he was assaulted only a few weeks ago, prior to coming to court this morning and pleading guilty.'

He maintained that he believed the assault had been an attempt 'to get at' Dutta because, he claimed, efforts had been made by Ben and me to find out which prison Dutta had been kept in.

Dutta's barrister, Mr David Bate, spoke of his client's character. 'Everyone who has come in contact with him, including the police, have found him to be charming, able, friendly and delightful. His probation officer called him a "thoughtful and resourceful man".'

Mr Bate argued that Dutta had fallen 'under the spell of Mr Guppy, a smooth-talking con man, who lives in a world of Concorde and millions, transatlantic journeys, huge profits and the like, and there is little doubt that this offence would never have occurred had it not been for the fact that he fell under this man's spell.' He contended that Dutta had been kept in ignorance of the scale of the plot and that, if he had known the extent of it, he would never have become involved as it was altogether outside anything that he could possibly have contemplated.

Mr Bate told the court, 'Mr Dutta knows very well that his life is in danger, because the people who have every reason to wish him out of the way have access to guns; they have access to huge sums of money and, it appears, will not hesitate to use that access to their advantage. Notwithstanding that fact, this defendant is determined to give evidence for the Crown.'

Inviting Judge Brooks to sentence Dutta, he explained most movingly why his client should be treated leniently: 'First, because he is in danger. He is at very much greater risk in prison, where his movements are known to other people. He is in constant risk of attack and one simply does not know how serious that attack will be. The first attack perhaps was a warning. It is apparent from what I have said that that will get back no doubt to Mr Guppy and his friends, and be quite apparent that that warning has not worked.'

In sentencing Dutta, Judge Brooks declared that the alleged insurance sting was 'an extremely well-planned and executed fraud' — which caused us a little concern coming from the man who was due to preside over our trial and who had heard none of the defence's arguments.

Dutta was sentenced to eighteen months' imprisonment, twelve months of which would be suspended. As he had already served six months on remand, he was released five days later.

Ben commented, 'Surely the Judge hasn't already made up his mind?'

'I hope not,' replied our lawyer.

I sat quietly for some minutes, thinking about events, which had clearly shown what lengths certain individuals were prepared to go to in order to ensure our convictions. It seemed that they were willing to indulge Dutta and Risdon and in the process to let Dutta off virtually scot-free and Risdon off completely scot-free. Now, some would say that the police and the criminal justice system must be beyond reproach, others that, no, the ends justify the means; in other words, that clever criminals would never be caught if the police and the courts did not allow a certain latitude. This is an argument I can easily understand and even sympathise with. But what is a little hard to swallow is when these very same people proclaim themselves to be whiter than white and come up with phrases such as 'our criminal justice system is the envy of the civilised world'.

But this was England in the 1990s and above all, this was reality.

Within hours of his release, an agitated Dutta phoned me at our offices in New Bond Street.

'Darry, listen,' he said, 'before you become angry I want to see you to explain everything.'

'Ishan,' I replied, 'I had a feeling that you'd call and I suspect you've had enormous pressure put on you.'

'You can say that again.'

Three days later, we met for afternoon tea at the Oxford and Cambridge Club in Pall Mall. We went downstairs to the dimly lit snooker room where we could talk in private.

'You're looking well, Ishan, considering you've just spent six months in Pentonville.'

Seeming down-hearted, Ishan told me, 'Darry, look, I'm really ashamed about what happened.'

'Yes, I can understand that,' I said. 'But what the hell was all that business in court about me having had you beaten up in prison?'

Ishan explained: 'In reality a black man thumped me because he thought I had jumped the breakfast queue. One day when the police came to visit me I casually mentioned what had happened. I then decided to put forward the story of you organising to have me beaten up in prison, thinking that the police would assist me in obtaining a lenient sentence in return, obviously, for my giving evidence against you and Ben.

'The police are absolutely desperate to convict you. They're literally behaving like little children. They ring me up every day to make sure I'm still on for giving evidence against you. They think this is going to be a high-profile case and they want to be known as the ones who brought you down. I'm just letting you know, Darius. You'd better

218

prepare yourself.'

He went on, 'They tried every trick in the book. When they arrested me, for example, they did the classic "nice guy, nasty guy" routine with Ellis playing the nice guy and Avery the not-so-nice guy. They kept coming into my cell and making it clear that I'd be on the next plane back to India if I didn't co-operate.

'I know I shouldn't have caved in but I just couldn't face the prospect of returning to India. It's not like this country. The authorities over there can do anything they want to you.'

Although I was angry with him, Dutta did have one particularly strong argument. 'Do you realise how well the whole business in court worked for us all? The important point is that I'm out of prison now, so I'm free to disappear. I've got no intention of giving any evidence against you or Ben. If I hadn't used this ploy, then I would still be languishing in Pentonville and I'd be forced to testify against you.'

'So you're going to disappear?'

'Yes, of course I am. They won't see me for dust.'

'Great,' I replied. 'But how can you leave the country? What about your false passport?'

'That's the beauty of it,' Dutta answered. 'They returned it to me as soon as I was released from jail.'

'Ishan,' I said, hardly able to believe what he was saying. 'Are you telling me that the police actually returned your false passport to you?'

'Darry,' he replied. 'You don't know how desperate these guys are to convict you and Ben. Incidentally, they also told me that Risdon wasn't exactly an angel but that they'd done a deal with him.'

Having explained his plan to leave Britain and settle for a while in Cyprus, Dutta then asked me if I would loan him £20,000 so that he had some money to live on. I knew that all his assets in India had been frozen and he was broke. Moreover, I had trusted him in the past with hundreds of thousands of pounds and he had never let me down. But I told him, 'I must impress on you that this £20,000 is only a loan. If people find out that I've given you this money, they'll immediately think I've bribed you to leave the country. So you must understand that when you've sorted yourself out, I want the money back. OK?'

'I agree. Thanks,' he said.

On the morning of 21 April, 1992, Ben and I arrived at Redbridge Magistrates' Court for the start of the committal proceedings. As we entered the building, we noticed clusters of lawyers and police in the hallway. They were engaged in heated discussion. Suddenly, Detective-Inspector Peter Avery hurried towards me.

'What's up Mr Avery?' Ben asked, with a touch of sarcasm in his voice.

'Your mate's done a runner, as you know perfectly well.'

'Well, he shouldn't have had his false passport returned then, should he?' I replied.

Avery rushed out of the building, yelling instructions down his portable telephone.

Later that evening, Dutta telephoned me at a friend's home. Ever since our arrest, I had been careful never to use my home or office telephones for anything other than routine calls, convinced that the police were bugging all my calls.

'I received the money,' Dutta said. 'Thanks a lot. I'm in Cyprus. I've no idea when I'll see you again, but I'll keep in touch on this number. Good luck.'

A week later, Ben and I were committed for trial at Snaresbrook Crown Court on various conspiracy charges. We did, however, score one victory during the committal. The Stipendiary Magistrate who oversaw the proceedings threw out the charge accusing us of conspiring to pervert the cause of justice.

A few months later, early one morning in July 1992 Ishan Dutta arrived, totally unexpectedly, at my mother's Chelsea home. Through tears he introduced himself to her and begged her to give me a message to contact him at 7.30 that evening on a telephone number that he left with her. Then he departed, as quickly as he had appeared.

My mother's message from Dutta sounded all the alarm bells and, after discussing the matter with Ben, we decided that I should tape-record every conversation that I was to have with him from that point on. Something must have gone very wrong for Dutta to risk returning to London, having failed to attend the committal proceedings as he had promised the police and Judge Brooks he would do.

During the course of the next few weeks, Dutta would tell me in a number of telephone conversations that I taped that he had had no alternative but to return to England, as he needed to have his genuine Indian passport renewed and the only places he could do this were in India or at the Indian High Commission in London. He had decided on London as the lesser of two evils.

However, unknown to him, the police had been following his movements by means of his credit card records. Within days of his returning to London, the police had been aware of his presence in the country and by keeping tabs on his expenditure had been able to ascertain which area of London he was living in.

One morning the police had called at the address in Notting Hill Gate where he usually stayed when in London and had found him still in his pyjamas. They had arrested him on a charge of conspiring to pervert the course of justice and, determined not to make the same mistake twice, had confiscated his false passport in order to prevent him from leaving the country. In one conversation, so desperate had Dutta become, he even asked me for a further £30,000 in the hope that with this money he would be able to purchase another false passport, as well as providing such incentives as were required to oil the wheels of justice in India so enabling him to return home as soon as possible.

After that phone call Dutta disappeared and Ben and I hoped that he would not re-surface until after our trial. We had no idea where he went.

Around this time our old friend, Tom McLaine, Risdon's ex-partner who had helped us in the early days, contacted me through our lawyers and Ben and I went round to see him at his south London home.

He recounted how he had been visited over two years before by Customs and Excise officers investigating our bullion venture.

Sitting in his shorts, beneath a signed painting of the Kray Brothers and an armoury of various weapons on the walls that included rifles, commando knives and the odd knuckle-duster, McLaine told us, 'After you were arrested Customs came round and said they wanted to talk to me about "a Darius Guppy". I had Samson, my Alsatian, by my side. He hates all official prats and can smell 'em a mile off, so they never dared come in. He was leaping at the door, growling and barking and biting at the letter box they were trying to speak through. I could hardly hear a word they said.

'Anyway, I told Samson to belt up and shouted at them "I don't know any fuckin' Delirious! Now fuck off out of 'ere before I set the dog on you!"

'They kept shouting through the box that it was a serious matter so I let Samson go and he leaped at the door barkin' and snappin' at them and trying to bite their faces through the letter box. I'll tell you, he went absolutely stark ravin' mad. I thought he was going to break the fuckin' door down. Anyway, they soon scarpered. Never heard another word.'

Then, offering proof, McLaine said, 'See the letter box? That's what he done; he's a good dog.' And, indeed, all around the letter box were claw and teeth marks. In fact, most of the door, that had once been painted with a layer of veneer, had been savaged through to the bare woodwork.

It was during our chat with McLaine that he brought up the question of Risdon's informing on us. We had lost touch over the past year or so but he had read about what had happened in the Press and, although it had not yet been reported in the newspapers, had heard through the grapevine that his former partner — who had run off allowing ETS to go bankrupt and owing Tom £150,000 — was the police's star witness against us.

'As soon as I heard that, I went looking for him; the slag,' he said. 'Fuckin' grass. He's been grassing everybody up. Not just you two. Twice I've just missed him. He keeps changing house every few weeks; one week in Clapham, one week in Mitcham. He's trying to stay one step ahead of some very heavy people who want to speak to him. OK, everyone pulls a few strokes, especially all the fuckin' politicians; we all want to make a quid or two, but there's a code and he's broken it. He'd sell his own mother. He's always tried to make out that he's tough, but he's weak. He's got no arsehole; that's the truth, Darius. But you wait 'til I catch him. He'll look even uglier than he does at the moment, I can tell you. Fuckin' slag.'

As we awaited our trial, a number of journalists from various national newspapers called at my house seeking an interview with Patricia and me after the trial had taken place and whatever the verdict. One reporter told us that Peter Risdon was trying to sell his story to the highest bidder.

In an attempt to jack up the price, the reporter informed us, Risdon had even claimed that I was madly in love with the Princess of Wales and that I had arranged for a team of mercenaries to hijack an oil-tanker in the Persian Gulf in order to gift the oil to the Islamic Republic of Iran!

I told him, 'No one can seriously believe such stories, can they?'

He replied, 'It's not a question of believing it or not. It's a question of what's going to make a good story and sell. We've discounted most of what Risdon's said as fantasy, but the point is that if you're sent down he'll make a lot of money for his story and the papers will reckon that no matter how outrageous the stories they print are, you'll be in no position to sue because you'll be in prison and you won't have much of a reputation to defend because you'll have been convicted. That's the way it works, I'm afraid.'

'But, at the risk of asking a slightly naïve question,' I said to the journalist, 'don't the newspapers have any regard for the truth?'

He paused before answering. 'You're right. Your question is a little naïve.'

Towards the end of September 1992, I was sitting in the restaurant Montpeliano's in Knightsbridge, waiting to meet Patricia for lunch. She had told me that she would be going on some errands in the morning, but it was now 1.30pm and she was half an hour late. I was beginning to get a little worried when one of the waiters came to my table and told me: 'Mr Guppy, there's a telephone call for you. It's your wife.'

Wondering what the matter could be, I accompanied him to the back of the restaurant, where I took the call.

'Darling,' Patricia said, 'I went to see the doctor this morning. I've got good news for you. You're going to be a daddy.'

'What?' I shouted. 'Fantastic news! Darling, come here straight away. We'll celebrate. And be careful, no sudden movements. And make sure you're warm!'

'I'll get a cab immediately,' she said, and I could hear the tears of happiness in her voice.

XV

The evening before our trial, on Sunday, 8 November, 1992, Ben and I went out for supper in Notting Hill Gate to make the final decision about whether or not to plead guilty the following day.

'Let's examine the evidence the police have got against us,' I said. 'They don't have the gun, they don't have any secret Swiss bank accounts, they don't have any evidence of high-living on our part and they don't have a single gemstone. But it doesn't exactly help matters that they do have the man who actually carried out the robbery.'

'Exactly,' said Ben, 'and what makes things worse is that the police, Customs, Lloyds, and of course the Press, are all absolutely determined that we should go down. Look what happened with Dutta. They'll stretch any rule they have to in order to get us.'

'It's almost as if the whole world were willing it to happen,' I added. 'Even some of our contemporaries at Oxford and in the City would love us to go to jail because they're envious of what we did and don't want to see us get away with it.'

'Let's face it,' I continued, 'this is going to be a show trial and if we lose they'll throw the book at us. Why don't we plead guilty?' I suggested. 'At least we'd get a lesser sentence for not wasting the court's time.'

'No way, Darry,' Ben replied. 'This case has become such a charade that I'm determined to fight them all the way. I just can't wait to get into that witness box.'

'You know I feel like you do, Ben, but I'm really torn,' I said. 'On the one hand, the single thing that has pissed me off more than anything else is the way they've indulged Risdon. But on the other hand, we're

225

guilty ourselves.'

'I know what you're saying, Darry,' Ben answered. 'If the police had told us, "come on, lads we know you did it; you had a go but tough luck; the game's up, come clean," then I would happily plead guilty and take the punishment. But all that crap about Risdon, the innocent dupe and you being the 'Godfather'; it just really gets to me.'

'I agree,' I said. 'This whole thing has got nothing to do with justice. So, I must admit, the urge in me to fight is stronger than the urge to throw the towel in.'

'Also, it's in Inca's interests that we fight and win,' I continued. 'If we lose, Lloyds will win their action against Inca and seize all its assets, bankrupting the company. If we win, however, almost certainly the company would survive.'

I paused and looked at Ben.

'So what do you say?'

'Shit or bust!' Ben replied.

'Shit or bust!' I repeated.

Patricia came to join us at the end of dinner and Ben left us alone to have a quiet chat before the opening day of the trial.

We returned home to find two messages on the answerphone. The first was from Charlie's mother, Frances Shand Kydd, who said, 'Patricia and Darry, I'm with you all the way. I want you to know that whatever happens, you can rely on my support because true friends are always there to stand up and be counted, even when the going gets tough. Lots of love to you both.'

The second message was a little less encouraging.

A deep Cockney voice, which I could not recognise, said, 'You're going away for five years; we know,' at which point the phone had clicked off.

'Who was that?' asked Patricia. 'Our number is ex-directory; we changed it again only last week.'

'I know who it is,' I replied. 'It's our charming friends, the same ones who phoned you at two in the morning after my arrest last year.'

The following morning, dressed in a dark suit, white shirt and a sober tie, I stood with Ben in the dock of court number twelve at Snaresbrook Crown Court near Epping, as His Honour Judge Andrew Brooks, in his wig and purple gown, walked from his chambers into the courtroom. A short, rather plump man with spectacles and a ruddy complexion, he appeared to exude self-importance as he bowed to the court and took his seat.

The courtroom was small. In front of the dock were several rows of benches and desks; the back rows for the defence team and the rows in front of that for the prosecution. Beyond this, were the desks belonging to the clerk and the court stenographer. At the back of the Court, raised on a dais, and facing the dock, was the bench where Judge Brooks presided. To his right, or our left, were the seats for the Press and members of the public who included a number of 'Snaresbrook regulars', old-age pensioners who lived locally and who came to court on a daily basis for entertainment. To the right of the dock were the jurors' seats and just behind where we sat was a wooden door with a spyhole that led to the cells below via a labyrinth of concrete corridors. Occasionally, the door would 'clack, clack' with the wind and sometimes I would imagine a prison officer looking at us through the spyhole, examining his potential prey like a lion crouched in the savannah.

The room was packed, primarily with Snaresbrook regulars and members of the Press. I felt a little like a creature being examined on a David Attenborough wildlife programme.

Ben and I were formally asked by the clerk whether we intended to plead 'guilty' or 'not guilty' to the charges. We pleaded 'not guilty'.

The prosecution team was headed by James Curtis, a short, wiry man in his forties with a particular affectation that would cause us amusement. On virtually every occasion that he began speaking, he would clear his throat three of four times in a deliberate and exaggerated style, as if for dramatic effect. His junior, Peter Finnigan, was a tall, good-looking and polite man in his thirties who always appeared particularly professional and objective.

I was represented by Tim Langdale, QC, a suave, elegant and charming man in his forties. His junior, Anna Christofides, was an attractive, dark-haired and efficient young woman, who always did her best to appear optimistic. Ben's counsel was John Kelsey-Fry, a slim, handsome and urbane man in his mid-thirties, and he was assisted by Rachel Bright, a vivacious and pretty blonde who had a cheeky smile and a very engaging personality.

After the jury had been sworn in, Ben and I looked at each other and slowly shook our heads as James Curtis rose to his feet to address the Judge, bending almost double and slowly rubbing his hands in a convincing imitation of a deferential courtier.

'Ahem, ahem. This case, ladies and gentlemen of the jury,' he began, 'is far from boring. It involves an armed robbery in a top New York hotel, fabulous gems, rubies, emeralds and sapphires, trips on Concorde, smuggling gold into India, front companies, Swiss bank accounts and millions of pounds ...'

He continued, 'It is the Crown's case that the defendants' enterprise, in which they successfully defrauded Lloyds of London, was particularly bold in concept, well-researched and meticulously executed.'

Ben nudged me and whispered, 'I don't know, Darry, the things you old Etonians get up to. He's beginning to make me feel quite proud really.'

Curtis went on, 'When they were discovered bound in their hotel room, it is the Crown's case that the defendants were able to fool the New York police officers who were called in to investigate with what, one has to hand it to them, was a quite masterful performance, especially by Guppy.'

Again, Ben nudged me and whispered, 'Rubbish! That was the worst piece of over-acting I've ever seen in my life.'

In a loud voice, Brooks seized his opportunity and bellowed, 'Quiet in the dock! You're not in a nightclub now!'

At the end of Curtis' opening statement, Judge Brooks suggested a break for lunch and, with a broad smile, told the jury, 'Now you can go and have your cigarettes and your coffee and whatever else you do in that little room of yours.'

As we walked out of the courtroom, our solicitor Harry Travers, asked us, 'Well, what do you think of the Judge?'

To which Ben replied, 'I don't that there's an appropriate legal term.'

During the break Ben asked our lawyers, 'Why did Judge Brooks make that remark about not being "in a nightclub"? I'd whispered something to Darry but it was very quiet and no one else could possibly have heard.'

Our lawyer replied, 'This is his courtroom. The jury has been sworn in and he can conduct the trial pretty much as he likes. If you get convicted, you could bring up his comments at an appeal but I can tell you that it wouldn't count for anything.

'Snaresbrook has a higher rate of acquittal than any other Crown court in the London area because the jurors from this catchment area tend to mistrust the police. As a result, they seem to side more with defendants. The jury was being reminded that you are "gilded youths", or as the Press describe you, "toffs".'

He added, 'You mark my words. Throughout this trial, the prosecution will exploit such prejudices.'

Ben said, 'What you're saying is that we're fucked.'

'Not necessarily,' he replied, 'but there's no doubt that we're up against it. It will be tough. We've not discussed it in the past, but you can always plead guilty.'

'Never!' Ben and I replied together.

At the end of the break, as we all filed back into court, Harry Travers approached a group of a dozen or so Pressmen who were standing in the corridor organising a sweepstake. When Harry asked them what they were betting on, they replied that they were taking odds on how many years we would get. The bets placed ranged between three years and ten.

'What about an acquittal?' Ben asked. 'Are they taking bets on that?'

'No,' Harry answered. 'They don't see that as a possibility.'

To everyone's surprise, Ben and I laughed out loud.

At the end of that opening day, the prosecution announced that their first witness would be Ishan Dutta. This was certainly a blow. Ben and I had hoped, perhaps a little optimistically, that he had hidden himself away somewhere until the trial was over.

Throughout his three days in the witness box, Dutta, nervous and drawn, tried desperately never to look at Ben or me. Occasionally our eyes would meet and instantly he would turn away.

After giving evidence for a day and a half, Dutta appeared to have become used to being in the witness box and seemed quietly confident when my barrister Tim Langdale rose to cross-examine him.

'Mr Dutta,' he asked quietly. 'How many passports do you have?'

That simple question immediately threw Dutta and he never recovered, instead tying himself up in knots as he tried frantically to extricate himself with one lie after another. At first, he denied having both a British and an Indian passport; when this was disproved, he denied that the British passport was a forgery; once again this was shown to be untrue, so he denied knowing that it was false. When asked by Tim Langdale how it was, in that case, that the false British passport stated that he had been born in London while the genuine Indian one described his birthplace as Calcutta, he told the court that he wasn't sure whether he had been born in Calcutta or in London.

A number of members of the jury began to smile, while others laughed openly as Dutta became more and more entangled in his web of falsehoods. In short, if it was possible for a barrister to annihilate a witness in the box, Tim Langdale did it with Dutta.

Next, Dutta went on to deny that I had given him £20,000 prior to the committal proceedings; to deny that he knew £20,000 had been credited to his account; to deny that he had invented the story about my having had him beaten up in prison; to deny that he had been intimidated by the police and to deny that the police had pressurised him into saying that I had threatened him. He also denied pressuring me for an additional £30,000 and being in trouble with the Indian authorities over his gold-smuggling activities.

Once Dutta had committed himself with such bold assertions, Tim Langdale produced a cassette recorder and put it on the table in front of him. He began by playing a recording of a conversation between Dutta and me that had occurred on 7 July, 1992, and that I had secretly taped.

As soon as Dutta heard the sound of his own voice, he went white, staggered back and almost fainted. The court listened in silence, eager to catch every word on the tapes, as Dutta heard his own words destroy the testimony he had just given to the court. When asked to explain the discrepancies he replied, 'That's not my voice.'

The jury, the public gallery and many members of the Press burst out laughing. At that point, the proceedings were adjourned until the following day.

The next morning, as he stepped into the witness box to resume his evidence, Dutta looked a wreck. It seemed that he had not slept a wink. His eyes were bloodshot and his demeanour that of a broken man. To make matters worse for him, a number of his former Oxford friends had come to watch him testify.

By the time he had completed his evidence, it was obvious that he could face charges of perjury and we awaited with acute interest for Judge Brooks' reaction. For Judge Brooks had sentenced Dutta very leniently on the basis that he should be released immediately from jail in case of my having him killed in prison and because of his courageous willingness to testify despite fearing for his life. The judge now knew, however, that immediately upon his release he had contacted me, asked for £20,000, fled the country before the committal proceedings and returned to ask me for a further £30,000. Furthermore, he had revealed the extent to which the police had indulged in a number of practices, all of which had potentially damaged the prosecution's case irreparably.

Judge Brooks' response, however, was to say, 'Thank you so much for taking the time to come to this court and give evidence. We are most grateful.'

'Why don't we just plead guilty?' I said to Ben. 'At least we won't have to sit through all this bloody theatre.'

As Dutta left the witness box he walked past the dock, but kept his eyes to the floor. Patricia had come to collect me that day as it was a Friday and we were due to drive straight up to Sunderland to spend the weekend with her mother as soon as the Court's business had been concluded. As Dutta passed Patricia, who was sitting in the front row of the public seating area, he smiled at her sheepishly. She looked at him with contempt.

Although Ben had always despised Dutta because he considered him arrogant and pompous, I did not feel the same way about him. In fact, I was genuinely sorry for him as he left the courtroom. We had enjoyed many good times together and I realised that everyone, sooner or later, has a cracking point. It was just a pity that he had caved in from the very beginning, offering so little resistance to the machinations of the police and resorting instead to pressuring his friends.

Above all I felt embarrassed for him. He was not like Risdon, a man without pride or honour. I knew that he would have been ashamed for being exposed as weak and a traitor, especially in front of his friends from his Winchester and Oxford days who had turned up to see him give evidence. The code of not informing on one's friends and colleagues is as strong in boarding-schools as it is in the Italian Mafia.

As it turned out, Dutta's evidence had been very helpful for us. Indeed, as we would learn later, by the end of his testimony a number of the jurors had considered the case against us so weak that had they been required at that stage to reach a verdict, they would have acquitted us.

Moreover, after we had finished for the day, we could hear heated arguments taking place in the rooms on the ground floor of the court building that had been reserved for the prosecution team.

However, two weeks into the trial our lawyers had to contend with perhaps the single most critical feature of the entire case, namely the question of the deal that Risdon had struck with the police, in particular the circumstances under which it had come about and whether in fact Risdon was a regular 'police informer'.

Our lawyers were convinced that if they were permitted by Judge Brooks to explore this vital issue, the defence would be able to expose the inconsistencies between the evidence given by Risdon in his statements and that given by the police under cross-examination at the earlier committal proceedings.

To this end, my barrister, Tim Langdale, supported by Ben's barrister, John Kelsey-Fry, made an application to Judge Brooks to be permitted to cross-examine Risdon on the question of whether he was a police informer. So crucial was this application, that our lawyers considered that the outcome of our trial could well hinge on whether it was allowed or not.

It was also clear that both the prosecution and Brooks knew of the importance of our application as the legal arguments concerning it would involve the best part of a day and Brooks' judgement would be reserved until the following morning.

At the committal proceedings, D/C Ellis had produced his 'duty statements', at the request of our lawyers. These 'duty statements' are effectively the diaries that all police officers must write up regularly, giving details of the duties they have performed during each day. The entries made by D/C Ellis in his statements under the heading of 'Operation Athene' showed that he and other officers working on our case had met Risdon on a number of occasions during the two months prior to Risdon making a formal statement against us on 10 May, 1991. Most of these meetings had taken place at a wine bar on the Embankment.

The prosecution's evidence rested on the single fact that the details contained in Risdon's statement of 10 May could only have been known by someone who had been present in Room 1207 of the

Halloran House Hotel in New York at the time of the alleged robbery.

Police codes of practice state that when a particular witness has evidence to give, his statement should be taken down as soon as possible, one of the principal reasons being to avoid any future suggestion of the police having influenced the witness or schooled him in making a statement tailored to the prosecution's case.

Our lawyers wanted to know what exactly had been said during the meetings that had taken place on the Embankment, and to explore the whole nature of the rather cosy relationship that had clearly developed between Risdon and the police. If, for example, during those meetings, Risdon had been shown the photographs taken by the New York Police's Crime Scene Unit of our room in the Halloran House Hotel before making his statement to them on 10 May, 1991, the prosecution's case would be in real danger of collapsing.

Of particular relevance in this regard was the fact that at the committal proceedings D/C Ellis had given evidence in which he had stated that the conversations that had taken place between him and Risdon on the Embankment, prior to Risdon giving his statement on 10 May, had concerned allegations that Risdon had made against other individuals and had had nothing whatsoever to do with our case. According to him, the very first he had known of Risdon's allegations about the New York robbery had been immediately prior to the statement he had given on 10 May.

The obvious inference of such a statement was that Risdon was a police informer.

Not for one moment did we believe that the first time Risdon had mentioned the New York robbery to the police had been just before his statement of 10 May.

Risdon's evidence at the committal proceedings had, however, been vague about these various unexplained meetings and he had suggested, contradicting D/C Ellis' testimony and duty statements, that only one meeting had taken place prior to making his formal police statement on 10 May.

When asked in cross-examination why it had taken him fourteen months to unburden his conscience and make a statement to the police about the robbery, Risdon had replied, incredulously, that he been unaware of the procedure for making such a statement. Such testimony flatly contradicted, of course, the evidence of D/C Ellis that seemed to suggest that Risdon was a regular police informer.

In short, had we been allowed to explore this whole question of Risdon's status of police informer and thereby been able to illustrate how it revealed the inconsistencies between the police's and Risdon's version of events, there could have been only a very limited number of inferences for the jury to draw — either the police, or Risdon, or both had lied in the witness box.

Such inferences, in turn, could have been fatal to the prosecution's case. Not surprisingly, Curtis vigorously opposed the application to pursue this line of questioning and stated that the defence team would no doubt find it very satisfying to see Risdon 'squirm in the witness box' for fear of the consequences for himself and his family.

Clearly, having seen Ishan Dutta squirming in the witness box, the prosecution were determined not to see their star witness torn to shreds as well. Curtis, therefore, requested the Judge to deny our application on the grounds of 'Public Interest Immunity', arguing that if Risdon was indeed a police informer he could be placed in danger if this fact emerged in open court.

This argument took no account of the fact that, first, Risdon's identity as the informer in our case had been extensively reported in the Press and second, that far from fearing the consequences of his identity being widely known, Risdon had actually admitted in the witness box that he stood a lot to gain in the event of our conviction, having negotiated to sell his story to a major national newspaper.

However, the disingenuousness of such reasoning seemed somehow to be lost on Judge Brooks. Instead, he asked the prosecution, 'Are you really concerned that this sort of evidence would harm the prosecution case? I mean there's enough evidence here to sink a battleship.'

Realising that his remark could indicate bias against the defence, Brooks came back to the point some time later and stated that he wished to withdraw his comment about the 'battleship'.

My barrister, none too pleased by some of Curtis' accusations, made his objections clear. 'I really do think it is most unfortunate when my friend starts to talk of people deriving pleasure from seeing witnesses "squirming in the witness box"!' Tim Langdale protested.

Curtis, who was seated as my barrister addressed the judge, was visibly agitated by this rebuke, his wig quivering with indignation as he mumbled wildly to himself a string of legal expressions in Latin, only to be further rebuked by Tim Langdale.

There was clear relief among the prosecution team when Judge Brooks announced his decision the following morning. 'After careful consideration of the powerful and persuasive arguments advanced by Mr Langdale and Mr Kelsey-Fry, I have decided that the defence will not be allowed to pursue this line of questioning.'

I whispered to Ben, 'Surprise, surprise!'

At that moment we realised that our trial had basically ended and that nothing short of a miracle would save us. Any qualms I had had about pleading 'not guilty' had by now evaporated.

In the witness box Peter Risdon appeared nervous and accounted for this by explaining to the judge that he was suffering from an injured back, strained playing football a few days before. Throughout his evidence, Risdon stuck to the innocent dupe line he had adopted in his statements to the police, stating that he had been utterly shocked and appalled to discover the extent of what he had become unwittingly involved in.

When asked to account for the long delay between the New York robbery and his giving evidence to the police, and only after having been caught attempting to commit an insurance fraud over the large rough diamond, Risdon replied, 'Above all, I have come here out of a sense of responsibility. I had been meaning to report the matter for a long time, but I simply didn't know the procedure. My meeting the police in March 1991 when they arrested me on a totally unconnected matter gave me the perfect opportunity of clearing my conscience.'

As an afterthought, he added, 'I want you to understand that there is nothing personal in my giving evidence against Guppy and Marsh. In fact, although I was misled, I'm still very fond of them.'

One of the younger women jurors put her finger down her throat, as if to be sick.

On another occasion, Risdon was asked what my reaction had been to certain Press reports that had called into doubt the authenticity of the robbery. He told the jury, 'I remember it clearly; Darius said, "Damn! There goes my peerage!"'

Two members of the jury actually burst out laughing and Risdon, realising that he had over-egged the pudding somewhat, looked decidedly embarrassed.

When asked about the artist's impression of the alleged robber, Risdon replied, 'It bears a remarkable similarity to me.' In reality, for obvious reasons Ben and I had been very careful to ensure that the photofit did not remotely resemble him and, indeed, I saw one of the jurors comment to the juror sitting next to him, 'It looks nothing like him!'

In fact, the very man whose face we had imagined when describing the robber to the New York police, Radek Sikorski, my old friend from Oxford, had come to court only a few days before and had even sat for hours next to the police officers investigating our case. When he had originally walked in, Ben and I had felt a little uneasy, especially as the photofit of the robber was widely exhibited throughout the courtroom, but no one had noticed.

When Risdon was asked about the attempt by his girlfriend, Frances, to ask me for money, he replied, 'That was a silly mistake on her part. I would never dream of doing anything like that.' He continued, looking vulnerable, 'Sadly, Frances and I are no longer together.'

I whispered to Ben, 'What a creep! He'd been planning to leave her for years. He just used her and he thought he was too good for her.'

'Can you imagine Risdon being too good for anyone?' Ben asked.

Towards the end of his evidence, Tim Langdale asked Risdon, 'Have you approached any newspapers with a view to selling your story?'

'Yes,' he replied.

'Anyone in particular?'

'I have been talking to The London *Evening Standard*.'

'So it could be said, Mr Risdon, that you have a financial interest in these two defendants being found guilty?'

Risdon paused before replying. 'Yes, that could be said. But above all, I have come here to clear my conscience,' he quickly added.

The day after Risdon had finished giving evidence, Curtis asked Judge Brooks whether Risdon's passport, which had been an exhibit in the trial, could be returned to him as he wished to take a holiday in Australia.

'Of course,' replied the judge. 'And please thank Mr Risdon for sparing the time to come and give evidence.'

As I walked from court for the Christmas break on 18 December, I saw an Indian woman lying on the floor of one of the building's corridors being comforted by her two sons. She had run from one of the courts, crashing through a glass door and causing a severe gash in her arm. Blood covered the floor around her.

'My boy, my poor boy,' she moaned.

I asked a security guard what had happened.

'We get this all the time, Sir,' he replied. 'Her son was just found guilty of manslaughter. Killed someone in a fight. Some family feud, I think. She ran out of the court when the jury gave the verdict and smashed straight into the door. Anyway, the ambulance should be here soon.'

I felt enormous pity for the poor woman lying on the floor. She had invested so much love in her son and now she would not see him as a free man for many years. In becoming so absorbed in my own problems, I had failed to appreciate properly the anguish that I had brought to my own parents and to many others. And, although those close to me had kept a dignified silence about their feelings, it was obvious how much sadness and anxiety they must have been experiencing. Ben and I, and indeed the whole defence team, had coped with the tension with much laughter and 'gallows' humour but the truth was that events, not simply in our own trial, but occurring at the same time in the many other courtrooms nearby, were the source of great misery.

I feared that I would be sent down for some years and I wanted to prepare Patricia, then four months pregnant, for the fate that I was certain awaited me. I also felt guilty that, over the past few months, I had been so embroiled in my trial that I had been unable to devote to her the attention she deserved. So, I decided to take her for one last holiday and we spent a week together over the Christmas break at the Lucknam Park Hotel, where we had honeymooned some eighteen months before.

Although I am sure that Patricia had formed her own views about whether Ben and I were guilty, not even during those seven days, however, did she ask me directly what had really happened in New York, preferring instead to enjoy the peace of our time together.

One evening, as I lay on the sofa of our room with my head in her lap, I told her: 'Sweetheart, we're going to be found guilty. I'm just warning you, it's going to be a media circus.'

I paused. 'What happens if I'm sent to prison?'

'I'll wait, Darling,' she replied, placing my hand on her stomach. I felt our baby kick for the first time. 'All that matters to me is our future together and our child. Whatever happens I know that one day we'll be together again.'

Throughout the Christmas break, I became increasingly concerned that when the court re-opened I would have to go into the witness box and give evidence. I did not wish to lie under oath and I resolved, therefore, as was my right, not to testify.

When the trial re-commenced in early January 1993 and I told my lawyers of my decision, they were alarmed and a crisis meeting was called in the defence room outside the court.

Tim Langdale told me, 'You simply must go into the box, otherwise you will definitely be found guilty. If you don't give evidence, then the jury will take it as admission of your guilt. It's that clear cut.'

He went on: 'Listen Darius, it's not as if this is a case where there's hardly any prosecution evidence. You have to do the running. You have to convince the jury that you are innocent. There is a witness who has stated under oath that he tied you up and shot the gun. Now, that's an allegation you simply must answer if you are to stand a chance. You can't just ignore it and say nothing.'

Another of my lawyers added, 'Risdon and Dutta were in this crime up to their necks and look how much the police and the prosecution have bent over backwards to protect them and convict you.'

Here was the truth and, although we were guilty, I had become more and more angry with every day that passed at the whole charade. It was this anger, more than any other factor, that drove me into the witness box.

For the following two weeks I found myself giving evidence and, to my surprise, not once did I feel that the prosecution caught me out.

Throughout this time I was in fact spurred on by my two friends — D/I Avery, with his dark suit, his Hush Puppies and his menacing stare, and the ever suntanned D/C Ellis with his grey suit and his new hair cut — who made it their business to sit only four feet away from where I was standing in the witness box.

By the time it came for me to be cross-examined, James Curtis' affectation of clearing his throat with a series of rising 'ahems' became even more exaggerated than usual. As he rose to begin his questioning, he struggled with a particularly obstinate 'ahem' that seemed to be lodged even more deeply in his imagination than his throat. For a full minute, the court was treated to sounds rather like that of a car on a cold winter's morning that struggles to start when the ignition key is turned.

Eventually he began, 'Are you a victim, Mr Guppy?'

'It depends what you mean by victim,' I replied.

'Are you a victim of a police conspiracy?' he asked. 'Is it your suggestion that the police officers in this case went to any lengths simply to convict you? Are you suggesting that they are corrupt?'

'I suppose it depends on what you consider to be corruption,' I answered. 'If you mean that the police have resorted to bending the rules and on occasion even breaking them, then the answer is yes.'

'I see,' he said and cleared his throat again. 'Ahem. And why do you think the police have pursued you with such vigour?'

'Because we refused to yield to them,' I answered. 'And if I was given the chance to prove the police's corruption ...'

'It is not for you to prove anything, let alone your innocence,' Curtis interrupted with the *gravitas* of Cato the elder rallying the Roman Senate before the destruction of Carthage. 'It is for us, the prosecution, to prove your guilt. No! no! no!' he cried, his voice rising, his chest inflating, his chin jutting towards the ceiling, his 'ahems' instantly cured. 'It must never be said that you have come here to prove your innocence. The law presumes your innocence. It is for the jury to decide; it is for them to convict you or acquit you on behalf of civilised society.'

Expecting a spontaneous explosion of applause and forgetting for a brief instant that he was not at the London Palladium, Curtis appeared visibly disappointed when none materialised, but he was soon recompensed by one or two admiring glances from members of the Press.

In fact, I rather enjoyed my five days of cross-examination by James Curtis and no doubt he did as well. Sometimes he came very close to catching me out and then, inexplicably, would change the direction of his line of questioning, letting me off the hook. But I never became complacent, for I respected the fact that this man was a highly experienced barrister.

After finishing my evidence, one day as I was standing outside the courtroom waiting to go back in after a lunch break, I overheard a solicitor who was acting for Lloyds and a journalist, who I had not seen before, discussing the case and, in particular, my role in the whole affair.

'He could have had such a brilliant career,' one of them remarked in a deliberately loud voice intending that I should hear him.

'He might even have been knighted one day,' added the other.

I smiled to myself, amused at their acceptance of the clichés that they had so obviously read about me in the Press.

It brought to mind a remark that Napoleon Bonaparte had made when handing out 'Légion d'honneur' medals to a group of veterans of his campaigns.

One of his aides had whispered to him, 'But Sire, these medals are mere baubles!'

To which Napoleon had replied, 'Yes, but it is with baubles that men are ruled.'

From the moment Ben began his cross-examination evidence, he ran rings round James Curtis.

At first Curtis attempted, as he had done with me, to cast Ben in the role of self-appointed victim.

'Why do you think these people have come to testify against you?' he asked.

'I'll tell you why,' Ben replied. 'Every single witness you've produced is totally dodgy and has got something to lose by not testifying against us and a lot to gain by doing so. You've not produced one witness of any importance who this does not apply to. Dutta is in trouble with the authorities in India; he's living here with a false passport and the police have used every trick to intimidate him into giving evidence.

'Risdon is as bent as they come and you know it! He was caught red-handed, taking a diamond out of a bank with a false passport and you're trying to claim that this was some sort of a coincidence and that his evidence against us was inspired by a sense of civic responsibility.'

Ben paused, then added, 'Come on, Mr Curtis, pull the other one.'

The more Ben argued, the more Curtis responded in incomprehensible Latin expressions.

At one point, Ben almost yelled at Curtis, 'Listen, Mr Curtis. The so-called unbiased police even offered me a deal to betray my friend.'

Pointing at D/C Ellis, he continued, 'That man gave me his personal pager number after I was given bail at Redbridge Magistrates' Court and told me that I was a "better sort" than Darius and that if I contacted him on the side he would see that I was looked after. But I didn't accept his offer.' He paused before resuming. 'So don't forget, I could be out of this! I could be sitting on some beach in Australia, like Risdon!'

At which, Judge Brooks, who had been writing out his notes, looked up and said, 'Be quiet, Mr Marsh! We're not interested in what you've got to say! Just answer the questions!'

But every time Curtis tried to ensnare Ben, he came off the worse for the confrontation and very soon seemed lost for words.

So, by the end of his cross-examination, he resorted to the one line of attack left open to him — the appeal to prejudice, emphasising that Ben and I were two privileged, well-educated and wealthy young men.

Ben's father, Peter Marsh, had once given his son a new Jaguar as a birthday present a few years before. Curtis sought to capitalise on this totally innocuous fact.

'So, Mr Marsh,' he said, 'when you arrived at your offices that day you were driving your Jaguar, eh?'

'Yes,' Ben replied. 'So what?'

'A Jaguar, eh? I see.' He paused. 'A Jaguar,' he whispered loudly. 'Ah.'

During one of the breaks towards the end of the trial, a reporter approached me and introduced himself, saying that he was from the *Daily Mirror*. He asked for an exclusive interview using a standard expression that, by now, I was very accustomed to and had come to realise was the signal for an intended character assassination: 'I promise you, Mr Guppy, the article will be very sympathetic.'

I told the man, 'Do I look stupid? Is that the problem? I've been following your newspaper's coverage of this trial. Now, every time the prosecution have seemingly scored a point, your newspaper has made a big song and dance about it. However, not one telling point that the defence has made has been reported by you, unless I've missed something. So, if you're willing to redress some of the balance then we'll see. Otherwise, please don't bother to ask me again.'

I never heard from the reporter again.

In his summing up, Curtis began, 'Ladies and gentlemen of the jury, you have seen two very strong men in the witness box. I was surprised by their performances, which were really very impressive. I don't know about you but I was also surprised by the fact that Guppy appeared the more artistic of the two and Marsh the more aggressive.'

Ben, a little miffed, turned to me in the dock: 'I always thought I was rather artistic. From now on, I shall have to turn up to court in my toga.'

Curtis continued by praising, as he put it, our remarkable attention to detail in carrying out the crime. 'I put it to you that their clear mastery of the tiniest details in this case suggests that these two defendants are men of exceptional cunning.' He continued, 'It might be very tempting for you to think, well so what? It's only an insurance company. But you must not be persuaded by such an argument. A civilised society has its laws and it is your duty, members of the jury, if you consider these two young men to have broken those laws, to return a verdict of guilty. What happens thereafter is the court's concern and not yours.'

One by one Curtis produced more than a dozen points that, he maintained, could be construed as proving our guilt beyond any reasonable doubt.

For the defence, Tim Langdale began his address by telling the jury, 'This is a most extraordinary case. It is extraordinary if the prosecution's allegations are true and it is extraordinary even if they are not.'

Langdale also dealt with the twelve or more points that Curtis had suggested proved our guilt and one by one dismantled them.

At the end of both speeches, Ben and I believed that there was every chance of the jury acquitting us. Tim Langdale's speech had gone very well it seemed and we had noticed that a number of the jury had taken copious notes during it, something they had not done when Curtis had spoken. For the first time in weeks we dared to hope.

It even seemed that the prosecution were feeling the same way as us.

In particular, after Tim Langdale had finished his address to the jury and we had adjourned for a lunch break, D/C Ellis, instead of engaging in the friendly banter that had become almost habitual between us during the three month trial, stormed past us with an expression of fury on his face. When I asked him, 'What's up, Mick?' He replied, 'I'm sick of you two; I thought you were men of honour!'

While we had lunch in the Court canteen on the ground floor, one of the Snaresbrook regulars, a short, elderly woman with glasses who had turned up to our trial every day, approached me as I sat eating a sandwich at one of the tables.

'Mr Guppy, I thought you might like to know,' she told me. 'I couldn't help overhearing some of the police officers talking in the corridor. They're convinced you're going to get off. Your chap, Mr Langdale, I think he did awfully well.'

'Thank you very much,' I replied.

'I hope you don't mind my saying so,' she continued, having by now joined me at my table and, looking over her shoulder from time to time, 'but I think those police officers in your case look simply dreadful. It must be so unpleasant for you having to deal with them.'

'Some of them are all right,' I said, wanting to change the subject.

'Listen, Darius. You don't mind if I call you that, do you? I want you to know that whatever happens, society will not reject you. I mean, these things are terribly important, aren't they? It's not as if you've murdered anyone, after all. In fact, if you go to prison, when you get out you and your friend, Marsh, will be *lions de salon*.' The woman looked at me.

'It's very reassuring to know that our status in society is guaranteed,' I remarked. 'So thank you for your kind words, but I can assure you that whatever the verdict, polite society will hold as little interest for me as it has ever done. And now, if you'll excuse me,' I added, getting up to leave, 'I think we have to get back to Court.'

Before Judge Brooks began his summing up, I noticed that the tape recorder, which had been running throughout our trial, was switched off. Instead, exclusive use would be made of the Court stenographer.

Judge Brooks' summing up lasted a little over one day and in that time, the record showed, he outlined the prosecution case in just over 22,000 words. He dealt with my defence in just one thousand words and Ben's defence in about the same.

He advised the jury, 'I say in this case, in broad terms: keep your eye on the ball and the ball in this case, members of the jury, is the money. Keep your eyes on the money and see where the money goes. You may find that will help you in reaching a proper verdict.'

He went on, 'The prosecution allege that these two defendants pocketed, if I may use that word, all the money or certainly part of the money as represented on invoices relating to gem deals amounting to approximately £2.75 million.'

He continued, 'Before you can convict you must be sure that these two defendants agreed with each other to commit the crime in question. It follows that you can either convict both of them, or acquit both. What you cannot do is convict one and acquit the other. You have to convict both or acquit both.'

Judge Brooks also dealt with Risdon's credibility and in essence steered the jury to accept his evidence as truthful. 'Risdon's credibility in this case is, you may think, crucial when you come to consider his testimony, namely if he was telling the truth or lying about the fake robbery, because the defence say that he has made up the story completely.'

He went on, 'Perhaps this piece of evidence will assist you — it is a matter entirely for you. I do not know, but if Risdon was and is lying, why did he say to Mr Langdale, "Yes, I was planning to sell the story to the newspapers"? He could have just said, "I haven't even contemplated the idea of selling my story to the newspapers," and left it at that.'

When Brooks finally invited the jury to retire and consider their verdict, any mild feelings of confidence we had felt after the defence's speeches had completely vanished and our mood hit rock-bottom. We knew we were doomed.

D/C Ellis, an excellent barometer for how the trial was progressing, had forgotten any feelings of antipathy that he had shown us only the day before.

Outside the courtroom, he sidled up to us and chanted, 'Seven years, lads, seven years.'

As the jury filed past us to consider their verdict, one of the young male jurors winked at me and gave the 'thumbs up' sign, as if to indicate that he was on our side and that we should not worry. This gave me a little hope.

By the end of two days' deliberation, the jury still had not reached a verdict. On my way home that evening, I stopped off as I had done on many occasions in the past three months at a flower seller to buy a bunch of roses for Patricia. Somehow, something compelled me to buy a whole basketful that day. That evening, I did not feel like eating, nor did Patricia, but I forced her to for the sake of the baby and we went to bed early.

The following morning, Saturday, 13 February, I was convinced when I awoke that I would not be returning home that evening. With each day that had passed, our lawyers had become a little more optimistic as the delay in reaching a verdict was a clear indication of indecision among the members of the jury, something that should have boded well for us. But my premonition that morning was so powerful that I packed my bags for prison, which I had not done the previous two days. I hugged Patricia with all my strength, without telling her what I was feeling, except that I loved her.

Outside the Court building, teams of Press reporters and camera crews waited expectantly for the verdict. One television station even gave hourly updates. I felt certain, as I drove into court, that they would not be disappointed that day.

Just before lunch, the jury returned to announce that they could not reach a unanimous verdict, whereupon Judge Brooks told them that he would accept a majority verdict.

At around three o'clock in the afternoon, Katrina, Ben's girlfriend, rushed into the coffee room where Ben and I were waiting. 'They're back, the jury's back,' she exclaimed. 'The usher told me they've reached a verdict!'

Patricia grabbed hold of me and I hugged her before walking into court. She told me: 'Don't worry. Whatever happens, it'll be all right. I love you and always will. Just be strong for both of us.'

As the jury returned, I scanned their faces to see if I could glean a clue about the verdict. Two of the younger women were in tears.

When the foreman of the jury stood up, and was asked for the verdict he replied in a low voice, 'Guilty'.

I looked immediately at Patricia. She was sobbing quietly, trying to retain her composure. For myself I felt not one iota of fear but for Patricia I was in turmoil, although I showed no emotion in the dock.

As soon as the foreman had pronounced the verdict, D/C Ellis, who was only a couple of yards away from where I was standing, jumped to his feet and punched the air exclaiming, 'Yeah! Yeah!' He turned to the other police officers, shaking some by the hand, patting others on the back.

There was pandemonium as Press men rushed outside with their portable phones to relay the verdict back to their editors while others jostled for the best position to accost Patricia and other family members when they would be ready to leave. Among the fifty or so reporters who had crowded into the small courtroom, a female journalist, who had attended the trial with almost obsessive regularity and that day had positioned herself near the dock, leaned forward, placing her face within inches of mine as she scribbled away in her notebook, desperately trying to detect some sign of emotion on my face.

'I won't give you the satisfaction,' I thought to myself, looking directly at Judge Brooks.

Brooks, looked at the jury and told them, 'Ladies and gentlemen of the jury; if it is any consolation, I would like you to know that you have come to exactly the right decision.'

Deferring sentencing for some weeks, he looked first at Patricia and then straight at Ben and me, and said, 'I want you to be in no doubt that you will be going to prison for a very long time.'

At that moment I saw Katrina jump from her seat and rush across to James Curtis, her face contorted with rage as she virtually assaulted him, wagging her finger in front of his face and shouting, 'You should be ashamed of yourself; you've sent two innocent men to jail!'

According to nearly every national newspaper I was supposed, at that moment, to have turned to my prison guard and said, 'Well, I suppose prison will be just like Eton.' Such a remark, as with so much one reads in the Press these days, was pure fiction.

The wooden door that led from the dock was opened and we walked into darkness. As we made our way along the maze of cold concrete and dimly lit corridors that led to the cells below, I commented to Ben, 'That was amazing acting on Katrina's part. She seemed genuinely to believe that we were innocent. Didn't you say anything to her?'

'Of course I didn't tell her point blank that we were guilty,' he replied. 'I assumed that like everyone else she would read between the lines and understand.'

He added, 'She seems to have been the only person in the entire country who thought we were innocent. If only she'd been on the jury!'

Darius' father, Nicholas, a guest on the Venezuelan ranch of billionaire Daniel K Ludwig, c. 1955.

Darius' mother, Shusha.

Top: Darius at Eton, aged thirteen.

Below: Family photograph, London, early 1970s. Left to right: Constantine, Shusha, Nicholas and Darius.

Darius' great-grandfather (right), a senior Iranian cleric, with his private secretary. Tehran, early 20th century.

Top: Darius' great aunt, Yseult Guppy, Port of Spain, Trinidad.

Below: Piedmont Cottage – Robert Guppy's home in San Fernando, Trinidad.

Darius with his philosopher grandfather, Tehran 1969.

Top: Tom McLaine, aged 53, with Samson, July 1991.

Below left: Darius at his Chelsea home at the height of his gold-smuggling operation. In the foreground, out of the sight of the camera, are aluminium crates packed with exhaust gas analysers and gold bars.

Below right: Darius in tails at a London Society ball.

Above: Darius, Patricia, Victoria and Charles Spencer and close friends at Darius' wedding day two weeks after his arrest, San Lorenzo restaurant, London, July 1991.

Right: Darius and Charles at Darius and Patricia's civil wedding ceremony, Chelsea Registry office, July 1991.

XVI

In the cells downstairs, we were greeted by a reception party of eight prison officers. In total silence, Ben and I emptied our pockets in turn and their various contents were then itemised on a property sheet, numbered and put into plastic bags that were subsequently sealed. It was all very clinical.

One of the officers, a rather pleasant-looking man of average height and with very short dark hair, broke the silence: 'All right, lads,' he said in a cockney accent, 'you're going to Brixton. Now listen to me; just keep your heads down, keep yourselves to yourselves, say nothing to anybody and remember this if you remember nothing else I'm telling you, give your home telephone numbers and addresses to no one.' He added, 'Brixton's rough but you'll survive. You'll probably be there a few months under observation before being transferred. OK?'

Ben and I nodded.

We were each handcuffed to a prison warder and marched out to an enclosed parking bay where we were told to climb into a minibus with large, clear windows, rather than the more usual type of prison van, or 'sweat box', with its tiny cubicles and blacked-out windows that is generally used to transport prisoners to and from court. As we drove out of the bay and wheeled round onto the gravel path that leads out of the Court's grounds and on to the main road, rows of photographers and television cameramen were waiting for us. It had all been perfectly stage-managed.

'Why aren't we in the usual type of prison van?' I asked the driver.

'They laid this van on especially,' he replied. 'They wanted the Press to get some good photos of you.'

A perceptive man, he added: 'I think it's what you call justice being seen to be done.'

It was night by the time we arrived at Brixton prison.

As soon as I walked into the dark, depressing, Victorian building, I was struck by an overwhelming feeling that I was underground. And, immediately, as my sense of hearing and of smell took over, I could tell that I would rely far less on my vision than in the outside world.

Brixton was a castle of jangling keys, steel doors clanking shut, swearing intermingled with the barking of orders from 'screws', and the smell of stale tobacco and disinfectant.

As we waited in the reception area, a young screw, who must have been no more than twenty-three, snapped: 'Are you Guppy and Marsh?'

'Yes,' I replied.

'Well, you won't be getting any fucking caviar in here! You may think you're toffs but in here we're the bosses so don't you fucking forget it.'

We made no reply.

'He obviously went to the same finishing school as Avery,' Ben whispered to me.

Having been ordered to strip, squat on a small wooden platform and hand over my clothes, I was given my prison number — NA0008. We were then weighed and led into a small, windowless holding cell, wearing nothing but short, purple-coloured towelling dressing-gowns.

Three hours later, we were still waiting.

Suddenly, Ben got up. 'Right, I've had enough. I don't think much of this place. I'm going home,' he said, as he rang the buzzer on the wall.

It seemed to do the trick, for after a couple of minutes the door swung open and we were taken in turn to see the prison doctor. As I walked into the room, a man at a desk looked up at me and said, sounding bored, 'Are you suicidal?'

'Not yet.'

'Next,' he said, scribbling on a piece of paper. I left the room.

I was marched by a couple of prison officers along several yellow brick corridors to the Clothing Exchange Store, which was run by a trusted prisoner.

'Hello, mate,' he greeted me. 'I know who you are; heard about you on the radio. 'Ere, you're a bit of a rough diamond, ain't you?' And he chuckled at his joke.

'Not really,' I replied, 'highly polished, but slightly flawed.'

He laughed aloud. 'Like it, like it.'

After being kitted out with a pair of jeans, a mauve sweatshirt, some underwear, a pair of black plastic shoes, a toothbrush and a set of plastic cutlery, Ben and I were led to yet another holding cell.

One hour later we were marched across an open courtyard to 'G' wing. News of our arrival had obviously travelled fast, for we were greeted with cries from the tiny cell windows that echoed in the night air: 'Oi! Guppy, mate! Nice one! Don't give 'em the fucking money back!' and ' 'Ere! Lend us a tenner! Ha ha ha!'

The yard was covered with litter, principally old milk cartons and slices of stale bread, and white pigeon droppings decorated the depressing dark-brown brick walls. Overhead was a criss-cross of wires with fluorescent orange balls spaced out at regular intervals, designed to prevent prisoners escaping by helicopter during their exercise breaks. Teams of guards patrolled along the yard's fence with their Alsatians.

I looked at my watch. Six hours ago, I had been a free man.

In 'G' wing, a tough, well-built screw with grey hair in his mid-forties was waiting for us on the ground floor.

'All right, Guppy and Marsh! Your cell's on the "threes". This is the "ones", the first floor's the "twos", the floor above that's the "threes", where you are. Got that? You'll be banged up now 'til 7.30. Then it's slop out. Breakfast at 7.45. Applications to the office on your landing 8.00 to 8.15. Got that? Bang up 8.15 'til 10.00. 10 o'clock, exercise for one hour. Got that? Lunch, 12.00 to 12.30. Bang up 12.30 to 4.00. Tea 4.00 to 4.30. Got that? Then bang up 'til the following morning. On the "threes" there's one hour's association Mondays and Thursdays, 4.30 to 5.30. Got that? You're on your own.'

Our cell was originally built for one man but had held up to four prisoners at a time until very recently. It was equipped with two bunks, a blue formica table, a wooden chair and a plastic bucket in the corner with a couple of inches of disinfectant in the bottom of it.

On the walls were various graffiti scrawlings. Written in black above the door were the words 'Pain has no memory'.

The door slammed behind us and a few minutes later the lights went out and I was lying on the top bunk bed. The first few hours in a prison cell are a test for any man and, although Ben was with me on the bunk below mine, we lay in silence, alone with nothing but our spirits. Through the small barred window above my head I could see the moon and the lights of Brixton. Only a hundred or so yards away people were walking along the streets, some happy, some sad, but all of them free. I drifted in and out of sleep, my thoughts always returning to Patricia.

At 7.30 the following morning, the door opened and I jumped up from bed, put my clothes on and went out on to the landing. I quickly learned the definition of prison life, a queue; a queue to brush your teeth, to 'slop out', to make an application, to see the doctor, a queue for every meal.

Downstairs, on the ground floor, Ben and I waited in line for breakfast. I had already had a taste of prison food during the twenty-four hours that I had spent in Wormwood Scrubs waiting to raise my bail sureties, so I knew what to expect, but I suspected it would be a shock for Ben.

As new arrivals with some celebrity status, we realised that all eyes were on us.

As Ben collected his food from the hot plate — porridge, heated tinned tomatoes and flaccid toast — he looked at it, sniffed it and remarked in a loud voice, 'This must be illegal. I mean this food simply has to be against the European Convention of Human Rights.'

The prisoner who was serving the meal, a Cockney of about twenty-five called Colin, immediately cracked up laughing. 'He's priceless, he is! The geezer thinks the food's illegal!'

'This is good, this is,' he added. 'You should've seen it a few months ago, mate.' Nudging the rather overweight screw who was standing next to him behind the hot-plate, he told him, ''Ere, he don't think much of your grub.'

The officer, wearing a dirty white hat and apron, failed to

appreciate the joke and protested, 'But I cooked that myself.'

Colin rolled his eyes in disbelief. 'Don't worry about him, mate,' he told Ben. 'He's not all there. Kick him in the balls and you might agitate his brain cell.'

Ben then asked the officer whether there was any sugar to sprinkle on his very runny porridge, but his enquiry was greeted with a vapid stare. Colin, who had not stopped laughing, chipped in, 'Gawd all mighty! You might as well ask him for his wife and a loan on top of that! You're priceless, you really are!'

A few minutes later, as we picked our way through our breakfast in our cell, the door swung open and Colin popped in and took two boiled eggs from under his tunic. ''Ere you are; I thought you'd better 'ave something to eat; I nicked 'em from the kitchen. Anything else you want, butter, milk, cheese, you just let me know and I'll see what I can do.'

Over the next few days, Colin befriended us, supplying us with a steady stream of provisions from the kitchens and persuading the screws on duty to allow him to stay in our cell for chats over a cup of tea. He never asked for anything in return and was always optimistic, invariably seeing the amusing side of everything that happened in the prison. The more I got to know him, the more I admired his determination not to allow his terrible predicament to break him.

I soon discovered that Colin was on remand, facing a murder charge. One day, he asked me if I would look at his legal papers and give him some advice. I was happy to be able to do something for him and that night I read through his depositions. It transpired that Colin had gone to a barbecue almost a year before and a fight had broken out between him and a man who had been constantly persecuting him on the housing estate where he lived. Either he or this man, for there was conflicting evidence from the witnesses on the subject, had produced a penknife and Colin had ended up stabbing the man through the heart.

The harrowing witness statements described how the victim had been lying on the ground, blood bubbling from his chest and how they had seen the fear in his eyes as he realised he was dying. A girl at the party had tried desperately to stem the flow of blood, screaming at him not to lose consciousness, 'Don't die, you bastard, please don't die!'

The psychiatric and social enquiry reports on Colin made for painful reading. Colin had been brought up in abject poverty in the East End of London. He had never known his father and when still a child his mother had faced trial, at which she was acquitted, for murdering a man who had raped her. For weeks on end, Colin had gone to school without shoes and only tatty, second-hand clothes. He had survived on scraps of unhealthy food with hardly a square meal throughout his childhood.

Teased and bullied at school for being so poor he had played truant for most of his school days, running errands and trying to earn money for his mother and himself. Having already served a three-year sentence for another offence, now he faced the prospect of a life behind bars, never knowing the son his girlfriend had given birth to shortly after he had been locked up in prison awaiting trial.

I felt nothing but pity for both the victim and Colin. Two lives and the happiness of their loved ones had been destroyed for ever.

As a boy and then as a young man, unlike many of my contemporaries, I had always suspected that the clichés one heard about the tremendous social injustices that plague this country had more than a grain of truth in them. In this respect, my years in prison were to prove not so much a learning experience for me as a period in which long-held suspicions were confirmed. As I read Colin's depositions, I found myself despising even more than I already did the party-going Ascot and Henley set whose obliviousness to the misery of so many people around them was actually less obnoxious than their inability to even imagine it.

Having finished reading through his legal papers, it seemed to me that Colin stood a distinct possibility of being found guilty of manslaughter instead of murder, but three months later I would see him when he returned from his trial, facing a life sentence.

Even then, though, he refused to allow his spirit to be broken and all he could think of was his baby boy and his girlfriend and what would happen to them.

'I'm going to do my time, Darius,' he told me. 'I'm going to keep fit in the gym and go on education so that when I get out one day, my son's going to have one fit and strong dad and I'll be able to get a job and look after him. You'll see.'

During our first few days in Brixton, a number of friendly inmates would slip various newspaper articles that had been written about us under our cell door. Two days after our conviction, I was surprised to see reproduced in full in the *Daily Star* the letter that Charles Spencer had written to me inviting me for a weekend's shooting, and that the police had seized when they had searched my house at the time of my arrest.

Charlie eventually sued the *Daily Star*, successfully, for breach of copyright.

As I read the numerous pieces that had been written about us, I learned an important lesson — vindictiveness, which has come to be associated as a matter of course with so much of this country's media reporting, is perhaps less a hallmark of the Press than sheer incompetence.

Indeed, the majority of the articles were so exaggerated and so ludicrously inaccurate in even the most basic of details that, inadvertently, they provided the best form of entertainment for Ben and me as we awaited the date of our sentencing. Often, we would lie on our bunk beds reading them out loud to each other and laughing heartily.

We had already been informed by a *Today* journalist some time before that Risdon, whose anonymity as a police informer had been so thoughtfully protected by the court, had been touring the offices of the national newspapers in an effort to sell his story to the highest bidder, fabricating the most fantastical stories — even by the standards of certain of the more unscrupulous elements of the Press —in a bid to raise the price.

One story concerned an alleged plot of mine, apparently deadly serious, to hijack an oil tanker in the Persian Gulf and gift the oil contained therein to the Islamic Republic of Iran. In purchasing this story from Risdon, however, the newspaper concerned had failed to appreciate that the one commodity that Iran has precious little need of is oil!

Another allegation stated that I had planned to have the media mogul, Rupert Murdoch, assassinated. Apparently, the article continued, Mr Murdoch took this suggestion so seriously that, now that I had been jailed, he could once more sleep soundly at night!

On reading such stories it was difficult to decide whether it had been pure gullibility that had led the newspapers to part with their money when purchasing them from the likes of Risdon, or whether they had known that the allegations were untrue and, therefore, libellous, but had published them nevertheless.

Perhaps the most amusing story of all concerned a large black man's alleged interest in me. Supposedly, this man once offered me cornflakes at breakfast instead of the habitual porridge in return for sexual favours. This offer, the article continued, had caused such terror in me that I had fled to my cell and hidden there for several days, refusing even to have a shower in case the black man should try to force himself on me.

While Ben and I saw the funny side of this story and actually cut it out of the newspaper and stuck it on to the wall of our cell, there was one person who flew into a rage over it.

'Woody', as he was called — a cheerful West Indian, personal fitness instructor whose leanings were of a distinctly heterosexual variety — took great exception to this story, being the only black man on the landing and, therefore, the only person to whom it could have referred.

At first, an incensed Woody threatened to burn down the newspaper's offices as soon as he was released from prison, but eventually he, too, along with the other inmates and several screws, would laugh each morning as I paraded for breakfast and asked him if he had any cornflakes on offer!

But while it was a combination of vindictiveness and ignorance that led to the manufacture of such falsehoods, it was sheer laziness that led to their repetition. It soon became clear that, after the original spate of reports that followed our conviction had passed, a pattern was developing in which those journalists who sought to write second or third generation articles would simply consult old, erroneous Press clippings, without bothering to check their validity, and would repeat the inaccuracies contained in them, having juggled around a few paragraphs on their word-processors.

In this way falsehoods become myths and myths acquire the status of truth.

While the consequences of such a process were insignificant as far as my own fifteen minutes of fame were concerned, my experience made me appreciate just how dangerous such practices could be when it comes to genuinely important issues.

Another myth that seemed to circulate in most of the Press reports concerning our case was that Ben and I had boasted to our friends of our 'perfect' crime and that this fatal act of arrogance had been one of the principal factors that had led to our eventual conviction. In fact, Ben and I had made it a cardinal rule from the outset never to talk about what had happened in New York. It had been for precisely this reason that, despite two years of tapping our telephones, putting pressure on potential witnesses, hiding tape recorders on accomplices in an effort to entrap us, and keeping us under constant surveillance, the police had never been able to find one single witness, apart from our co-conspirators Risdon and Dutta, to confirm that we had ever admitted to having committed any crime, let alone 'the perfect crime'.

The reality is that since our families and our close friends had refused to talk to the Press, despite all manner of financial inducement, the newspapers, so desperate had they become to write about our story, had had to rely on their imagination instead of the facts. In this way Old Etonians, such as myself, sat around in their offices all day wearing fancy waistcoats and sipping champagne and were the sort of people who played chess in the dock when facing criminal charges; people educated at Oxford were 'upper crust' and 'arrogant' and spent their lives womanising, and so on and so forth. In the end, such clichéd notions revealed far more about the second-rate minds of those who penned them than they did about Ben or me.

In particular, though, it was the moral lecturing on the part of certain of these newspapers that was so sickening for, while they accused me of arrogance, principally because they interpreted a desire for privacy and a distaste for their methods as 'arrogant', these very newspapers daily treat their readers as imbeciles who will only be satisfied with a diet of lies and trivia. Their justification for this is that they are only giving their readership 'what they want'. Such an attitude, it seems to me, is the ultimate arrogance.

While I was able to treat the majority of the articles that were written about my case with a degree of humour, one particular variety of report did not amuse me. Before I was sent to prison I had ensured that, in the event of my conviction, Patricia would be looked after. In this regard, Charlie had been particularly generous with his offer to put her up in one of his estate's houses. I had, however, always had a nagging doubt that the Press might harass her. However, I had assumed that there was a certain line that even they would draw. In such an estimation, I was too generous. For, from the moment of my conviction, a number of the papers that had managed to obtain private photographs of her — for example, when she had been topless on a beach during a holiday as a teenager — reproduced these photographs in various 'splashes' on their front pages and subjected her to a barrage of harassment.

The articles written about her also revealed the latent snobbery and obsession with class of those who had penned them, almost invariably portraying Patricia as some sort of Elisa Doolittle figure who had been thrown into the world of the privileged and had found herself out of her depth. One journalist even expressed surprise that I had not married some Duke's daughter.

Picking on an innocent, pregnant woman in this way, whose husband had just been sent to jail and was, therefore, unable to defend her, shocked even some of the most hardened criminals in one of England's toughest jails. It seemed that these men had a keener moral sense than many of the newspapers that delight in lecturing their readers on issues of morality.

After two weeks, Patricia came to visit. Although seven months pregnant, she looked relaxed, pale and beautiful, but I could tell that she was trying to remain cheerful despite her feelings of loneliness. After the visit, in which I held her hand throughout and reassured her that I was coping fine, I kissed her goodbye and, as I did so, felt a surge of determination to complete my sentence, get out of prison and look after her and our unborn child. I looked across at Ben who had been chatting with his girlfriend, Katrina. He was clearly upset.

As I left the visiting hall I was told to stand on a wooden block to be searched. After frisking me in the routine way, the young officer said quietly to me, 'Don't worry, mate, your missus looks fine.'

He tapped me on the shoulder indicating for me to leave. 'He's clean,' he said to the other screw on duty.

'Guppy!' this second officer barked. 'Not so fast; strip-search for you.' And he subjected me to a full strip-search. As I undressed, he said, 'You're going down for a long stretch; you're going to get ten years. Just think, by the time you get out, you'll be able to start paying your child's university fees.'

Seeing the anger on my face, the first officer came up to me and, when his colleague had turned away, gently whispered, 'Hold it down, Guppy. Don't do anything stupid; ignore him. He's just like that. You'll be all right.'

I was more concerned with Ben than myself. That night, Ben recounted to me how Katrina had ended their relationship during his visit. She had told him that she felt let down because he had not confided in her the truth about the events in New York. Even if he had wanted to protect her and had assumed that she would be able to work out the truth for herself, she still felt a fool.

It was very sad for me to see Ben suffering from such a cruel blow and I realised just how lucky I was to have Patricia.

Many friends wrote to me in jail, some from my days at Eton and Oxford, including my old porters at Magdalen, wishing me the best of luck. In fact, during my first three months in prison I received more than a thousand letters of support from strangers — men and women, young and old, who wrote to me from all over Britain, and even from places like Canada, Zimbabwe and Nepal. Indeed, throughout my three years inside, I never received one hate letter.

I also received support and encouragement from another quarter.

While Brixton was a miserable place to live for most of the inmates, the various priests and nuns, such as Brother Philip, Father Carmelo and Sister Stephanie, the imam, Sheikh Jannah, and prison visitors such as Lady Giles, with whom I became friends, did their best to relieve a lot of that misery and devoted much of their time to showing genuine sympathy and understanding towards the prisoners. Some of them even telephoned Patricia from time to time to enquire how she was coping and to let her know that I was well. I hate to imagine what the prison would have been like without them.

After a few weeks, when Ben and I were still awaiting sentencing, we were suddenly moved to Pentonville for ten days before returning to Brixton. It was on our first day in Pentonville that Ben made his decision to plead guilty before the sentencing and to hand back his ill-gotten gains.

'What?' I shouted as soon as he told me. 'Ben, if you do this then my appeal will be totally stuffed!' I was furious.

'Darry,' he said, 'do you honestly think we stand a chance at appeal?'

He went on, 'Our barristers may think we have good grounds for an appeal but you know how the appeal judges hate to go against what their colleagues have done. No matter how biased Brooks may have been, or what tricks the police got up to, they'll find some way round it because they think we're guilty as hell and they'll use that infallible weapon of theirs, intellectual dishonesty, to justify their decision. Come on, Darry. You've seen the system. We don't have a prayer. Let's face it; we're perceived as part of the Establishment and if there's one thing the Establishment doesn't like it's to be made to look stupid, especially by its own. It's all about appearances. We've just got to be *seen* to grovel. Otherwise they'll throw the book at us.'

I let Ben continue.

'I don't know what you did with your money,' he said, 'so I can't harm you.'

For an hour we discussed the pros and cons of Ben's decision and my anger turned to resignation. I realised that if Ben pleaded guilty, I would have no choice but to follow suit. He would be grilled by the police for several days, who would be determined to wring every piece of information from him. It was also clear that following Ben's interviews, I would be made to undergo a similar process myself.

Towards the end of March 1993, Ben was taken to a secure unit at Woodford Green police station and spent five days providing D/I Avery and D/C Ellis with details of our bogus robbery from its planning stage to its execution. He also arranged for £540,000 to be returned to Lloyds of London.

As soon as Ben had completed his interviews with the police, I was taken in turn to Woodford Green police station. Understandably, Ben and I had not been allowed to see each other again before I was questioned.

As I walked into the interview suite at Woodford Green, D/I Avery stood up and shook me by the hand. 'Hello mate, how are you?'

He went on, 'Before we begin, Darius, I want you to know that it gives me no pleasure to see you in prison. We just want to sort out some details. As you know, Ben told us his version of what happened and we just want to make sure that your two stories tie up.'

He told me that they would begin the formal interview process with tape recorders the following morning.

Avery then left the room and I found myself alone with D/C Ellis.

'You know, Darius,' Ellis began, 'you might have fooled Lloyds and the New York police, but as soon as the South East Regional Crime Squad came on the scene the case was as good as solved.'

'Wait a minute, Mick,' I told him. 'While I'm sure you deserve to be congratulated on your deft detective work, there's no need to be so smug. Let's not forget that you happened, quite by chance, to bump into Risdon a year after the robbery. It was sheer luck for you and bad luck for us and it's got nothing to do with you being Sherlock Holmes.'

Ellis looked hurt. 'Maybe Risdon gave us a start, but it was our detective work that brought you two to justice.'

I made no reply.

He continued, 'At one point, you know, we really thought you had won that trial. Mind you, after the guilty verdict one of the male jurors came up to us and told us that he'd made up his mind you were guilty from the minute he saw you in the dock, before the trial had even started.'

'That's life, Mick,' I replied, eager to end the conversation.

The following morning, before switching on the tape recorder, D/C Ellis told me, 'Now, before we begin, Darius, you must know that you have to tell us everything. You cannot be seen to beat the system; you cannot be seen to have the last laugh.'

During the following few days I went through, in great detail, everything that had happened, from the initial idea of the sting, through to the planning stage, the bogus robbery itself and what we did afterwards. Understandably, the police were particularly interested to learn what had happened to the money after we had been paid out by Lloyds.

'As you know,' D/C Ellis began, 'we've had some success in freezing one or two of your accounts, but the trail has gone cold because it appears you withdrew all your funds in cash before we got to those accounts. We're especially keen to trace an account of yours called Selon International Rescue. Can you tell us where this account is located?'

'Selon International Rescue?' I asked, genuinely puzzled. 'I have no idea what you're talking about. Sounds like something out of *Thunderbirds*.'

D/C Ellis then handed me a wad of my bank statements that showed a number of transfers coming into my account from Geneva with the phrase *Selon Instructions Reçues* written at the bottom of the various transaction slips.

'Well, what's this then, Darius, eh?' he challenged me.

I replied, 'This, Mick, is French. It means "according to instructions received" and is the standard term that you will find included in virtually every single bank transfer that is recorded in the French language.'

Another officer who was present laughed. Ellis looked a little embarrassed.

'Well, how the fuck was I supposed to know?' he said. 'I didn't go to fucking Eton.'

D/I Avery then asked, 'Well, where's the money, Darius?'

I explained that a substantial part of the money had been spent in legal fees, various VAT reimbursements to the Customs & Excise and general living expenses and that all that remained was approximately £200,000 in cash, which I had handed over some time before to a trusted Middle-Eastern business associate for safe keeping.

D/I Avery and D/C Ellis, who it seemed clear did not believe my reply, tried various different ways to urge me to give them more details.

'I have nothing more to add,' I would repeat every time they attempted to draw me out on the matter. 'That's what happened. You asked what happened to the money and I've told you. There's nothing more to add.'

Later on in the interview I commented, 'One reason that I'm not prepared to give you any further details about third parties is because, with respect, there has been a considerable amount of indiscretion involved in this case. I don't want you harassing any innocent third parties or leaking stories about them to the Press.'

'Let me give you just one example,' I went on. 'That letter from Charles Spencer to me that you confiscated when you searched my home. Two days after our conviction, I see it reproduced in the *Daily Star*. Now, how do you explain that?'

Both officers looked very awkward. D/I Avery stammered a reply, 'We saw that letter, too, but I can assure you that it had nothing to do with us.'

I looked with scepticism at both of them.

'There have been certain people who have been indiscreet,' D/I Avery continued, 'I must admit.'

I said nothing more about the matter.

Throughout the four days that I spent at Woodford Green police station I gained a certain respect for D/I Avery. Although he was a strong, tough, even intimidating police officer, in many ways he was more direct than his colleague D/C Ellis who seemed insufferably smug.

One day, when the tape recorder was switched off, D/I Avery and I had a private chat. He told me that his favourite pastime was duck shooting at night and I explained how I used to enjoy the same sport in Scotland.

'Darius,' he said, 'just to be on your own crouching in the cold wind, watching the duck coming towards you at dusk and being at peace with the world; it's the best feeling of all.'

He paused, looked me in the eye and said with remarkable sincerity, 'Don't take all this personally, mate. All of it, the whole thing, it's just a game.'

Any feelings of animosity I had held towards the man vanished completely with the honesty of that remark and in that instant, I felt nothing but respect for him.

'What you must understand,' he went on, 'is that you had to get clobbered. I know there was a lot of pressure from above with Lloyds pulling strings with their mates in the Home Office. They needed to be seen to be doing something in a high-profile case like this. It's just your bad luck, mate.'

When I was taken back to Brixton my new cell mate was a fifty-year-old Cockney called Terry, who owned a scrap yard. Finding 'Darius' a bit of a mouthful, he decided to call me 'Del' instead.

The day before my sentencing Terry spoke to me in confidence. 'Listen Del. I'm going to tell you something that no one 'ere knows anything about because basically I think you're an all right geezer.

It's top secret, so remember to thank me when you get out and write your memoirs. Listen 'ere; what you've got to understand is that all them judges and all them police are Masons, the lot of 'em, I'm tellin' ya. Don't care what no one says, they're all bang at it, mate, believe me.'

Terry then put the index and second finger of his right hand together and wiped them a couple of times slowly and deliberately across his forehead. 'See that? That there is a secret sign from one Mason to another. It means "help me, I'm in distress." '

'Make sure,' he continued, 'that when you're in the dock you do it just like I've done it there, and make sure the judge sees you doin' it, all right? Then he'll know that like him you're a Mason and he'll 'ave to help you out otherwise he'll get into big trouble with his Lodge. He'll have no choice, I'm tellin' ya. I promise ya, it's guaranteed to work. 'Undred per cent. You'll get one or two years, top whack.' He then made me practise the gesture a few times to check that I was making the sign correctly.

The following morning at Snaresbrook Crown Court I decided to take Terry's advice, believing that at worse it could hardly harm my chances. As Judge Brooks took his seat on the bench and looked at us in the dock, twice I gave him Terry's secret Masonic sign, wiping my two fingers across my brow. During counsel's speeches in mitigation, I repeated the sign whenever Judge Brooks looked at me.

The entire court was crowded that day with members of the Press and Brooks had given them permission to sit in the jury's seats.

I nudged Ben and whispered, 'Look over at the jury's bench; that's a fitting metaphor if ever there was one for this charade — the Press as the jury.'

Throughout the hearing, Brooks seemed the epitome of the supreme Judge, the champion of the people, the defender of Justice, the hero of the popular Press, moody and magnificent — a bit like the Wizard of Oz.

In sentencing us, he said, 'This case has cost the taxpayer more than a million pounds.'

In fact, as the accounts would later show, the defence's proportion of the bill amounted to under 15 per cent of the total.

'Well, next time the police should travel on package tours for their investigations,' Ben remarked to me in the dock.

Brooks went on, 'It is not my practice to lecture defendants when sentencing and I am not going to depart from that practice in your case, suffice to say the offences were in my view extremely well-planned and very carefully executed. Offences committed upon insurance companies are extremely prevalent nowadays and I have a clear duty to protect such companies. Of late, insurance companies have sustained losses of millions of pounds through fraudulent activities by people like you. This has inevitably resulted in the insured having to pay considerably higher premiums.'

He added, 'In your case, Marsh, I am satisfied that you have gone all the way and admitted the whole lot and indeed identified the money and led the police to the money. In your case, Guppy, it is only partial.'

He then sentenced us to five years' imprisonment and imposed a fine of £539,000 each, in default of which we would have to serve an extra three years. What appeared a five-year sentence, therefore, amounted in reality to a 'global' term of eight years.

As the judge walked out of court, Patricia ran towards the dock. As I bent forward to kiss her one of the prison officers tried to hold me back and I kept him away as I snatched one final kiss before being taken below.

As Ben and I came back through the reception area into Brixton prison we bumped into my cell-mate, Terry.

'Well Del, how'd it go?' he asked enthusiastically.

When I told him the news he was clearly surprised. 'I can't understand it, Del; are you sure you gave the right sign?'

'Yes, of course I did,' I told him. 'I must have used it five or six times.'

'I can't think what went wrong,' he said, scratching his head. 'That judge of yours, must 'ave been in the wrong Lodge, mate. Oh well, bad luck.'

For a week or so, Ben and I were cell mates once again.

One day we were informed that we would both be transferred to Ford prison in West Sussex within a few days. However, forty-eight hours before we were due to leave Brixton, a senior officer came to my cell and announced that, while Ben's relocation to Ford would go ahead as planned, I would be sent to HMP Kirkham in

Lancashire instead.

'Why?' I protested.

The officer replied, 'The service has come under a lot of flak recently over high-profile prisoners, like the Guinness lot. As a result, certain politicians and ministers now interfere more than ever in the running of the prison service. There's nothing we can do about it. We hate it and so do the governors.'

'But why Kirkham?' I asked again. 'It's hundreds of miles away from my wife, who is heavily pregnant, and the rest of my family. I thought policy stated that prisoners should be located as near as possible to their families so that they can receive regular visits.'

'I know all that, Guppy, and I'm sorry,' he replied, 'but they're making an exception in your case. You've got no idea just how paranoid the politicians are about the prison service. They poke their noses in it all the time. If there's anything in the Press about a particular prison or inmate, those wimps in the Home Office panic and the shit hits the fan. The governor, us lot and you lot all have to suffer, I'm afraid.'

He went on, 'Off the record, I think you'll find they want to move you as far away from London as possible to keep you away from the Press. When it's all calmed down they'll probably move you down south again so you can be near your family.'

The day they came to take Ben away to Ford, I felt sad. From the very beginning the authorities had tried everything to destroy our friendship and, on occasions, it had almost worked.

At 6am the cell door opened. 'Marsh, pack your kit; you've got fifteen minutes.'

I made a couple of cups of tea and we toasted each other. 'Ben, whatever happens, we mustn't let the system beat us. There are people out there who would love us to end up enemies. We've had a lot of pressure and it would have broken most friendships but we've known each other since those days in the playground at the Lyceé and we must never let them win.'

'Darry, say no more. I'm with you all the way. In two or three years this will all be over and we'll look back and laugh. Listen, I love you like a brother. No regrets.'

It would be more than a year before I saw Ben again, in the cells below the Court of Appeal, and it would be almost three years before we would be able to sit down and have a good chat about all that we had been through.

Now I was on my own.

XVII

The visiting-room of HMP Kirkham, near Preston in Lancashire, was full that sunny afternoon in mid-May 1993 when I saw my daughter Isabella for the first time.

I was dressed in the standard prison uniform, consisting of blue jeans and a blue and white striped cotton shirt and was waiting at the table that had been allocated for my visit.

Patricia would be coming up by train from London. Isabella had been born about ten days earlier on 8 May. That day, I had been working in the kitchens and the Principal Officer had been kind enough to allow me to make telephone calls to Patricia at the hospital where she was in labour in order to check on her progress. Every half hour or so, I would go to the telephone boxes in the middle of the prison compound and obtain an up-to-date report from the midwife.

For some reason we had all been convinced that Patricia would give birth to a baby boy so when, at 2.40pm, the midwife told me: 'Congratulations, Mr Guppy, your wife has had a little girl,' I was a little surprised as well as being overjoyed because, although I would have been delighted whatever the sex of the child, secretly I had always yearned for a daughter.

Immediately I had informed the two inmates who had accompanied me and they had congratulated me and slapped me on the back. The midwife had then passed the phone on to Patricia who, although she had had an easy labour of only two hours' duration, was understandably exhausted as well as being immensely happy. She put the receiver next to the baby's face so that I could hear the sound of her breathing and at that instant I had relaxed for the first time that day.

'What does she look like?' I had asked Patricia.

'She's got masses of dark hair. She's got green eyes and olive skin and she's very much a little girl.'

We had both decided that in the event of our having a daughter we would call her 'Isabella', assuming of course that the name seemed to suit her.

'Does she look like an Isabella?' I had asked.

'Very much.'

The prison authorities had not allowed me a compassionate leave in order to be at Patricia's side, a privilege afforded to nearly all prisoners considered not to be dangerous to the public, on account of my so-called 'high profile'. In embarrassed terms, the Prison Governor had informed me that Prison Service Headquarters had vetoed my application for a Temporary Release licence for fear of possible media coverage — yet further evidence, as far as I was concerned, of the extent to which prison service policy was being dictated by considerations of public relations.

'Sorry, Guppy,' the Governor had informed me. 'If you were an ordinary prisoner, there'd be no problem at all, but my hands are tied. It's called "politics".'

'It's called pathetic,' I had replied.

When Patricia entered the visiting hall she looked more serene and beautiful than I had ever seen her. In her arms was a bundle wrapped in white. She walked over, kissed me and passed Isabella to me. I looked at my little girl, surprised at how tiny and light she seemed. Her eyes were closed and she was sleeping. I kept my head lowered, not wishing anyone to see the tears that had come to my eyes. An almost unbearable desire to break free welled up inside me, but I controlled my feelings and sat down.

For two hours, Patricia and I chatted while I held Isabella in my arms.

'Darling, promise me you'll never get used to this,' Patricia pleaded with me.

'How can you possibly think I would?' I asked her.

'It's a natural self-defence mechanism,' she answered, 'to ease the pain. Most people would get used to it sooner or later.'

'You don't understand, Patricia,' I said. 'I'll never get used to this because I'll never allow myself to, even if it means that each day goes by more slowly. You and Isabella are the most important things to me now and I'll not allow myself to forget it.'

When it was time to leave, I kissed them both goodbye and determined that I would do whatever I could to get transferred to a prison further south where it would be easier for Patricia and Isabella to visit. In the meantime, I counted the days until I would see my beautiful daughter again.

After a couple of months the transfer I had been seeking came through, in large part because the Press seemed to have forgotten about me and, as a result, the authorities had become a little less nervous. After travelling south via a number of prisons, including Liverpool and Wandsworth, I arrived at Standford Hill, a prison on the Isle of Sheppey in Kent.

It was at Standford Hill that I became deeply involved in the religion of my Persian forebears, Islam.

In prison, inmates usually move from one job to another every so often. After working on the farms for a few weeks, I was allocated a job tending the prison's gardens. One sunny August afternoon, quite by chance I was standing by a beautiful bed of flowers admiring some magnificent roses when I said out loud to myself: 'How can a man view such an object and not believe in God? He would have to be a fool.'

At that moment an inmate named Mohammad, a lawyer from Pakistan, happened to be walking by and he invited me to his cell for a cup of tea after work.

In his cell later that day, he told me: 'Darius, that remark you made next to the rosebush — you didn't know that anyone was near you. It proves to me that you have a love of God. I know a little about your case from what I have read in the papers and I believe that one side of your family is Muslim. What do you know about Islam?'

'I often used to go to Friday prayers at various mosques in London before I was sent to prison and, ever since I was a little boy, I have been fascinated by all religions,' I replied.

'Have you read the Koran?' he went on.

'Yes,' I replied, 'though only in the English translation.'

'And what did you think?'

'I thought it was sublime,' I answered.

271

'Then I will teach you to read it in Arabic, which is the only way to truly appreciate it. Then you will realise that it is sublime precisely because it is the very word of God.'

'Of that, already, I have no doubt.'

For the next few months Mohammad and I were inseparable. He became a great friend and remains one to this day. In the evenings, when work had finished, he would teach me to read the Koran in Arabic and after some practice I became reasonably proficient at it. I also read Martin Ling's excellent biography of the Holy Prophet of Islam and buried myself in a variety of Islamic works.

I had always had an open mind about all religions, which I had considered to be different ways of approaching the same issue, but the more I studied the more I came to appreciate the incredible purity of the religion of the Persian side of my family. Its tolerance and its emphasis on the complete equality of all mankind appealed to me immensely. Islam's portrayal at the hands of the Western media, I realised, had been a total misrepresentation borne of lack of understanding, fear and outright propaganda, the last of which made me wonder whether our so-called 'independent' Press really is as independent as it likes to boast.

Since the Revolution in Iran in 1979 and the Iran/Iraq war that had begun a year earlier, I had always been especially proud of the way the Iranian Muslims had conducted themselves. My sympathies had been entirely pro-revolution from the outset and while it saddened me to think that the beautiful country of my youth had been ravaged by a bitterly fought eight-year war, I was filled with pride by the exemplary bravery of the young Iranian Revolutionary soldiers who had simply refused to yield when so many of the Western powers had ganged up against their country by blockading it and giving almost limitless financial and military support to the Iraqi war machine. Nearly every observer had predicted the collapse of the revolutionary regime within months of Saddam Hussein's invasion of Iran and nearly every Western Government had conspired to achieve this goal, but the Islamic Republic of Iran had steadfastly defied such an onslaught. That indomitable spirit, that refusal to succumb to a much stronger, evil force, has manifested itself in the various wars that Mujaheddin (Muslim warriors) have fought in recent years and continue to fight today, in places such as Bosnia, Chechenya and Afghanistan.

272

Although I was unhappy at being separated from Patricia and Isabella, I was determined to make the best use of my time in prison. Ever since I was a young boy, I have always had a Spartan streak and so I found any physical discomforts the easiest aspect of prison life to cope with. Indeed, I thrived on the rather monastic existence. The routine, the chance to study, exercise and focus my mind in contemplation all appealed to me.

Also, throughout my three years in prison, I was given the opportunity of making friends with prisoners from all sorts of different backgrounds. Prison is a great leveller and while, as in the outside world, there were the occasional idiots who liked to made life difficult for those around them, I had little problem with the vast majority of those I came into contact with, whether they were West Indians, Cockneys, Scousers, Geordies, Asians or whatever.

At Standford Hill, apart from my religious studies, my other pastimes included teaching autistic children, who would come into the prison from outside to swim in the jail's swimming-pool, and working out and boxing in the gym, which I did with a group of black armed robbers and a 'lifer' who had been in custody for twenty-six years.

After a couple of months or so at Standford Hill, I was called up by the prison's Sentence Planning Officer. 'Sentence planning' is a system whereby prisoners set down various objectives that they wish to achieve during their sentences, whether in the field of education, of sport, employment in the prison, or whatever. A review of the inmate's progress is made by the Sentence Planning Officer every six months.

The Sentence Planning Office was a small, sparsely furnished room in one of the prison compound's many prefab huts. On one side of a formica-top desk sat the Sentence Planning Officer, a short, exceptionally thin, bespectacled woman in her mid-fifties. I was seated opposite her on a red plastic chair.

I couldn't help but notice that on the desk was an old paperback entitled *Elementary Psychoanalysis*.

The woman officer looked sternly at me.

'Are you learning about psychology, then?' I asked, in an attempt to break the ice.

'You could say that, Mr Guppy. In fact, although I say so myself, I've become something of an expert,' she replied. A slight smile had come to her narrow purple lips.

After running through a number of standard questions on the form in front of her, she came to a section entitled 'Offending Behaviour'.

'Ah, ha,' she said, ominously.

'Now, Mr Guppy,' she went on, 'I assume that you accept responsibility for the events that led to your conviction. Is that correct?'

'Yes,' I replied.

'Good. Because, clearly the prisoner's acceptance of his crime is a fundamental consideration when it comes to the Parole Board's assessment of his eligibility for early release.'

'I understand the logic of that,' I said, 'and I accept my guilt entirely, but do you mind if I ask you what would happen if someone was genuinely innocent of a crime of which he'd been convicted? I mean, statistically, there must be some innocent people in jail. What about them? Will their applications for parole be prejudiced unless they admit to having done something that they haven't done?'

The woman officer seemed uncomfortable at my line of questioning. 'A prisoner is expected to show ...' and she paused, looking for the right word, '... remorse.'

'If we're entirely honest, Miss,' I said, 'is it not the case that the showing of remorse is, in fact, far more important nowadays than the actual feeling of it? What you're basically saying, it seems to me, is that even if the prisoner is innocent or if he feels not an iota of regret, so long as he's clever enough to work out the answers you want to hear and you then put those answers into the appropriate boxes on that form, then even if those answers are a pack of lies, that'll be good enough for those who have to consider his release.'

The woman looked angrily at me: 'Mr Guppy! These forms have been designed by experts.'

'Now,' she continued, 'judging from your attitude, I think that an Offending Behaviour course may well be appropriate. Let me see ... we have an Anger Management course, a Stress Management course ...'

'Why do you think an Offending Behaviour course would be appropriate?' I enquired.

'Well, Mr Guppy. Your offending behaviour has been noted.' At this she drew out a dark blue file from her bag that was lying on the floor. She removed a page with some scribbles in red ink on it and looked at me over the frame of her spectacles. 'Take, for example, your use of phone cards.'

'My use of phone cards?' I asked, genuinely bemused.

'Yes, Mr Guppy. As you know, Standford Hill prison regulations permit the purchase of a maximum of ten phone cards weekly, per inmate. Now, the landing officers have been timing your telephone conversations and estimate that last week you must have spent at least fourteen cards' worth on your calls.'

'Perhaps I just borrowed four cards from some friends,' I explained.

There was a look of disapproval on her face followed by a beam of triumph. 'Are you not aware that the borrowing of phone cards is not permitted under prison regulations?'

For the first time in my prison sentence I experienced fear; not at the prospect of being caught for some minor offence but at the realisation that such people, people about whom I had only read in novels such as George Orwell's *1984, actually* existed. Worse still, such people had power over me. Was I dreaming this? Was this a human or a robot in front of me? What made her wake up in the morning? Was there any passion in her life? Did she have children? A husband? A lover, perhaps? Surely not, unless, O God no, it couldn't be — another Sentence Planning Officer.

'No, I didn't,' I replied, controlling myself.

'Well, I won't put it on your record on this occasion.'

I hated myself for feeling almost grateful for this clear sign of magnanimity.

'Yeeessss ...' she went on looking at another sheet of paper, 'I have just the course for you — a Money Management course.'

I wanted to laugh. An ex-investment banker on a Money Management course. Still, when I thought of it that way, perhaps she had a point.

Hoping to end the meeting on a good note, and not wishing to have a black mark put against my name on account of my independent thinking, I remembered how Winston Smith in Orwell's *1984* had eventually been made to love Big Brother despite all his initial defiance. Perhaps I should try accepting defeat in some way.

'Miss, I would like to make my position clear. I accept full responsibility for my actions,' I told her in automatic tones. 'What I did with the phone cards was an act of stupidity and wanton rebellion. I recognise the need to address my offending behaviour and, accordingly, am happy to attend the Money Management course that you have so thoughtfully recommended. I realise how insignificant I am next to the system and I am truly grateful for the opportunity that the prison service has given me to assess my whole life and to prioritise those things which are truly important to me.'

Incredibly, she replied, 'Very good, Mr Guppy. That's much better.'

I never heard from her again about the Money Management course.

*   *   *

In early September 1993, one of the Prison Governors, an exceptionally pleasant man called Mr Ashworth, asked to see me in his office.

'We've received these documents from Lloyds' lawyers, Clyde and Co. They're for you,' he told me.

As I read through the papers that had been served on Mr Ashworth, I became more and more incensed for it became clear that Mr David Reynolds, the solicitor acting for Lloyds, had obtained a warrant to search my wife's home and freeze her assets on the basis of representations that he had made to the Court. His affidavit, which he had presented to the High Court *ex parte* (without my wife's knowledge) and which had enabled him to obtain the necessary orders, stated, *inter alia*:

'It is equally clear that Mrs Guppy knows of, and holds some or all of those assets as nominee or as trustee for Mr Guppy' and that 'I verily believe that documents must exist at Mrs Guppy's address which will reveal the existence of assets and property which Mr and Mrs Guppy hold but which he has not disclosed.'

Reynolds' affidavit had gone on to ask that I be prevented from communicating with Patricia for a seven-day period allocated for her to provide an affidavit setting out her financial position, a request which was granted by the Court.

Over the next few days, as I spoke to Patricia and her lawyers, a picture began to emerge of what had happened.

Reynolds, aware that my appeal was approaching, seemed to me to be concerned that the fine that had originally been imposed by Judge Brooks against me might either be completely quashed at the Court of Appeal or else would remain as a fine and not be replaced by a compensation order. This latter scenario would mean that any ill-gotten gains that I then paid back would be returned to the State and not to Lloyds. In a bid to pre-empt such an eventuality, Reynolds seemed to have gambled on my having left details of secret accounts or business dealings lying around in Patricia's home, which would lead him to any hidden moneys and allow him to freeze them before my appeal. However, in order to justify obtaining an order to search Patricia's residence, Reynolds had had to swear an affidavit before the court giving very compelling reasons for the granting of such a Draconian order.

In his legal advice, Patricia's barrister summed up the veracity of Reynolds' affidavit: 'Mr Reynolds' affidavit, it seems to me, is capable of serious criticism.'

In particular, Reynolds' assertion that Patricia 'must' have been living off the proceeds of my crime was misleading, considering that he should have known all along of legitimately earned funds that were quite clearly her own and off which she had been living.

It seemed to me that some light was shed on the motives for his action against Patricia when I read copies of the minutes of various meetings which he had had with Patricia's solicitors after searching her house. In a meeting which took place in December 1993, he had expressed his concern that 'his clients were being made to look foolish'. 'For this,' Reynolds had continued, his clients would 'make life as difficult as they could,' and 'keep him inside for as long as possible.'

When it transpired, having searched Patricia's home and investigated her finances, that his allegations had been wholly without foundation and that no documents revealing hidden stashes of ill-gotten gains had been discovered, Reynolds agreed to discontinue his action against Patricia and even pay the bulk of her legal costs. Poor Patricia had been so traumatised by the false accusations and by the search of her house, which had extended to rummaging through Isabella's nappies, that she had even stopped lactating. She agreed to Reynolds' offer, wishing to put the whole matter behind her.

This single episode more than any other that had occurred since my arrest made me determined to frustrate Lloyds and their solicitors to the maximum extent.

As I made clear to my lawyers in a telephone call a few weeks after

Patricia's home had been searched:

'What I did may well have been wrong and I accept that, but to pick on a woman is not acceptable. I have met many very bad people in jail, but all know one golden rule — that you can do anything to a man, but you do not touch his family. Even if it costs me extra time, my policy as regards Lloyds will be one of total and utter non co-operation.'

My lawyer replied: 'This is a classic case of professionals not actually sitting down and doing the mathematics. They have actually spent far more than they could possibly hope to get out of you. The problem is that the more they struggle, the more they seem to add to their embarrassment.'

'It's little wonder these people have reduced so many of their "names" to virtual penury,' I commented.

A couple of months later, the number one Governor, Mr Twiner, summoned me to his offices and had me put in the prison's punishment block. After an hour, he came into my cell accompanied by a couple of officers and said: 'We have received information from the Passport Office that you have put in an application to renew your passport.'

'Yes, Governor. So what?' I responded.

'Well, we have fears that you may be planning to abscond.'

'That's ridiculous,' I protested. 'This is an open prison. I've had ample opportunity to abscond. Apart from anything else, it's not as if I'm called John Smith. I must have one of the most distinctive names in the country, perhaps unfortunately for me. If I was planning to escape do you really think I'd be so unsubtle as to do it in my own name by making an application to renew my passport through the Passport Office? With respect, there are about a hundred inmates in your prison who would be able to get me false documentation under a different name within twenty-four hours and for very little money.'

I continued: 'All you have to do is to check with my solicitors. They made the application on my behalf because lawyers acting for Lloyds confiscated my passport during a search of my wife's home a couple of months ago and, although they're supposed to have returned it ages ago, they've been messing us around, keeping hold of it for as long as possible, not returning my solicitors' calls, and so on. My lawyers simply decided to get a new passport on my behalf since Lloyds' lawyers were being so difficult.'

Mr Twiner, a weak-looking man of average height and thinning black hair, looked puzzled.

'Look, Mr Twiner,' I went on, 'it's very simple. My lawyers actually cleared all of this with the Prison Service before submitting the application. They even wrote to the Home Office informing them that we were making this application. Just phone my solicitors and ask them to fax through copies of all their correspondence to this effect.'

'We'll do that,' he replied, whereupon he left the cell accompanied by the two officers. The door clanged shut behind him.

Twenty-four hours later, Mr Twiner returned and informed me that, although he had received the faxes from my lawyers, he had no alternative but to transfer me to a closed prison.

'Why?' I protested. 'Have I committed any disciplinary offence?'

'No, you haven't,' he replied, 'and you're not being charged with one either.'

At this point he hesitated, and said, 'The decision is not mine.'

I later discovered that the Press had been camped outside the prison while all this was happening. The penny dropped. Of course! The inmates had obviously heard that I had been arrested and placed in the cells and one or more of them had tipped off the Press in return for £50. The Prison Service could not be seen to back down. If it was admitted that a mistake had been made in apprehending me without investigating facts, the Service would be made to look stupid in front of prisoners and, more importantly, in front of the Press.

'Let me get this right, Mr Twiner,' I said, by now feeling depressed and angry. 'Your employers are effectively going to punish me when I have done nothing wrong. I am not even being charged with an offence.'

I never saw the man again.

I was handcuffed and transported by four officers in a van to the high-security prison a couple of miles down the road from Standford Hill, HMP Elmley.

I felt particularly sad for Patricia as we would no longer be able to enjoy our six-hour family visits once a month, a privilege that is available to inmates of open prisons and that had become so important for us. I also knew that I would miss Mohammad.

Although Elmley was a closed prison and much tougher than

Standford Hill, in many respects it was actually a better prison; better organised and with better facilities. For the next five months I shared a cell with a marvellous character, Del Roy, or 'Lips' as he was better known, a black armed robber from Battersea. Lips was fit, strong, about my age, incredibly cheeky with the officers though at the same time popular with them, in short, a highly amusing and very charming man.

During the days I would study Farsi (the language of Iran), Islamic studies and computing and, when all the prisoners were locked up at 8pm, I would chat with Lips for a few hours, invariably laughing my head off at his various anecdotes.

One night, a couple of weeks after arriving at Elmley, when Lips was sitting on the edge of his bed rolling a cigarette, he explained to me that his 'trade' involved robbing drug dealers of their money.

I asked him: 'How often have you been arrested by armed police?'

Lips rolled his eyes heavenward at the sheer naïvety of such a question.

'Tcha! Thousands of times, man! What you talkin' 'bout? Fuck about! Thousands of times!'

He went on to explain: 'Oi, Gopi. On this sentence, right, I was walkin' down the street to my place in Brixton and I seez this red Vauxhall rush past me and turn and stop and I think — it's on top, man. Then, outta nowhere, I mean nowhere, theez guns are flashing all over the place. "Del Roy!" they yell and people's screamin' and runnin' everywhere. "Del Roy! Armed police!" I look around and they're all pointing guns at me, guns everywhere, man. And I've got a bag of shoppin' in my arms, for fuck's sake. I mean, I ain't goin' nowhere.

' "Put the bag down, keep your hands in the air and lie face down on the pavement!" So I do it. Then two of 'em come, one points his gun at me while the other searches me and I'm lookin' at 'em from the ground and then the geezer who's frisked me shouts to his mates: "He's clean!" And then all the guns go away and everyone relaxes. Know what I mean? I mean, what's happening, man?

'Anyway, they tie my hands behind my back with this plastic cord and they take me back home to search the premises and they miss my fuckin' revolver man. They couldn't organise a piss-up in a brewery, those wankers. I'd put it in the bin outside in the garden, but *everyone* keeps their guns in the bin outside, they should know that, and they missed it, man. Tcha! God smiled on me that day, man.'

At this point, Lips sprang up from his bed and did a hundred press-ups in one go. After he had finished, he banged a battery on the ceiling and called out of the window to the cell above him: 'Oi! Chewy! Any burn?'

''Ow much?' Chewy yelled back from above.

'Just enough for two cigarettes, man. And pass us four Rizlas while you're at it!'

Eventually, a plastic cup on the end of a line made out of cord from an old blanket was dangling out of the window from above and Lips retrieved the tobacco and cigarette papers from it before Chewy pulled it back up.

'Thanks, Chewy.'

As Lips rolled his cigarette, he noticed an old issue of *Hello!* magazine on my shelf. A picture of Patricia holding Isabella a few days after her birth was on the front cover and the magazine also contained an eight-page interview with her and me.

'Can I have a read?' he asked me.

'Sure,' I replied.

After looking at it he asked: 'Gopi, is this your wife? She's beautiful. Wicked.' A short while later, having read the whole article, he added, 'Tell her I don't even know her, man, but she's been loyal to you and I like that. Tell her I like her. Tell her: respect. Wicked.'

He then jumped up and did another hundred press-ups. By now we were both laughing so loudly, the rest of the wing could hear us.

'Gopi, man. You're a rude boy. D'ya know that? I mean, when I get out and all them people ask me, "Hey, what was it like sharing a cell with Gopi?" I'll tell 'em straight, 'cos I don't need all this bollocks yuppy talkin', I'll tell 'em straight: "Gopi's sweet, man, sweet. 'E's safe." You know, Gopi, you're a rebel, man. Some people here probably think you're posh because you went to Eton and that but I'm tellin' ya, you're a rude boy. Rude. You and me's goin' to run this gaff.'

The article in *Hello!* magazine that Lips had read had been the subject of a complaint made to the Press Complaints Commission.

The Commission had adjudicated against *Hello!* on the grounds that, in paying me for an interview, the magazine had breached clause 9 of the Commission's Code of Conduct concerning the payment of people convicted of criminal offences. An outcry had ensued in the national press in which various newspapers had expressed nothing but moral outrage at *Hello!*'s 'flagrant breach' of the Commission's Code. However, these same newspapers had somehow forgotten to mention that, almost without exception, they, too, had offered me and my family substantial sums of money in return for interviews. In fact, shortly after Isabella had been born, one of the large tabloids had even offered Patricia's brother, Tony, £10,000 in return for a photograph of Isabella. Needless to say, Tony, a manager of a small electrical company in the North East who could well have done with the money, declined the invitation to betray his sister.

In February 1994, Lips got into a fight with a young lifer who was serving food from the hot plate at lunch. After the situation had been defused, the lifer became angry with one of the officers, who pushed him. When he pushed the man back, the officer blew his whistle and nine other officers rushed to the scene while the alarms went off. What ensued came the closest to developing into a full-scale riot that I witnessed during my three years in jail. All the prisoners were locked behind the iron gates at the end of their various 'spurs', or landings, but they could still see what was happening through the gates' bars. About ten officers piled on top of the lifer who did his best to fend them off, fighting them with all his strength.

The watching prisoners, Lips and myself included, became incensed at the sight of the man being beaten up. I could see the fear in the officers' eyes as the inmates screamed abuse and started rattling the gates with such force that they threatened to come off their hinges. The noise was deafening but it was also exhilarating to witness human nature taking over and compelling these men to come to the aid of one of their comrades.

Eventually, the lifer was subdued and was led away in a headlock to the punishment block. Four other officers came to take Lips away to the 'block' as well.

Having seen how close the prison had come to mutiny, one of the Governors, a level-headed and tactful man, defused the situation entirely by avoiding handing out any punishment, either to Lips or the lifer, and allowing them both to return to the wing after they had cooled down a couple of hours later.

The Governors I met at Elmley were able to combine a sense of order and discipline with humanity. A number of them would joke with the men and walk round the wings at night having private chats with many of them. They seemed genuinely interested in the inmates' various problems, most of which involved their families, and showed compassion wherever possible while at the same time never giving the impression of being soft touches. I suspect that one of the reasons the men seemed to like and respect these Governors was that they were 'men's men', not bureaucrats in suits who had no idea about prisons or prisoners, but people who had worked their way up the system instead of simply being appointed from outside and who, above all, sympathised with the inmates as fellow human beings. One of them was a karate expert who refused to be accompanied on his rounds by any officers. He was capable of looking after himself and the men respected him for this.

With one of the Governors, in particular, I formed a good relationship. Every so often, he would call me into his offices for private chats and I admired his forthrightness and honesty.

One day, when we were talking, he said to me: 'You know, Darius, you and your co-defendant, you're like the Great Train Robbers in a way. You've embarrassed the system and you're being punished as much for what you represent as for what you actually did.'

'The Establishment has a very neat way of protecting itself,' he continued. 'You must have noticed it on the outside and I'm sure that in prison the same thing is true. Basically, in prison, we have absolute power over you. We can do what we want with you. OK, there are one or two complaints procedures but everyone knows that there's no such thing as objectivity when it comes to considering an inmate's complaints. Very rarely will the system side with the prisoner. It's the same throughout the country in all walks of life. The Press investigates complaints against the Press. The police investigate complaints against the police, the Medical Council against doctors, judges against judges, solicitors against solicitors, politicians against politicians.'

Since being transferred from Standford Hill I had been applying for a move to HMP Ford. The Governor now got round to the subject of my application: 'We all know you were angry over that passport incident but it's better for you not to complain. Let the dust settle and then you'll be rewarded. Don't buck the system. Let it save face and then, you'll see, you'll get your transfer.'

I was amazed that the Governor was so direct in expressing his views.

'Do you think prison works?' I asked.

The Governor laughed. 'Of course it doesn't bloody work, at least not the way it's run at the moment. No one in the prison service thinks that.'

A few weeks later, in March 1994, I was transferred to HMP Ford in West Sussex. Before leaving, I said goodbye to Lips and to various other friends I had made.

Lips shook me by the hand. 'Gopi, it's been good knowin' you. You make me laugh, man.'

'Likewise, Lips. It's been good to know you. Keep in touch,' I told him.

'You know, when I get out there, Gopi, I hope God gives me a break. Just one break, man. That's all I need,' he said, 'then I'll never come back to one of these shit holes again.'

Largely owing to the Press coverage of the Guinness defendants when they had been there, Ford, perhaps more than any other prison in the land, has acquired the reputation of being a holiday camp. In fact, there are many closed prisons that have far better facilities than open ones. Perhaps the single biggest benefit of being a prisoner in a jail like Ford is the joy of being able to see the sky above one rather than experiencing the constant sense of living underground that goes with residing in a high-security prison.

It has become the aim of certain tabloids, for some reason, to do away with open prisons. In every single one of them that I visited, because cameras could be smuggled in more easily than into closed prisons, the biggest racket among inmates was to negotiate with the Press a deal whereby they would obtain a story and photographs to illustrate in some way that the prison concerned was like a Butlins holiday camp. To this end, many a prisoner has posed for the tabloids with bottles of booze in their arms, joints dangling from their lips, and so on. In reality, all prisons are pretty grim and boring places and the greatest punishment comes not with the physical deprivations, but with being separated from one's family.

Shortly before my appeal in April 1994, Express Newspapers started a campaign to suggest that Charles Spencer had been involved in laundering the ill-gotten gains of the New York sting.

The suggestion was that, having been a Trustee of the Spencer Estate and a director of a number of Charlie's farming companies, I had somehow used these various companies as vehicles for syphoning off millions of pounds! These allegations were so absurd that, if they had not been so serious, Charlie would probably have laughed them off. What was immediately apparent, however, was that the *Express* had desperately wanted to believe that their allegations were true and that this desire had been based on pure malice.

Just as depressing as the realisation of the *Express'* malice was to understand the thought processes in the minds of those on the newspaper who had masterminded the campaign against Charlie.

Nearly every comment that I had read in the Press regarding Charlie's 'loyalty' to me had described such loyalty as 'extraordinary' or 'incredible', implying that, somehow, he should have been disloyal and dropped me as a friend once I was convicted. What a sad indictment it is of our times that qualities such as friendship and loyalty should be considered 'extraordinary' or 'incredible' instead of the norm. The *Express* could not conceive that perhaps, just perhaps, Charlie had been loyal for honourable reasons. To them, it simply had to be the case that he had been involved in my crime. Such an attitude in fact revealed a lot more about the *Express* than it did about either Charlie or me.

In the end the *Express'* ambitions for a sensational 'scoop' would backfire disastrously.

About a week before going to the Court of Appeal, I telephoned Charlie and asked him what he was going to do about the *Express'* libellous allegations.

'Darry,' he told me, 'Wormleighton and Nobottle farms must be the most boring companies in the whole of England. The idea that they're part of some money-laundering syndicate is laughable. But I'm not laughing. The Press in this country have done their best to ruin me and my family, printing lie upon lie about us and sooner or later they were going to go too far with me. Well, now it's happened. I'm minded to sue. What do you think?'

'Charlie, I'm glad you said that,' I replied, 'because not only do I think you should sue, I think you have a duty to do so. The Press in this country have become far too powerful, basically because our politicians are so terrified of them that they will allow them to run riot and ruin people's lives. The Tories are absolutely desperate to hang on to power and so will fawn like the spineless wimps they are before the media. People like you who are rich enough to do something about it, therefore, should do what they can.'

'You're absolutely right, Darry. At least I'm in a position to take them on. But can you imagine what it must be like for those who can't afford to do so?'

'That's precisely why you have a responsibility to stand up to these bullies, Charlie. In this country, 99 per cent of people are prohibited from doing so because of the massive expense involved in litigation against a newspaper. This effectively means that the papers can call the vast majority of this country's inhabitants child-molesting murderers and there is absolutely nothing they can do about it. The Press Complaints Commission is a toothless organisation as everyone knows, which is basically run by members of the Press — a classic example of that great British tradition of self-policing for purely cosmetic purposes. You must sue, Charlie. And I bet you'll win.'

'Darry, you'll see, I will sue and what's more I'll win.'

Charlie was right. Two years later, the *Express* would make a humiliating public apology in Court, pay Charlie £50,000 in damages and also pay the entire legal costs of the proceedings, amounting to several hundred thousand pounds.

My appeal took place at the Royal Courts of Justice on the Strand, London, on 28 April, 1994. Lord Justice Rose presided.

I was cross-examined for several hours in the witness box by James Curtis about my finances, a very unusual procedure during an appeal. At the end of the hearing, the judges quashed my original fine of £539,000 and replaced it with a Compensation Order payable to Lloyds to the sum £227,000, in default of which I was to serve an extra three years on top of my substantive five-year sentence.

Their Lordship's judgement stated that the figure of £227,000 was 'the only sum in relation to which there is evidence of availability to Guppy'.

'You were lucky, Darius,' my barrister Tim Langdale told me after the appeal. 'Despite whatever suspicions they may have had about your evidence, at least their Lordships were honest enough to concede that there was no evidence against you. It could so easily have gone the other way. Often judges can and will apply intellectual dishonesty to justify the judgement they give, whatever the evidence. You've had a result.'

While I was pleased with the outcome, I was still furious about what Lloyds' lawyers had done to Patricia.

Many people would argue that I am in no position to feel aggrieved by the action of Lloyds' lawyers. But, as I have explained, to attack an innocent woman with a tiny baby who is highly vulnerable and whose husband is in jail and, therefore, unable to protect her, simply to 'get at' her husband is unacceptable. I was determined to make Reynolds pay for his behaviour in the only way I could — by adopting a policy of total non co-operation, even if this meant I had to spend longer in jail.

Over the next six months, while at HMP Ford, I worked on the farms during the day and continued my religious and other studies as well as my physical training with a number of fellow inmates in my spare time.

In October 1994, almost two years after my trial had begun, I enjoyed my first home leave with Patricia and Isabella. It lasted three days and I spent it at the Garden House on the Althorp Estate, a beautiful small Georgian house where Charlie's sister and brother-in-law Jane and Robert Fellowes had once lived. From the day I had been convicted, Charlie had offered to ensure that Patricia and Isabella would have somewhere to live in private and I was truly grateful for this mark of his friendship. Although at first, I had been concerned about the prospect of Patricia living alone in such an isolated spot, within a week of her moving there I could tell that she loved the country life far more than living in London. It soon became clear that her taking up of Charlie's offer had been one of the best decisions of her life.

Those three days were magical. Isabella was now eighteen months old. Patricia had brought her up to know about me, even though she had rarely seen me, by constantly showing her photographs of me and making her listen to my voice on the end of the telephone whenever I called from prison. As soon as I walked through the front door, she threw herself into my arms and giggled. It was wonderful to get to know my beautiful daughter, to feed her, bathe her, play with her and do what most fathers take for granted. I was also very proud to see what an exceptional mother Patricia had turned out to be. During the day the three of us would go for walks in the Northamptonshire countryside and during the evenings, Patricia and I would sit by the log fire until late into the night and catch up on almost two years apart from each other.

When I returned to Ford after the home leave, a Governor called me into his office. I had applied for a 'town visit', a monthly six-hour family visit in the local town, which prisoners could choose to take on any day of the month. I was due to take my visit the following day and Patricia had driven me back to the prison and had booked a hotel for the night, because the visit had already been approved by the prison.

'I'm sorry to say this,' he informed me, 'but your town visit has been cancelled by Prison Service Headquarters.'

'For what reason?' I asked, perplexed.

'The official line is that you've just completed a home leave and so it would be inappropriate for you to have a town visit so soon after it.'

'But, Governor,' I protested, 'we both know that's not true. The prison rules state clearly that I can take my visit whenever I choose to. Certainly, that's the rule that applies to every other prisoner in the jail.'

'I understand, Darius,' he replied. 'And I don't like it any more than you do, but because of the Home Secretary's paranoia about the Press you've been branded a notorious prisoner and every single application you make has to be approved at the highest level.'

'How high?' I asked.

'As high as you can get,' he answered. 'I shouldn't be telling you this, but the decision is entirely political. Do a little digging and you'll find out for yourself.'

Patricia was naturally upset when I told her on the phone about what had happened and we resolved to get to the bottom of this interesting mystery.

I wrote to Mr Alan Rayfield, the Area Manager responsible for dealing with Ford, querying why my visit had been blocked.

He replied in writing: 'Your visit was postponed because you had just come back from home leave and there was not sufficient justification for you to need to see your family again so soon. Your visit was not cancelled, but merely delayed to take place after an appropriate interval.'

Refusing to let the matter lie, Patricia then visited my MP, Nicholas Scott (the member for Chelsea), whose secretary had seemed to recoil at the idea of me, a common prisoner, being seen to visit her master and had insisted that Patricia attend his offices on her own. Patricia left her eventual meeting with Mr Scott with a vague promise from him that he would enquire further into the matter.

Such enquiries elicited a written response from the Minister for Prisons, Mr Michael Forsyth, which reiterated the official line that had been adopted by Mr Rayfield.

Despite the responses given by Messrs Rayfield, Scott and Forsyth, a subsequent investigation by the Prison's Ombudsman, Sir Peter Woodhead, would reveal that the prison service had lied about the real reasons for blocking my visit.

When looking through my files at Prison Service Headquarters, the Ombudsman discovered a number of secret memos that showed clearly that my visit had been vetoed in order to save the Home Secretary's blushes, for the very week in which I had been scheduled to take my visit, Mr Howard had been due to deliver a speech on law and order at the Tory Party conference in nearby Bournemouth.

One of the memos discovered by the Ombudsman, written by Ms Philippa Drew, the Director of Custody, read: 'I said that there was no way Mr Guppy should be granted a town visit during the week of the Conservative Party conference as the resultant publicity would be damaging to the prison service and to Ministers.' In short, a photograph of me in a tabloid on a visit with my family would look bad for Mr Howard who was desperate to be seen as the apostle of law and order.

It goes without saying that I had had no intention of joining the party faithful in Bournemouth on the occasion of my town visit.

As a result of the Ombudsman's report, the then Director-General of the Prison Service, Mr Derek Lewis, was ordered to apologise to me, no doubt a little humiliating for him, although to this day I suspect the man really responsible to have been further up the ladder.

More importantly, for it would affect other prisoners, the Ombudsman's report into my complaint was to prompt a very sinister response from the Home Office, for, approximately a year later, the Home Secretary ruled that in the event of an investigation by the Prison's Ombudsman uncovering memos involving Ministers, such memos were not to be disclosed in future. In other words, had such a rule been in place at the time of my complaint, the Ombudsman would never have been able to disclose to me the real reasons for my visit having been blocked.

This, it seemed, was an example of the depth to which Mr Howard would sink in an effort to protect his reputation.

Now, while I accept that the example of the political machinations that I have just illustrated refers to a relatively trivial incident, it does make one wonder just what lengths certain people in positions of power will go to regarding matters that are not so trivial.

I also accept that England is one of the few countries in the world in which a prisoner with a complaint such as mine could have been able to uncover such machinations and to expose them in the Press. But this, of course, makes it doubly important to ensure that such protections of our civil liberties as we have should not be allowed to be eroded by those in positions of authority who would seek to abuse their power.

Many people, particularly in the media, have accused me of being anti-authority, largely on account of the defiance that I showed towards the police and Lloyds.

My answer to this criticism is that my record both during my school and university days and also during my time in prison shows that I have been willing to comply with authority where the people who hold it command my respect. For example, I had every respect for the vast majority of the Governors and officers I met during my three years in prison, for while of course there were exceptions, most of them were decent people simply doing their jobs who were quite happy to treat the prisoners in their custody as human beings. Such problems as I encountered during my time in prison were only with those above them who controlled the prison service at the very highest levels.

It has never been in my nature to take orders from people I do not respect, nor will such a thing ever come easily to me. How could I, or indeed any of my fellow prisoners, respect a system that so clearly has no interest in rehabilitating offenders and far less interest, it would seem, in protecting the public, than in protecting the reputations and positions of those who control it?

In January 1995, I left Ford to go to HMP Sudbury in Derbyshire, which was closer for Patricia and Isabella who were living on Charlie's estate in Northamptonshire to visit. Up until that time, Patricia had been required to drive a two-hundred-and-fifty mile round-trip to see me, which she had been happy to do on every single occasion that I had been due a visit.

There, as in the other prisons I had resided at, I formed a good relationship with most of the prisoners and staff. The attitude was very much that if the prisoners did their work properly and caused no trouble they would be left alone and allowed to get on with their lives.

I also got on well with the number one Governor, Mr Peter Salter.

Mr Salter was a Welshman, of average height with dark hair and a pleasant face, who was courteous to everyone. One day, in June 1995, a few days before I was due to be transferred to HMP Latchmere House in London, where Ben Marsh had been an inmate and where I would be allowed to work in the community for the last few months of my sentence, Mr Salter called me into his office.

'Bad news, Darius,' he informed me.

'Don't tell me, Governor,' I replied. 'The Head Office has blocked my transfer to Latchmere House on account of the article that appeared a few days ago in the *Express*.'

'You've guessed it.'

A few days earlier, the *Express* had published a short article about my prospective transfer to Latchmere House. I was to discover subsequently, from a contact on the *Express*, that the Home Office itself had deliberately leaked this story to the newspaper so that when an article appeared criticising my prospective transfer, the Prison Service would be given an excuse to veto it. In short, a photograph in a newspaper of me working in the community, even if I only had a few months left of my sentence to serve, would be embarrassing.

Mr Salter remarked: 'I'm sorry, but you've no idea just what pressure we Governors are being put under by Prison Service Headquarters and certain Ministers to toe the line. If we don't we've been told that we'll lose our jobs.' He went on: 'It's silly, but you've no idea how terrified they are about you in the Home Office.'

'Poor things,' I muttered.

Once again, I refused to be beaten and I asked the Prison's Ombudsman to investigate and once again he upheld my complaint.

His report, completed a few months later, stated: 'It cannot be just for prisoners to receive differential treatment — either positive or negative — according to their degree of notoriety. If a decision about a notorious prisoner is correct but would be unpopular, the Prison Service must be prepared to explain and defend it rather than change its mind for fear of the media reaction.'

In one respect, however, I was fortunate in not being transferred to Latchmere House for in late June a new inmate arrived at Sudbury named Abu Hamza, with whom I immediately struck up a strong friendship that continues to this day.

Abu Hamza was a tall, powerfully built Pakistani of eighteen stone who came from a poor background in Birmingham. He had been British Tae Kwon Do champion and had defrauded the DHSS of some £10,000, which he had subsequently donated to the orphans of Bosnia where he had also fought with the Mujaheddin against the Serbs.

Abu Hamza and I would train every day in the prison gym, after I had finished working in the prison workshops where I made industrial boots. Every morning, we would wake at 4am for morning prayers that we would attend with a group of fellow Muslims. I admired and respected these men enormously. I was truly impressed by their devotion and their puritanical streaks and would regularly spend hours in their company discussing religious topics.

In the summer of 1995 I was granted parole and was due to be released on 18 August. However, in July, Redbridge Magistrates' court, which had been responsible for enforcing the Compensation Order made against me by the Court of Appeal, had imposed on me an extra sentence of two years and nine months for non-payment. However, the Magistrates' order had made clear that as soon as I paid the compensation due to Lloyds, which was to be reduced by some £200 for everyday I spent in prison, I would be released.

I began this extra sentence on 19 August, having lodged an appeal.

Some time later, while I was waiting for my barristers to finalise their advice on that appeal, I walked into Sudbury's education building one afternoon. I was surprised by shouts of: 'What a wanker! That toss-pot doesn't know what the fuck he's talking about!'

There was uproar coming from one of the rooms.

'You smarmy twat! Who d'ya think you're connin'?'

I entered the room. A group of inmates, prison officers, teachers and even a Governor had gathered round a television set to watch Michael Howard deliver his speech at the Tory Party conference in Blackpool. To my amazement, the invective was coming not from the inmates but from the prison staff.

'He's the worst fuckin' Home Secretary this country's ever had!' one of the officers, a rather blunt Yorkshireman, shouted. 'He doesn't give a fuck about anybody except himself. He visits one or two prisons in America and he thinks he's an expert! Fuckin' nancy boy! He should ask the Yanks what's happened to their prison service!'

'He's just saying all this bollocks for the Press!' yelled another officer. 'It's a soddin' disgrace!'

I smiled to myself. Perhaps not everyone was quite so stupid as certain politicians imagined them to be. I took a seat and for the next half hour or so watched one of the most disgusting displays of fraudulent rhetoric and rabble-rousing that I have ever witnessed.

What worried me was not so much the patently insincere Niagara of platitudes issued by the Home Secretary, but the fact that a lot of the people at the Party Conference seemed to believe him.

Perhaps even less appealing was the sight of large numbers of self-righteous and complacent middle-class people, together with certain frustrated members of the Primrose League, in a state of undignified excitement at Mr Howard's ill-thought-out schemes to lock prisoners up and throw away the key.

I was reminded of my studies of the French Revolution and the *tricoteuses* — the women who would queue for days to enjoy a close view of people being guillotined. I was also reminded of a Tory MP who had recently suggested, apparently in earnest, that criminals should be whipped on live television just before the announcement of the National Lottery results.

And I wondered who society actually needed protecting from more, Mr Howard's so-called hordes of criminals rampaging through the country or people with such unsavoury, almost perverted, instincts.

A few days after the Home Secretary had delivered his speech, Abu Hamza was released from prison.

'What do you want to do now?' I asked him just before he left.

'Anything to help oppressed Muslims throughout the world. I'll probably go back to Bosnia or the Middle East.'

I was proud to have this man as my friend and we promised to keep in touch.

In December 1995, my legal advisers lodged my appeal against the extra sentence at the High Court and made an application for me to be released on bail pending that appeal.

The application for bail was successful and on the evening of 8 December, I was suddenly released from prison.

However, my freedom was to be short-lived, for on the following Monday Lloyds' lawyers made an application for my bail to be revoked. Interestingly, the judge at the hearing, the same judge who had originally granted me bail, refused to hear Lloyds' lawyers' submissions in Court on the grounds that Lloyds were not a party to my appeal. Nevertheless, and despite my not having broken any bail condition, my bail was revoked and I found myself back in Brixton prison over Christmas. There was nothing I could do to contest the judge's decision as the granting of bail by a Judge in Chambers is entirely a discretionary matter.

Having tasted freedom and been reunited with Patricia and Isabella only to have my freedom taken away again for no apparent reason, made the first few days after landing back in Brixton without doubt the most depressing time for me in the whole of my prison sentence. However, such feelings only lasted a week or so and I soon found myself determined to fight on.

On 21 December, I was back in the High Court for my appeal. I wasn't surprised to lose it. The one consolation was that I was granted a 'certificate of public importance' by the High Court, effectively enabling me to appeal on to the House of Lords, a very rare event in a case such as mine and one that illustrated the strength of my lawyers' arguments.

I was determined to fight all the way and gave my solicitors instructions to this effect.

However, on 29 December, David Reynolds, Lloyds' solicitor, wrote to Patricia offering me a deal. His letter stated:

'I write to remind you that on several occasions during this lengthy litigation, I have sought to engineer settlement of my clients' dispute with your husband. These initiatives have, to date, effectively been ignored by your husband. My clients and I object to your suggestion in the Press that Lloyds is no longer interested in a monetary claim. The reverse is quite the case: my clients have no wish to be involved in the expensive litigation that your husband has forced them, through his actions, to fight. I am willing to work with you and/or your husband's lawyers to try to arrange a satisfactory resolution of the case, provided there is good faith on your husband's part in recognition, if nothing else, of his responsibilities to you and your daughter. The matter remains, as it always has, in his hands. I look forward to a positive response rather than continuing litigation.'

Patricia came to visit me at Brixton and gave me a copy of Reynolds' letter. My initial reaction was to remain defiant to the bitter end, but I saw the look on Patricia's face.

'Isabella needs her father and I also need you. Perhaps Reynolds allowed things to get too personal but now he's just doing his job. He has to do his best for his clients and to show them that he's justified his fees. You've fought him tooth and nail. He's looking for a way out. Just give it to him and come home. Enough is enough.'

She had tears in her eyes and I knew that she was right. If I did a deal with Lloyds, I would be released immediately.

'All right, darling. Leave it to me.'

After Patricia left, I telephoned my Bankruptcy Trustee, John Alexander, a partner of the accountancy firm Pannell, Kerr Forster and a more pragmatic and commercially minded man than David Reynolds. Over the next couple of weeks, he masterminded and negotiated a settlement between myself and Lloyds.

Under the terms of the deal I would pay Lloyds approximately £156,000, which I would borrow from a number of friends who would remain anonymous, plus a proportion of my income above a fixed level once I had reimbursed the third parties who had loaned me this sum, over the next three years. This would constitute full and final settlement of Lloyds' claim of some three million pounds against me and it would also secure my immediate release from prison.

In January 1996, I was transferred from Brixton to Ford. The £156,000 arrived in the prison's bank account on Friday, 2 February.

That Friday afternoon I was called into the Governor's office where the Governor told me: 'Your Compensation Order has been paid and you'll be released on Monday at 9am. Good luck, Guppy.'

He paused. 'Well, how do you feel?' he asked.

So many different thoughts were racing through my head.

'I don't really know,' I replied.

XVIII

On the evening before my release, Sunday, 4 February, I said my goodbyes and went to the 'hut' where I resided — a twenty-man wooden dormitory with partitions that separated the bed spaces.

There I did my packing, putting all my belongings into a black plastic bin liner, said a few more farewells and lay on my bed. Patricia was staying in a nearby hotel and would be meeting me in the morning.

Looking at the ceiling, I thought back over the past few years. In bed spaces all around me were people who would be far less fortunate than me when they were released. In my years in prison, I had been aware of countless prisoners' marriages breaking down, of prisoners losing their homes as they failed to keep up their mortgage payments while in custody and unable to work, of prisoners losing their children to the social services, indeed losing everything they had, and I realised how easy it would be for people to become bitter in such circumstances and to seek revenge on an unforgiving society, becoming trapped in a cycle of crime.

How lucky I was to have been blessed with a loyal family and friends and to have remained unbroken by events. I remembered certain of the more hysterical articles that had been written about me after my conviction that had described me as 'dangerous'. Had my ordeal broken me, as many hoped it would, it is precisely at that point that I would have become genuinely dangerous.

If I left prison with nothing, no family, no support, no home, no stake in society, unable to find employment owing to my criminal record, with no prospect of improving myself and in such circumstances still, nevertheless, having to provide three meals a day for my daughter, I would stop at very little to achieve this. And so would any man — even the revoltingly self-satisfied people I had seen on television frenziedly cheering Mr Howard at Blackpool. I remembered the words of a Bob Dylan song: if you have nothing, you have nothing to lose.

What a waste of time the prison system is and how damaging for society as a whole, at least in the direction along which it is currently being steered. It seemed almost as if those responsible for running the system were determined to create more crime. The supreme irony for me was that virtually every member of staff, probation officer and prison visitor with whom I had come into contact during the past three years had thought the same.

'What about the victim?' goes the popular refrain. Fair enough. Punish the culprit. But in doing so make the culprit a better, less anti-social, more productive person for his punishment. In short, in remembering past victims, do not forget the future victims, for in creating a sub-culture of criminal desperadoes you will be doing nothing for them.

It seems fashionable in the pages of the Press at the present time to describe Britain's penal system as being far too 'soft'. To this end prisons are compared to holiday-camps. That had not been my experience, having been an inmate of ten jails, some of them reputedly the 'hardest' in the land and some of them the 'softest'. I had seen mentally ill prisoners locked up in their cells, lying in their own excrement all day because the prison hospitals were too full to accommodate them. I had witnessed numerous fights, stabbings and 'juggings' (whereby a jug of boiling water into which sugar has been dissolved is thrown on to someone's face), and had also witnessed several attempted suicides. In my first few months in Brixton jail, a number of such attempts had been successful. Britain's prisons are places of much misery and the public should not be fooled by the more irresponsible reports that they may read in certain newspapers.

All that aside, people would do well to remember that even a room in the Ritz is hell if you do not have the key to get out of it and that there is no loneliness worse than the loneliness of being apart from one's family. I am amazed that so many in a nation that prides itself on its history of loving freedom should seemingly have such little appreciation for freedom.

As I began to fall asleep I thought of the acquaintances I had made in prison, most of whom I would probably never see again. Very rarely in three years in jail had I met anyone irredeemably evil. Granted, there had been some who were distinctly dangerous men, but they were far fewer in number than most people would imagine. And, while there were certainly some prisoners who should never see the light of day again, the majority had been men who had made mistakes and who in different circumstances would have led perfectly honourable lives. Indeed, in certain circumstances some of these people would even have been called upon to fight and die for their country, like so many of their forebears who had fought wars and done the dirty work of gentlemen and kings. And to those who deny the link between poverty and crime, my response is simple — exceptionally few of those I met in prison were rich or even comfortably off.

In the morning, at 9am, having completed my discharge routine, in order to avoid the attentions of the waiting paparazzi, one of the Governors smuggled me out of the prison in the boot of his car to the Bailiff's Court Hotel a few miles from the jail where Patricia was waiting for me. After getting out of the boot, I shook hands with the Governor who wished me luck before driving off. Patricia and I embraced and we sat and chatted for half an hour in the hotel lobby where a fire was burning.

In order to avoid the Press who, by now, had discovered where we were to be found, I hitched a ride with the driver of a Q8 petrol tanker who had been delivering oil to the hotel. I hid beneath a blanket under the front seat while Patricia drove away separately, creating a diversion. We met up five miles away at a petrol station where I was dropped off and from there we made our way to the farm in Northamptonshire on Charlie's estate where Patricia had been living for the past year.

As I opened the front door, Isabella, who was being looked after by a friend, ran into my arms and I played a game with her, chasing her round the kitchen table. Ben, who had been free for almost a year, had warned me that the last thing I would feel like doing upon my release would be to celebrate with a mass of friends. He was right. Charlie telephoned me the following day from South Africa, where he was now living, to offer his congratulations and I spoke to a number of other friends on the phone. But for the next week or so, I simply stayed at home, enjoying my reunion with my wife and daughter while it snowed outside.

About a week after that, Ben drove down to see me. He was looking fit and well, though a little slimmer than when I had last seen him and he had lost none of his habitual cheer. It was immediately obvious that the events of the past few years had not affected our friendship remotely.

We went for a walk through the white countryside.

'Darry,' he told me, 'although I wish it had been a shorter experience, in many ways I'm almost grateful for what happened. I'm far less concerned with the trivial things in life that used to occupy so much of my time and I feel a stronger person.'

'I agree,' I replied. 'Although like you, I wish it hadn't been for quite so long.'

'Well, next time we'll just have to make sure we hire a different gunman,' he quipped.

A few days after Ben left, I drove to Cambridge to visit my father. He had moved into a friend's house, a tiny cottage in the centre of the town.

We hugged and he embraced Patricia and Isabella. After lunch we talked in the cottage's small garden. His hair, from being silver, had turned completely white since I had last seen him before going to prison. He had aged and I was very sad that the man I had looked up to in my youth and whose adventures had so captured my imagination had lost his home and his possessions. I also knew that, despite his being too tactful to mention it, he had been very hurt by what I had done.

I admired him for his pride and dignity. He showed me a mountain of paperwork that Lloyds had sent him, demands for yet more money that he could never hope to pay, threatening letters and complicated proposals for a settlement that would leave him with even less than he had somehow managed to hang on to.

'At least I have a roof over my head and have managed to create a sort of tropical garden here,' he said. 'Lloyds have now offered me a deal whereby I'd be left with not a penny to my name in exchange for a pension for the rest of my life, amounting to £225 per week before tax.'

'Perhaps I wasn't meant to be a millionaire,' he reflected. 'Looking on the bright side, however, a deal would put an end to the avalanche of paperwork that arrives by post each day from Lloyds.'

With a smile, he continued, 'Remember that I'm now in my seventies and I have to set about finishing the books I've been unable to complete since this nonsense began.'

Then he joked about how he would live to be a hundred and get everything back again.

When we said goodbye and I waved to him as I walked with Patricia and Isabella up the tiny concrete lane that led from his cottage to the road, one part of me felt very sad. Then I thought about the life that we had once enjoyed in better times and about what I had done. And another part of me felt glad.

EPILOGUE

When I first sat down to write this book, I asked a number of people for their advice about how to conclude it. One friend's advice, in particular, stood out:

'Darius,' he told me, 'you must remember that you have become a symbol and that this has nothing whatsoever to do with what you actually did. In fact, nobody really gives a damn what you did because in the scheme of things it is trivial. What counts is what you have come to represent. The evidence for this is obvious. Look at Ben Marsh, your partner and friend. He received exactly the same sentence as you from exactly the same judge in respect of exactly the same charges. His role was considered by the prosecution to have been identical to yours and yet the amount of coverage that he has received in comparison to you can be fitted on to the back of a postage stamp. So something, some extra ingredient, must have distinguished you from him to have warranted such disproportionate attention. That extra ingredient, is of course, your friendship with Diana's brother and the fact that you went to Eton. It is amazing, isn't it? In fact, it's actually very sad that so-called grown-up people — MPs, Ministers, civil servants, editors of newspapers and others — should have been so dazzled by this fact, so in awe of it almost, that they lost all sense of what they were actually doing.

'So, above all, in writing your epilogue, you must remember the psychology of this culture. Be aware that in this country, they love to write scripts and people get very annoyed if those scripts are not followed.

'The script that has been written for you, no matter how ludicrous it sounds, goes like this: "Darius Guppy, the man who had everything and was born into immense privilege, decided to pit himself against the system. He lost — how could he possibly have hoped to win? — and was punished, severely. Society demanded it. Now the whole world can see how fair our society is because here we have proof that it simply will not tolerate such behaviour, especially from the ranks of the privileged. In short, that great British maxim has been applied, for not only has justice been done, it has been seen to be done."

'That is the clichéd morality tale that has been written for you, Darius. That is the story people want to hear because it gives them a right, or so they believe, to criticise others and in the process to feel good about themselves, for nothing feels quite so good as righteous indignation. You have pissed a lot of people off, particularly certain hypocritical elements of the media, by showing defiance in not subscribing to the script that has been so carefully prepared for you. The fact that you seem to have emerged unscathed from your ordeal, unbroken, with a beautiful wife and daughter, a wonderful family and loyal friends has really grated with such people.

'Also you must remember that you are dangerous, for if a man such as you can be glamorised and seen in some way to have won, then the system itself is threatened. After all, many people might consider three years in jail for almost £2m to be a fair deal.

'But the script can have a happy ending if you want it to and for that you need do only one thing: say you're sorry, even if you don't mean it. Do you honestly think they give a damn whether you mean it or not? Say you're sorry. Bare your soul. Grovel. Let the world know that the "system", whatever that word means, has beaten you and that, like everybody else, you are a mere nothing next to it. Then, they will forgive you. What is more, and here is the ultimate irony, they will not only forgive you, they will love you. In fact, people will bend over backwards to give you a hand, to help lift you back out of the gutter while they bask in their own magnanimity.'

My friend, a barrister, paused and added: 'Somehow I don't see you doing this, Darius.'

He was right.

I have always thought that if ever I was a judge and I heard endless expressions of remorse from defendants who had been found guilty and whose remorse was generated for precisely that reason, I would actually give them a stiffer sentence for their hypocrisy than to those defendants who simply accepted what they had done and took their sentence on the chin. However, as in so many things, I seem to be in the minority on this issue.

For me, there is only one type of remorse that actually means anything and that is the type that is felt as a result of analysing your actions for yourself and reaching certain conclusions by yourself from such analysis. To express remorse, parrot fashion, simply because you have been pressurised into doing so or because you feel that it is the 'right thing to do', in other words to follow the script without considering its contents, counts for nothing. And yet, this type of remorse would seem to count an awful lot for an awful lot of people.

To feel the genuine type of remorse, you have to sense that your actions have been 'wrong' and while, arguably, it should not be the case, human nature is such that a cardinal part of the process of appreciating that you have done 'wrong', is to accept that those who have punished you are somehow 'right'. In short, those who dispense and administer justice have to occupy the moral high ground. If they do not, if the punishers are, and are perceived to be, no better than the punished then the whole question of punishment ceases to be a matter of right versus wrong and becomes instead an arbitrary exercise — those in positions of strength oppressing those who are not so strong.

Of course, right and wrong should not be about the morality of those who judge you. If you have genuinely done wrong, then you have done wrong, full stop. There is no relativity when it comes to morality. I accept this entirely.

What I did was wrong and there is no debating the fact. My motives may even have been justified. No doubt some — I suspect more than would openly admit — would privately agree. But there is no question that the method I chose should have been different. No doubt, too, when confronted by the police I should have bowed to the inevitable and put my hands up without a fight but, as I have explained in this book, the reasons I did not do so had nothing to do with the question of my guilt but were motivated by my anger, which I believe was justified, at the way the authorities acted and the dishonest charade that they put on for the benefit of the public and the media.

However, while my respect for the 'system' has diminished considerably as a result of my experiences, it has increased enormously for those working within it who genuinely seek to improve it, whether they are police officers determined to root out corruption within the force, or prison governors and staff who work to transform a prison service that has become the plaything of certain power-hungry ministers into an institution that truly improves society by rehabilitating prisoners, or the rare honest voice in the media that is still interested in the unfashionable concept of truth, or legal professionals who strive to overhaul an antiquated and inequitable system of justice.

Where my defiance has entered the equation is in refusing to be lectured to by those whom I consider to be hypocrites and who I consider to be in no position to lecture anybody:

- By certain police officers whose methods I have highlighted
- By a Crown Prosecution Service that was so obsessed with securing a high-profile victory in court and thereby a feather in its cap, that it was prepared to indulge misdemeanours by others, such as Risdon and Dutta, simply to achieve its goal
- By a judge who appeared to me to make it clear to the jury that he believed we were guilty
- By a prison service that pays lip service to protecting the public and to 'helping prisoners lead law-abiding lives', to use its own words, but has, at its highest levels, become so politicised and so taken over by spineless bureaucrats that, when it comes to applying its principles, will run terrified from any possible criticism in the media
- By certain sanctimonious and pompous MPs whose own private

rackets make them far more unscrupulous than any prisoner I
have met in three years in jail

- By a Home Secretary who dares to claim to represent the
  morality of the people but whose own agenda is so
  transparently insincere that it will mutate according to
  wherever he perceives the votes to be
- By certain publications that have the arrogance to pontificate to
  their readership on questions of morality and yet daily defraud
  these same readers on a massive scale, peddling lies,
  propaganda and filth
- Finally, by those who would love to see me under Waterloo
  arches, poor and broken, and yet, given half the chance, had
  they had the guts or my motives or thought that they could
  have got away with it, would have done exactly what I did. The
  posturings of such people have precious little to do with ethics
  and everything to do with envy and hypocrisy.

In fact, of all those who played some part in putting me in jail, the
police officers were the only ones who privately admitted the truth
to me and for that they have my respect. One of the investigating
officers hit the nail on the head when he said to me, 'You cannot
be seen to have the last laugh.' So, while I accept full responsibility
for my actions, I will listen not to the aforementioned but only
to my own conscience and to those whose opinions I respect. This,
I maintain, is the only type of self-realisation that actually
means anything.

Do I feel sorry for the pain I have caused to those I love? Yes,
deeply. Do I feel sorry for Lloyds? No. Do Lloyds feel sorry for
the countless 'names' they have ruined and driven to suicide? I
doubt it. Do I accept the moral authority of those who have
punished me? No.

What is done is done. The question remains about what to do in
the future.

No doubt it is supposed to be the case that once a man has 'done
his time' and paid his debt to society, he should be free to move on.
However, I am under no illusions that while this may be the theory,
in practice, and in particular in a culture where envy and hypocrisy

have become institutionalised, this may prove difficult. However, I look forward to the challenge.

As for the various protagonists in this story?

Lloyds of London is currently preparing a settlement package for its 'names', a package that seems likely to win general approval, although in many cases the worst-hit 'names', my father included, will be asked to sign an agreement before receiving full details of what they are actually being offered and how exactly their losses will be mitigated. Whatever happens, Lloyds seems likely to be changed for ever, with individual 'names' playing much smaller roles in the future and capital being provided principally by financial institutions. Although a number of judgements in the High Court have been made against various Lloyds' syndicates involving hundreds of millions of pounds, somehow Lloyds has avoided the perils of an investigation into the numerous allegations that have been levelled against it or indeed a public enquiry — a classic case, a cynic might argue, of the Establishment having protected itself.

My father is living in straitened circumstances in Cambridge at a friend's house.

Enquiries with the police records department have revealed that D/C Ellis has resigned from the force and that D/I Avery is, at the time of writing, absent on long-term sick-leave.

The last I heard of Ishan Dutta, the question of his immigration status was quietly swept under the carpet and he was working in Paris as a sales representative of a trading firm, waiting for the dust to settle before returning to India and keen to keep as low a profile as possible.

Peter Risdon, according to some of his ex-colleagues, went to ground after my conviction, eager to avoid bumping into a number of his former associates on whom he had informed and embarrassed by his status of 'grass' within the criminal community.

James Curtis was made a Queen's Counsel shortly after our conviction and, according to those who know him, is extremely proud of the fact.

Ben Marsh has remained himself — amusing, optimistic, caring not one jot about the opinions of the sanctimonious and generally getting on with life. We remain the best of friends.

As for me, it is easy to claim that I feel no bitterness about what has happened but this is the truth, for to feel bitterness you have to feel in some way defeated and clearly I have no such feeling. I have a wonderful wife and family, and my friends, much to the fury of certain elements of the media in particular, have remained steadfastly loyal.

In short, I have rejected the script that was offered to me. If it was the aim and hope of certain people that I should be broken as a consequence, then they will have to remain disappointed.

Murder, Madness and Marriage
Kate and Ronnie Kray

Ronnie Kray was one of the most legendary gangsters of all time. His ex-wife Kate is an effervescent blonde with a deadly sense of humour. This is a story of violence, bloodshed and passion. But it is also a strangely haunting and memorable love story.

The Nemesis File
Paul Bruce

The most controversial and sensational true story ever written about Britain's legendary special force, the SAS. Former Sergeant Paul Bruce tells the extraordinary story of his top-secret assignment in Northern Ireland. On the *Sunday Times* best-seller lists for fifteen weeks, this book will make history.

Lifers
Kate Kray

Kate Kray, the beautiful wife of killer Ronnie Kray, went behind the high walls and steel bars of Britain's jails to talk with eight deadly criminals about their crimes.

Psychic Cop
Keith Charles with Derek Shuff

The amazing story of Britain's only clairvoyant detective. Keith Charles brings the analytical skills of a seasoned policeman to examine the mystery of life after death. His verdict: that the spirits walk beside us ...

The Naked Spy
Yevgeny Ivanov

The sensational inside story of the Profumo scandal, written by the Russian spy who started it all. For the first time, this top Soviet undercover agent reveals the true story of the débâcle which brought down the Conservative Government of Harold Macmillan.

All prices include post and packing in the UK. Overseas and Eire, add £1.00 to the price of each book.
To order by credit card, telephone 0171 381 0666.
Alternatively, fill in the coupon below and send it, with your cheque or postal order made payable to
Blake Publishing Limited, to:

Blake Publishing Limited
Mail Order Department
3 Bramber Court, 2 Bramber Road
London W14 9PB

Please send me a copy of each of the titles ticked below:

☐ MURDER, MADNESS AND MARRIAGE   £14.99

☐ THE NEMESIS FILE   £5.99

☐ LIFERS   £14.99

☐ PSYCHIC COP   £14.99

☐ THE NAKED SPY   £14.99

Name _____

Address _____

_____

_____

Postcode _____

PLEASE ALLOW 14 DAYS FOR DELIVERY.